THE BRITISH ARMY IN BATTLE AND ITS IMAGE 1914–1918

Stephen Badsey is Reader in Conflict Studies at the University of Wolverhampton. He was educated at King Edward's School Birmingham, and Cambridge University, where he was awarded a PhD in 1982; he was elected a Fellow of the Royal Historical Society in 1995. Further information may be found at his website www.stephenbadsey.com

Series Editor: Gary Sheffield, Professor of War Studies, University of Birmingham.

Series Associate Editor: Dan Todman, Senior Lecturer, Queen Mary, University of London.

The British Army in Battle and Its Image 1914–1918

Stephen Badsey

University of Wolverhampton UK

BIRMINGHAM WAR STUDIES SERIES
Series Editor: Gary Sheffield

continuum

Continuum UK, The Tower Building, 11 York Road, London SE1 7NX
Continuum US, 80 Maiden Lane, Suite 704, New York, NY 10038

www.continuumbooks.com

First published 2009

British Library Cataloguing-in-Publication Data
A catalogue record for this book is available from the British Library.

ISBN 978 1 4411 5319 7

Typeset by Pindar NZ, Auckland, New Zealand
Printed and bound by MPG Books Ltd, Cornwall, Great Britain

Contents

Illustrations

Between Pages 110 and 111

All photographs copyright Imperial War Museum

1   A still from the film *The Battle of the Somme* (*see* page 126) showing the moment of the infantry attack on 1 July 1916, now believed to be one of the few outright fakes in the film. Imperial War Museum photograph Q70168.

2   The posed official photograph of Field Marshal Sir Douglas Haig taken on 12 September 1917 (*see* page 168) while the Third Battle of Ypres was being fought. Imperial War Museum photograph Q2879.

3   The official photograph of British stretcher-bearers in the Third Battle of Ypres taken by John Warwick Brooke on 1 August (*see* page 177) and published in the *Daily Mirror* on 6 September 1917. Imperial War Museum photograph Q5935.

4   The first of the sequence of aerial photographs taken by Lieutenant John Webster of the trench raid by 9th Durham Light Infantry on 15 September 1917 (*see* page 150). Narrow Trench runs across the lower part of the frame, intersected by a sunken lane on the left (compare with the map on pages 144–5) and running British infantry are just visible in no-man's land towards the top of the frame. Imperial War Museum photograph Q58653.

Acknowledgements

Professor Gary Sheffield as series editor of the *Birmingham War Studies* series first approached me to include this book in the series, and provided help along the way. Robin Baird-Smith of Continuum Books has seen the book through to publication. The index was compiled by Andrew Mikolajski. Acknowledgements and thanks are due to all those individuals and institutions who gave permission for the use of public and private documents that were quoted or cited in previously published versions of some of these essays. My thanks also, to every one of my colleagues at numerous institutions who helped along the way towards their production. Specific acknowledgements are as follows.

Introduction: An earlier version was given as a talk at a one-day conference 'The Future of the First World War', held at Queen Mary College, University of London, in 2005.

Douglas Haig and the Press 1914–1918: An earlier version appeared as 'Haig and the Press' in Brian Bond and Nigel Cave (eds). (1999) *Haig: A Reappraisal 70 Years On*. London: Leo Cooper. Copyright of the editors, material used with permission and with gratitude to two thoughtful historians of the First World War.

***Blackadder Goes Forth* and the 'Two Western Fronts' Debate 1914–1918:** An earlier version was first given as a paper 'Blackadder Goes Forth and the Image of the First World War' to the 18th International IAMHIST Conference held at Leeds University, July 1999; another version was published as '*Blackadder Goes Forth* and the "Two Western Fronts" Debate', in Graham Roberts and Philip M. Taylor (eds). (2000), *The Historian, Television, and Television History*. Luton:

University of Luton Press. Material copyright John Libby Publishing Ltd; used with permission.

Cavalry and the Development of Breakthrough Doctrine 1914–1918: An earlier version was published as 'Cavalry and the development of Breakthrough Doctrine', in Paddy Griffith (ed.) (1996), *British Fighting Methods in the Great War*. London: Frank Cass. Material copyright Taylor and Francis Books Ltd; used with permission.

The Battle of the Somme (1916): **The Film of the Battle:** An earlier version of this chapter was published as '*Battle of the Somme* (1916): British war propaganda', in *The Historical Journal of Film, Radio, and Television*, Volume 3, 2 Number 1983. Although retaining copyright as author, I am glad to acknowledge the original publication in a valuable and sometimes under-rated journal, and to thank the present editor, Professor David Culbert.

The Raid on Narrow Trench, 1917: An earlier version of this chapter was given as a paper to a meeting of the British Commission for Military History at the Imperial War Museum in 1984, and subsequently published as 'The trench raid at Chérisy, 1917', in *The Imperial War Museum Review*, 4 Issue 1984. Although retaining copyright as author, I am glad to acknowledge the original publication by the Trustees of the Imperial War Museum, London.

The Press, Propaganda, and Passchendaele 1917: A version of this chapter was published as 'Images of battle: The press, propaganda and Passchendaele' in Peter H. Liddle (ed.) (1997), *Passchendaele in Perspective: The Third Battle of Ypres*. London: Leo Cooper; copyright Peter H. Liddle. Original material used with the permission of the copyright holder, and my gratitude to my co-author, Professor Philip M. Taylor of the Institute for Communications Studies, University of Leeds (UK).

The Missing Western Front: Politics, Propaganda and Strategy in 1918: An earlier version of this chapter was published under the same title in Mark Connelly and David Welch (eds) (2005), *War and the Media: Reportage and Propaganda 1900–2003*. London: I. G. Tauris. Material copyright of the editors; used with permission, and with gratitude to Professor Mark Connelly and Professor David Welch, both of the University of Kent (UK).

To those who served in the British Army 1914–1918
pro mortuis loquimur

Series Editors' Preface

War Studies is an influential, popular and intellectually exciting discipline, characterized by the broad range of approaches it employs to understand a fundamental human activity. It has the history of war at its heart, but goes beyond operational military studies to draw on political, cultural and social history as well as strategy, literature, law, political theory, economics and social science. *Birmingham War Studies* celebrates this diversity by publishing examples of the discipline at its best, bringing the best academic scholarship on war to a wide audience. The remit of the series is deliberately ambitiously wide, ranging across periods, methodologies and geographic regions. In this, it takes its cue from the treatment of the subject by the War Studies Group (WSG) within the Department of Modern History at the University of Birmingham. The launch of the series as a joint venture between Continuum and the WSG marks the latter's emergence as a major force in the field, both in the UK and internationally.

That of the first three books to be published, one deals with military theory and doctrine, and another with social anthropology, indicates that, whilst 'traditional' military history has its place in *Birmingham War Studies*, the series' scope is very broad. The high quality of research, analysis and expression will make these books required reading for all those interested in the study of war in general as well as in the topic covered by each volume. In each case, the methodologies used in these specific studies will drive the field as a whole forward.

The British Army in Battle and Its Image 1914–1918 is a distinguished contribution to the history of both Britain's army and the First World War. This subject was once dominated, with some notable exceptions, by popular writers whose works ranged from the admirable to the abysmal. The historiography of the British Expeditionary Force (BEF) has been transformed in the last quarter-century as professional historians have exploited archival sources to produce a nuanced picture. Working at the Imperial War Museum, the Royal Military Academy Sandhurst, and latterly at the University of Wolverhampton, Dr Stephen Badsey has been a prominent member of the informal group of historians located across the English-speaking world who have effected this transformation. His contributions have largely taken the form of important conference papers and chapters in books: his major monograph *Doctrine and Reform in the British Cavalry 1880–1918*, although based on a doctoral thesis that appeared in the early 1980s, was not published until 2008. It is thus a pleasure, as well as a service to the historical community, to bring a selection of his work together in book form for the first time.

Here there is space to highlight just two facets of this excellent collection. As the title of this book suggests, the image of the Army is a very worthwhile area of study, and Dr Badsey's work represents a major advance in this area. His expertise in propaganda and the often uneasy relationship between the military and the media illuminates an aspect of British high command that has previously been cast in shadow, and significantly adds to our understanding of the career of Douglas Haig. Similarly, his seminal work on British cavalry in the war rescues this arm from the ignorance, prejudice and plain derision of contemporaries and historians, and consigns the myth that it was an utterly obsolete arm to the wastepaper basket. Instead, through meticulous research, Badsey places cavalry firmly into the evolution of British military thought and argues persuasively that previous historians, by ignoring the cavalry, have left our picture of the British Expeditionary Force (BEF) curiously incomplete.

The British Army in Battle and Its Image 1914–1918 is a major work by a first-class historian. Scholarly, provocative and highly readable, it is a very welcome addition to *Birmingham War Studies*.

Gary Sheffield, Editor, Birmingham War Studies
Dan Todman, Associate Editor, Birmingham War Studies
Birmingham and London
March 2009

Author's Preface

Sometimes you don't know what you're doing for some time, until you find out that you've done it; that is why we call it research.

These essays represent most of my short writings and publications about the British Army in the First World War over a period of about a quarter of a century. Some deal with high command and how battles were fought; some with the way that these battles were represented to the British people, particularly through the mass media; and some deal with the fusion between fighting and reporting – between the Army in battle and its image. All of them deal principally with the Western Front, which was the major land front on which the British Army fought, and remains an important focus for any study of the war in British history. Reading through the titles of these essays, I am conscious that there should be more about other countries, other fighting fronts, other services, and generally other experiences of the war. Perhaps in another collection in the future there will be; but I can only hope that the reader or reviewer will not be disappointed with what is here, rather than what is not.

People who open books like this one want to read about history, not about historians – at least I hope so. But it is impossible to explain these essays without some reference as to why they came to be written. Some owe their origins to my doctoral research at Cambridge University in the late 1970s, which was mainly concerned with what would now be called issues of military thought and doctrine, although those terms were used rarely (if at all) at the time that I was doing this work. The final product of this particular line of research into the British cavalry before and during the First World War was published in 2008 as *Doctrine and Reform in the British Cavalry 1880–1918*. A wide interest in military thought and doctrine has stayed with me throughout my career, but this was joined by an interest in propaganda and in media representations of warfare as a result of my first postdoctoral position, as a research assistant at the Imperial War Museum in London, chiefly working in cataloguing their collection of original films of the First World War. Some of these essays very obviously owe their origins to work done with the museum's collections. In studying both the military history of battles and the cultural history of the media and propaganda in warfare, by the 1990s I found myself also involved in an increasingly vocal dispute between military historians and historians of culture, which I later came to characterize as the 'Two Western Fronts' debate. Before long, I had reached the conclusion that the two sides should be working together rather than in opposition, to help towards a better explanation of the nature of the First World War.

My particular hypothesis for the British Army on the Western Front, which is reflected in these essays and which took almost three decades to formulate, sounds when articulated (like many far more profound academic insights) like a glaring statement of the obvious. It is that, during the First World War, there was an intimate connection between the way in which the Army fought, and the way in which its actions were perceived and understood through the mass media, both by the Army itself and by others, including civilians on the Home Front; and that in seeking to understand the history of the period we need to approach conventional military history and cultural or media history as conjoined rather than separate activities, and with the same rigorous standards of attention to facts and evidence. The last of the essays in this book, in particular, reflects my attempts to link British strategy and battles with media and propaganda, and show how they affected not only each other but also our historical understanding of events.

Earlier versions of most of these essays have appeared under various titles, often in journals or as collections which were not specifically dedicated to the First World War, and as a result they may have been missed by students of the war. Looking through them all again, the obvious temptation facing me as an author was to re-write each of them from scratch, to reflect either my own changing views, or changing fashions in the study of the history of the war, or both. On the whole I have managed to resist this, although I have modified some phrases or judgements to which I could not honestly put my own name today, whatever

I may have thought at the time, and in some cases I have added a new introductory paragraph. In places where one or more of the essays tells much the same story, or where one essay elaborates on another, I have tried to harmonize them rather than bore the reader with repetition. Otherwise, I have limited any changes to adding a few facts that I did not know at the time of first publication, or that have since come to light through further research, correcting as many factual errors as I could find, changing a few infelicities of style (including reversing some editorial decisions with which I did not agree in the first place), and harmonizing the styles employed, including in the end-notes. The result is, I hope, a better and more readable set of essays.

Stephen Badsey
University of Wolverhampton
March 2009

Introduction: The Western Front in Public History 1914–2014

Each of the essays in this collection studies a different aspect of the British Army's conduct of the First World War and some reflect how this was portrayed by the media of the time. But this introductory essay is different: it is an attempt to understand how the Army, the Western Front, and the war itself will probably be viewed and understood in the near future. Today, as this is being written, is 11 November 2008, the 90th anniversary of the Armistice that ended the First World War, at least as far as the British people and the Western Front were concerned. Almost certainly, by the time that you come to read this paragraph, we will have lost the last remaining combat veterans of the First World War, those whose adult lives were directly affected by the fighting. Also, and of much less importance to the general public at present, historians and others will have begun planning how to commemorate the four years starting in 2014 that mark the 100th anniversary of the war.

This in itself is something of a surprise. When the Imperial War Museum in London was established during the war, and its sister institution the Australian War Memorial in Canberra shortly afterwards, one view of their function was that they should remain open as memorials until the last of the veterans of the 'war to end war' had died, when their purpose would be at an end and they should close. Even today, there is an argument that, with the passing of the last of the veterans, public interest in the First World War may decline. Commemoration of Remembrance Day (originally Armistice Day, or Veterans Day as some other countries call it) came close to fading out of existence in the 1960s. But since then the need for modern society, in Great Britain and elsewhere, to remember and commemorate the dead of the First World War and many other wars has grown in strength and public importance. We may now look forward to the centenary of the years 1914–1918 as marking a unique opportunity to establish a new global understanding of the events of the war, both in itself and as the single most significant event in shaping the history of the last 100 years.

The term 'Public History' used in this opening essay may not be very familiar to British readers. The term was first popularized in the United States in the early 1980s, to reflect the increasing number of occasions on which the best historical research available needed to connect with aspects of public life rather than remain within academia, entering a domain 'where historians and their various publics collaborate in trying to make the past useful to the public', with the public use of history foremost in mind.[1] This includes the participation of historians in activities such as television history, the design and unveiling of memorials, the commemoration of historical events, and any other circumstances in which governments or other institutions might need to employ a specialist historian, just as they would employ a lawyer or a surveyor. In looking at how the First World War is likely to be commemorated in 2014, public history is concerned not only with the latest trends in historical research, but also with how these may interact with much wider political, economic and social issues. This is history for a wide audience, and for anyone interested in history, as a source of inspiration or ideas or simply as entertainment, as part of what the late and much admired novelist Michael Crichton called the 'flight into authenticity' from an increasingly mediated modern world.[2] In this, military history enjoys a rare privilege, in that it is one of the few forms of history that has a mass popular readership and following. This includes an increasing participation in study of the First World War from groups such as the Western Front Association (first founded in 1980), people whose interest in the war is less than a profession but more than just a hobby, and which can link cutting-edge scholarship on the war directly with the rest of society. This is why interest in the First World War is likely to continue: it is something about which a lot of people *care*.

Why this should have happened is a simple question with no very obvious answer, except through a combination of factors that all continue to work together. A broad-based public interest in the First World War and how it was fought is not confined to the British Isles, but it appears to be at its strongest presently in the English-speaking world. It has been pointed out that comedies about the war, such as the play *Oh! What a Lovely War* (1963) and the television series *Blackadder Goes Forth* (1989), could never have been made in France, where the events of the First World War are still not the subject for humour in any form. At least part of the explanation is surely the increasing number of British holidaymakers passing through northern France and Belgium, who cannot fail to notice the neat cemeteries preserved by the Commonwealth War Graves Commission. The increasing number of smaller wars and military operations in which the British have been involved since the early 1980s may also have brought home something of the experience of war to a wider public. Maybe also there is some nostalgia for a world that, with the passing of the last of the veterans, will be accessible to us only through history. This entire issue of the 'history of memory' has attracted considerable attention recently, as a way of looking at the war in which its memorials and how they have been interpreted since 1918 form as much a part of the story as the battles themselves.[3]

At least in Great Britain, through a number of factors that are quite beyond the control of professional historians (although not beyond their influence), the erosion of the distinction between academic and public history which is already evident in the study of the First World War will continue, to the benefit of the latter without lowering the standards of the former. One of the long-term consequences of this is that our view of the war, by the time it reaches its 100th anniversary, is likely to be more global and less narrowly national. For many centuries, if not millennia, there has been an international community of scholars who have sought to share knowledge; but in this respect, globalization has affected historians and the practice of history just as it has affected all other aspects of our society. The internet, relatively cheap air fares, and international publishing have all vastly increased our ability to combine and compare ideas about the war; in doing so, we have found that our old versions of its history will no longer do. In particular, one of the more evident discoveries from this new globalism is that frequently the respective versions of the First World War accepted in different countries – even countries with close historical and cultural ties – do not always match particularly well. Another is that, especially in the case of the countries of the former British Empire, so much of one country's military history is in another country's records and archives. It is also apparent that the British Army – the army about which we know the most due to the upsurge of interest in the Western Front – was the most untypical army of all. The British Army began as a small all-volunteer force of long-service soldiers; it expanded massively through wartime volunteerism, and even after conscription was introduced in January 1916 its soldiers remained strongly committed to the war and to victory. It was augmented by the Indian Army – itself at that time the largest all-volunteer army in history, as it remained until the end of the Second World War – and by contingents that came from all around the planet, in many cases men who had been originally born in the British Isles or their sons. This contrasts with the large conscript armies of continental Europe and the Ottoman Empire, all with long traditions of military involvement in politics and vice versa, and with very different social structures. This sets historians a puzzle and a challenge: how can any of the events of the war and the Western Front be truly understood without looking beyond the British horizon?

Historians, like other specialists, are sadly not immune from jargon, and one confusing example is our use of the word 'myth' to mean not what everyone else thinks it means – a falsehood or fiction – but as a (quite possibly) real event surrounded by layers of cultural meaning. In this way, historians write about 'national myths', of the stories that people tell themselves about their past, and this includes any modern myth of the First World War. The myth of the war that prevailed in historical scholarship until quite recently was very much a national history, with each country focusing on its own experience. For the English speaking world it was overwhelmingly about the Western Front, and the two great bloodbaths of the Somme in 1916 and Passchendaele in 1917, with the British Army 'defeated' in spring 1918 and the subsequent victory due to other causes. The Australian version of this myth elevated Gallipoli to a central event in the story of an independent nation, despite the fact that more soldiers of the French Army than Australians fought in the Dardanelles, that the Australian forces did by far their hardest and best fighting later on the Western Front, and that the distinction between English and Australian at the time was often far from clear.[4] A similar Canadian tradition has overlain the Battle of Vimy Ridge and the Canadian Corps's reputation as the 'storm troopers' of the British forces on the Western Front.[5]

Above all, this view of the war was one that refused to accept or understand its events, and that looked for someone to blame. It held that the war had begun by accident over nothing, had been fought by incompetents who had sacrificed a generation, and that nothing had been won by it that was worth winning. In the German version, an explanation was needed for how the war had been lost, and the ready answer was the 'Stab in the Back', that the German Army had not been defeated but betrayed by a collapsing Home Front. In British – but not French – history also, the superiority of the German fighting soldier was taken for granted and German generals were seen as slightly less stupid than those of the Allies. Again, the Australian variation – and those of Canada or the United States – was that any faults lay with the British, who had to be rescued from themselves by the superior fighting abilities of their newly arriving partners. This view of the war, or something quite like it, still remains strong in British popular culture, as the tone of so many public pronouncements during the 2008 commemoration of the Armistice showed, including those of some amateur historians. But the link between historical scholarship of the war and popular culture is now sufficiently strong that, on this occasion, there were many people around the country who understood that the events of the war could no longer be made to fit this traditional British myth.

It needs to be stated at once that this is not simply a new generation of historians promoting revisionist views of history for their own sake, especially now that the last of the veterans are no longer around to tell the truth. The attitude that the war was a bungled and futile disaster was held by some people in Great Britain and its Empire while it was being fought and immediately afterwards, but not by many, and certainly not by a majority. When, in 1917, Captain Siegfried Sassoon made his much-publicized protest against the war, if his views had been truly representative of the British Army it would have followed him by mutinying, which it never did for the entire length of the war other than on some minor occasions, in contrast to the large-scale mutinies of the French, Austro-Hungarian, Russian and, eventually, German armies. The view of the war as a completely futile waste emerged most strongly from the 1930s, with the unsavoury 'Battle of the Memoirs', as politicians and generals or their supporters struggled to dominate the historical record, and also when the combination of economic depression, the rise of totalitarianism and the increasing likelihood of another war appeared to contradict any idea of a victory in 1918. At a time when the First World War was already under question, there followed the archetypal 'good war' in the form of the Second World War to provide a contrast. Then the last stage of the process came with the social revolution of the 1960s, in which the entire structure of the societies that had fought the First World War was rejected and mocked. Only more recently have we returned to trying to understand them.

In seeking to make predictions about how the First World War might be commemorated even in a few years' time from now, no historian of the British Army should fail to reflect on Douglas Haig's statement in 1907, 'The role of cavalry will always go on increasing', about which he was in fact right in the long term (especially taking 'cavalry' to mean mobile troops, as they were the only form of mobility then available), but not for the specific conditions of the Western Front.[6] As historians and as human beings, we do not predict the future so much as project the present day's circumstances forward, and by definition we cannot include the unexpected, except to be confident that it will happen. Nevertheless, several trends seem strong enough to continue for at least a few years. Public interest in the First World War will increase, particularly through battlefield tourism, which is itself a product of several interacting factors since the 1980s. One of the turning points in public interest in the war was the success of the 75th anniversary commemoration of the Battle of the Somme in 1991, which convinced both tour and television companies that such events were worth promoting. It is also a near-certainty that battlefield tours will continue to grow in connection with university courses on the First World War. In future, having walked the ground will be an essential requirement not just for books about the land battles of the war, but also for any historian whose book attempts to explain the wider implications or meanings of those battles.[7]

For the study of the war in universities, one of the most significant developments of the next decade will be the final retirement of the 1960s generation of academics (historians and others), hopefully removing a strong prejudice against military history in general, and the First World War in particular. This prejudice may be compared with that famously shown against the serious study of science fiction in literary circles up until the 1960s: by definition, military history is seen as inferior, and if it is good then it cannot be military history. This prejudice is already waning considerably in Great Britain and Canada, but remains strong in Australia and especially in the United States.[8] Its end should permit, at last, the integration within First World War studies of military, cultural and political history, and their further integration with public history.

One of the most important dynamics of the study of the First World War has been the 'Two Western Fronts' phenomenon (also mentioned in other essays in this collection): the gap between new historical findings on one side, and not only British popular culture but also the analyses of cultural historians on the other. Like many academic disputes, this debate has not been very accessible to most people with an interest in the war, and sometimes its arguments have verged upon the bizarre, including suggestions that the Germans actually won the war on the Western Front, and that either this has been concealed from history by a vast conspiracy, or that culturally speaking they won because they have the most impressive and moving military cemeteries. But it is from the more serious contributions to this debate that a new consensus on the Western Front is emerging, and by 2014 this consensus should be visible in the public history of the war.[9]

Failing some radical change in wider society, the institutions that house and preserve historical artefacts and documents of the First World War should remain much the same, presenting a version of the war to the public that should be accessible and sensitive to contemporary sensibilities. These include national institutions like the Imperial War Museum, the Australian War Memorial, and the United States' National World War One Museum at the Liberty Memorial in Kansas City, but also other museums that have established reputations for scholarship, including the In Flanders Fields Museum at the Cloth Hall at Ypres, and the Historial de la Grande Guerre at Peronne on the Somme battlefield. Increasingly, the internet is making it possible for these and other institutions not only to disseminate new ideas and research, but also to make available to a much wider public the raw data of their collections. This is another trend that will continue, so that future writers of the history of the war will be expected to have looked at the photographic and film evidence, and the evidence from sound recordings, as well as the documents. Increasing computer power will make it more likely that at least some books will achieve what is now largely a science fiction ideal, by including both written text and electronic evidence together in one volume.

How the history of the First World War will be presented on television in the near future remains a problem, especially as the fusion of television with the internet becomes more likely. It is possible that increasing dissemination through the internet or its equivalent will make it commercially viable for specialist or niche channels to provide serious and high quality military history, of a standard comparable to those programmes on many subjects presently produced in Great Britain by the BBC in conjunction with the Open University. Only a few years ago, there was a serious attempt by British historians and programme makers to find common ground, and to bring cutting-edge history of the war to a wider television audience, in a way that has been done on British television for decades with the hard sciences, zoology and archaeology. But this has failed, chiefly through wider commercial pressures on television companies searching for a bigger share of the audience, but also partly because of a culture clash between programme makers and historians both insisting on control of the programme. It is significant that the most successful recent television history has been what is called 'presenter-led' history, made by historians who understand how to negotiate this difficult relationship and turn themselves into television personalities. But even this approach has recently succumbed, together with the rest of television history, to a wider commercial demand for programmes as entertainment, which has led to the increasing use of the 'host' as presenter, a recognizable television personality rather than an expert. At present, rather than experiencing history directly and at first hand, viewers are more often invited to watch and admire the host's performance, usually combined with poor quality dramatic reconstructions and camera or editing tricks. The results are sometimes entertaining, but they are not history even in the public sense. It is a reflection of this decline in quality that although major historical television documentary programmes of the recent past have themselves become part of the study of the history of memory of the war, most evidently the BBC series *The Great War* (1964), there is no prospect of this happening with any recent documentary productions on the First World War. Quite often television documentary programme makers have not wanted historians involved in their programmes at all, and the few programme makers who have troubled to consider the matter take the view that 'television history' is an activity completely divorced from history, that a television programme is a cultural artefact, or at best the retelling of a myth, and that they should be left alone to do this.

From the other side of this argument, just as many (if not most) historians still view military history with disdain, so the majority of historians continue to hold television as remote from, and beneath, any of their interests. Even among historians who regularly work with television (and so qualify as 'public historians'), there is a shared recognition of the immense limitations of the medium for presenting historical ideas. Even those who enjoy making programmes often share the view that ultimately television can do no more than entertain, and treat it as a source of revenue for their real historical work. Others, fewer in number and perhaps more idealistic, believe that given the right subject and enough talent television history can make a real contribution not just to public education but also to historical knowledge, and there have been rare cases of this happening, encouragingly well received by the public.

To return to the issue of a more globalized approach to the study of the First World War, and also regrettably to the subject of jargon and myth, what the public history of the First World War will look like in 2014–2018 may well depend on how that history interacts with the prevailing national and international myths of the war, what historians call the war's 'grand narratives', a term originally taken from the French. The prevailing grand narrative in Europe is driven by modern French and German preoccupations with a culturally and socially (if not politically) united Europe, and is reflected particularly in the museums and commemorative buildings of the Verdun battlefield and in the Historial at Peronne.

This is an interpretation of three wars – the Franco-Prussian War 1870–1871, the First World War 1914–1918, and the Second World War 1939–1945, all falling within one lifetime – as three episodes in a disastrous European civil war comparable to the Thirty Years War 1618–1648, wars in which there were no winners and Europe as an entity was the loser. This grand narrative sits awkwardly with the historical facts of the extreme nationalism of 1914–1918, especially in France and Germany. It also does not sit well with British sensibilities, but it does allow a way for British historians to co-operate with their European colleagues in studying the First World War and its consequences.

For the British, their own grand narrative of the First World War for many years was that it was the explanation for the decline and eclipse of the British Empire. It is this view of the war as a futile disaster, incompetently managed, that has been the subject of so much recent revisionism, and at least one factor behind this revisionism is that the British no longer need this particular myth. More than half a century after the Suez Crisis in 1956, modern British society has moved on in historical terms, and needs no explanations for any past decline of the Empire. Indeed, a part of this process has been a revived interest in the history of the British Empire and how it fought the First World War, an interest shared not just by Great Britain but by former member countries of the Empire around the world, including Australia, New Zealand, Canada and Ireland. The first historical re-evaluations are also starting to appear of the Indian Army in the war, not just from Indian scholars but from elsewhere within the old Empire. These countries, although mostly excluded from the European grand narrative, are linked by their Imperial past through Great Britain to European scholarship. It is only the United States, where the First World War remains remarkably under-studied despite its importance to American history, which has, at present, a national grand narrative of the war that fails to link it to Europe or the wider world. The American national myth remains that of the avenging cowboy of the Wild West, the stranger who arrives, resolves the problem by violence and then rides on; just as the United States in 1917 sent its soldiers 'over there' to fight, and then after the war withdrew into isolation. For the United States, the critical year of any commemoration of the First World War is likely to be 1917, marking not only its own entry into the war but also the Russian Revolution, and the decline of European power over the rest of the world.

If these national grand narratives cannot be easily reconciled, they nevertheless provide a strong starting point for a shared history of the First World War, and an awakening awareness of other possible perspectives. The military history of Russia and the Russian Empire in the war is still obscure in many of its aspects, as is the military history of the Ottoman Empire and its disintegration, or that of Austria-Hungary, despite the early work of some accomplished scholars, and these gaps in the global historical understanding of the war are becoming ever more apparent. Both increasing historical study and changing modern circumstances have led historians to understand that the experience of the British Army on the Western Front was one among many, to be understood and interpreted in a wide variety of ways. Perhaps by the 100th anniversary of the First World War some progress will have been made towards a genuine and public world history for what was truly a world war. That seems like a reasonable ambition.

NOTES

1 As defined by *The Public Historian*, the publication of the US National Council on Public History. *See* their website: www.ncph.org, and also *Public History Review* published by the University of Technology Sydney at www.epress.lib.uts.edu.au/ojs/index.php/phrj

2 Crichton, M. (1999), *Timeline*. New York: Ballantine.

3 The literature of the history of memory is large, but complex and not always accessible to the non-specialist reader. For a very good introduction *see* Todman, D. (2005), *The Great War: Myth and Memory*. London: Hambledon & London; and for the most thorough exposition in English *see* Winter, J. (1995), *Sites of Memory, Sites of Mourning: The Great War in European Cultural History*. Cambridge: Cambridge University Press.

4 Australian historians have themselves been at the forefront of challenging this Australian view of the war; *see*, for example, Blair, D. (2001), *Dinkum Diggers: An Australian Battalion at War*. Melbourne: Melbourne University Press.

5 *See*, for example, Cook, T. (2008), *Shock Troops. Canadians Fighting the Great War, 1917–1918*. Toronto: Canadian Penguin Group.

6 Haig, D. (1907), *Cavalry Studies*. London: Hugh Rees, p. 8.

7 Indeed, one scarily knowledgeable battlefield guide of the author's acquaintance is quite scathing on the subject of what she calls 'mere library theses'.

8 For a summary of the problems of American military historians, which might have been written about their British colleagues 20 years previously, *see* Shy, J. (2008), 'History, and the history of war', *The Journal of Military History*, 72, (4), 1033–1046. The situation in Great Britain is still far from satisfactory. For his inaugural lecture in 2008, my colleague at the University of Wolverhampton, Professor John Buckley, chose as his title for an overview of military history in academia Margaret Atwood's poem, 'The Loneliness of the Military Historian'.

9 The debate is well reviewed in Bond, B. (2002), *The Unquiet Western Front: Britain's Role in Literature and History*. Cambridge: Cambridge University Press.

2

Douglas Haig and the Press 1914–1918

Historians of the First World War, and of the military career of Douglas Haig (Commander-in-Chief of the British Army in France 1915–1918), have certainly not neglected the role played in both by the British Press. Robert Blake, in his introduction to the 1952 published edition of Haig's papers, noted the remarkable power exercised by Press magnates during the war, and the deference shown to them by politicians and generals.[1] According to several Liberal politicians of the time, Haig was, from even before the war, an arch intriguer against governments and a manipulator of the Press and public opinion from behind the scenes, behaviour which played a major role in a near-breakdown of British civil-military relations in 1918. In terms of hard evidence, though, this view is little more than conjecture.[2] Even after an entire media century has passed, a full account of the British Press in the First World War has yet to be written, and the extensive newspaper record of Haig's activities remains a misunderstood and under-used resource. Consequently, the manner in which Haig fought what is now often called the 'media war' is a neglected factor in assessing his achievements.

The remarkable powers attributed in Britain during the First World War to the Press and its owners arose directly from the failure of established institutions to adjust to the political and social changes of the preceding years. Despite the extension of the franchise by the Reform and Redistribution Acts of 1884–1885, Britain continued to be governed largely by patricians for another two decades. In 1914 many politicians whose fathers had feared both the Mob and the Revolution were still feeling their way towards understanding the new mass politics. In 1928, after two further extensions of the franchise had produced universal suffrage, Herbert Asquith wrote that 'The average party politician finds it difficult to realise the extent of the vague, floating, and dim formless elements which go to make up our vast electorate',[3] adding that things had become much worse since the granting of votes to women.

With the Press also, it was not until the early twentieth century that changes instituted decades earlier began to have their impact in Britain. The Education Acts (England and Wales) of 1870 and 1880 are now seen as the culmination, rather than the start, of the growth of working-class literacy and newspaper reading.[4] But despite the more populist 'New Journalism' style introduced in the 1880s by the *Pall Mall Gazette*, the major changes in newspaper ownership and sales came only in 1894, from the Harmsworth family, led by Alfred (created Lord Northcliffe in 1905), whose success in founding the first mass-circulation daily newspaper, the *Daily Mail*, in 1896, also enabled him to buy *The Times* in 1908.

In the nineteenth century, owners and editors of newspapers – and a few reporters – had been seen both as opinion formers and as essential conduits of communication between the various national elites and interest groups; the actual size of newspaper circulation was much less important. This older type was still well represented by one of Haig's guests at general headquarters (GHQ) in 1916, John St Loe Strachey, the owner-editor of the weekly *Spectator*, who was also Lord Lieutenant of Surrey.[5] Northcliffe, as the self-styled 'Ogre of Fleet Street', was himself very much a journalist, but his success began a new trend of businessmen with little background in journalism founding or acquiring newspapers, often in syndicates rather than outright, solely for financial gain and as a means of exercising political influence. From a market utterly dominated by *The Times* 50 years before, by 1914 there were about eight major daily national newspapers, all based in London with the exception of the *Manchester Guardian*, together with about twice that number of influential weeklies and lower-circulation London newspapers. A close association with this kind of Pressman was a mark of political radicals, including particularly Lloyd George, who surrounded himself with newspaper owners such as Sir Henry Dalziel, Sir George Riddell, Lord Cowdray, Lord Rothermere (Northcliffe's brother), and Sir Max Aitken (who became Lord Beaverbrook in 1917). Part of the story of Lloyd George's wartime rise to power and premiership was his eventual success in bringing such men into his government by 1918, progressively alienating others as he did so.[6]

The power exercised by these men derived partly from their being rich enough to own newspapers, but also from a basic dilemma among politicians of how to measure and interpret public opinion in the mass. A fusion of the older belief, that a newspaper report or editorial spoke for an important section of public opinion, with the fact of the mass sales of newspapers like the *Daily Mail* or Beaverbrook's *Daily Express*, produced the simplistic view that the Press somehow held direct control over the views and voting powers of the new mass electorate. Beaverbrook's later assessment of Northcliffe, that 'His power was so considerable that it was of the utmost importance in all matters of public interest to secure his assistance or at any rate his neutrality',[7] was widely held during the First World War, not least by Northcliffe himself. In one entirely characteristic outburst to Haig in January 1917, Northcliffe threatened, if they would not do his bidding, to bring down not only the British government but also the French government as well.[8] These beliefs were given formal expression as a weapon of war by Lloyd George in spring 1918, with the appointment of Northcliffe as Director of Propaganda in Enemy Countries and Beaverbrook as Chancellor of the Duchy of Lancaster, heading the new Ministry of Information. The patrician Lord Esher wrote to (the very plebeian) General Sir William ('Wully') Robertson that 'The [P]ress has taken over the powers that Parliament has abdicated', adding that this was 'a natural outcome of what is called "popular government"'.[9]

Chief in importance among the lower-circulation London newspapers was that bastion of die-hard Conservatism, the *Morning Post*, edited by H. A. 'Taffy' Gwynne, who was later associated with the early British fascist movement.[10] The most famous of the accredited war correspondents at Haig's GHQ, Philip Gibbs of the *Daily Chronicle*, wrote that he found it necessary to talk to most generals 'on the lines of leading articles in the *Morning Post*'.[11] During the Curragh Incident in spring 1914, Gwynne acted as an adviser to Field Marshal Sir John French;[12] other senior Army officers with whom he had at least some contact or correspondence included Henry Wilson, William Robertson, Horace Smith-Dorrien, Henry Rawlinson, Hubert Gough, Julian Byng, Philip Chetwode and Ivor Maxse, as well as Douglas Haig.[13] Although Gwynne visited Haig at GHQ, written communication between them, and also between Haig and other prominent members of the Press, took place through either Haig's Brigadier General General Staff Intelligence, John Charteris, or his suave and secretive private secretary, Captain Sir Philip Sassoon.[14] Reporters visiting GHQ were also usually seen by Charteris, (who had worked for *The Times* in the past),[15] or even by one of his staff officers,[16] while Haig might see editors and proprietors himself.

Other than Gwynne, the newsman who enjoyed the most privileged status among senior Army officers was the military correspondent of *The Times*, Lieutenant Colonel (Retired) Charles à Court Repington, whose involvement in the military politics of the war became notorious, not least through his own egotistical memoirs. In the early part of the war, Repington enjoyed the privilege of personal invitations to GHQ from Sir John French. Indeed, it was the sophistic claim that Repington was present at GHQ as a guest rather than a reporter that enabled both French and *The Times* to argue that Repington's 'Shell Scandal' report of 12 May 1915 was not a violation of military regulations.[17] Repington also listed French's two chiefs of staff, Archibald Murray and William Robertson, as 'two of my oldest and most valued soldier friends',[18] a relationship that deepened in significance when Robertson took over as Chief of the Imperial General Staff (CIGS) at the end of 1915. In contrast, Haig's dislike of Repington went back years before the First World War. When Repington asked to interview him at First Army Headquarters in May 1915, Haig declined on the grounds that 'neither I nor my staff had the authority to see any newspaper correspondents and that all information for the Press must be obtained from GHQ'.[19] This was followed by an incident a few days later when one of First Army's observation posts was heavily shelled, something which Haig and his staff attributed to a further report in *The Times* by Repington, which French had let pass uncensored.[20] Haig's first reaction was to demand from GHQ the exclusion of all reporters from First Army area, and the experience undoubtedly reinforced his underlying dislike of the Press.

In addition to the activities of proprietors, editors and reporters behind the scenes, described by Esher as having 'taken the place of the Jesuits of old',[21] the main political importance of the Press was the manner in which an otherwise hidden conflict or controversy could coalesce around a sudden public revelation or 'scoop' (a term which itself dates from the 1880s). In the course of the war, such episodes included the Mons Despatch in *The Times* of August 1914, Repington's 'Shell Scandal' report of May 1915, and the Maurice Letter of May 1918. The newspaper interview in particular was in 1914 still seen as a recent practice, introduced into Britain from the United States as part of the 'New Journalism' style. A willingness to grant interviews was an indicator of political populism, and Asquith eventually made it a rule to give no Press interviews at all.[22] A common compromise, which Haig himself adopted at GHQ, was to allow occasional interviews, but to forbid verbatim reporting, so that no actual quotations appeared. Brigadier General Charteris, who was usually present, contemptuously described the resulting pieces as '... "Union Jack over the door, cow grazing in the meadow, strong silent man, blue eyes, white moustache, raised [relief] maps", and such-like drivel'.[23] Given Haig's inarticulate style of speech, this was a wise precaution. In 1908 there had been a spectacular gaffe when an interview with Kaiser Wilhelm II intended to improve Anglo-German relations had appeared in the *Daily Telegraph* in verbatim form, beginning with the Kaiser's observation that 'You English are mad, mad, mad as March hares',[24] an incident which precipitated the fall of Chancellor von Bülow. Just as the assassination at Sarajevo was the occasion rather than the cause of the war itself, so during its course such newspaper dramas formed the occasions through which much wider issues found their particular form and substance.

By the First World War the convention was very well established that senior Army officers were permitted the same kind of informal contact with newspaper owners and editors as any other influential people. Even interviews were tolerated, although only rarely of the verbatim kind. But in their strict interpretation, military regulations made contact with the Press of virtually any kind an offence. Military censorship and tight control of the Press at the start of the war was not, as it is often portrayed, a personal whim of Lord Kitchener, (although he was deeply hostile towards war reporters), but a reflection of the most recent thinking on the subject, based on a genuine attempt to learn the lessons of previous wars.[25] Even the criticized use of Colonel Ernest Swinton as the military 'Eyewitness' from autumn 1914 to early summer 1915, producing a twice-weekly column of news from headquarters, was just a late manifestation of the nineteenth-century tradition of serving officers doubling as war correspondents. Military thinking on the Press reflected the views of civilian society: that what the war correspondent wrote was so powerfully influential that it must be rigorously controlled, not just to avoid giving secrets to the enemy, but to maintain civilian morale at home. In addition to wide-ranging government powers for control of the Press, starting in 1914 with the Defence of the Realm Act (DORA) and the creation of the Whitehall Press Bureau, the War Office had its own double censorship system for reports from the Western Front, which were censored first by the Press Section at GHQ (a part of the Intelligence Branch known as Id) and then again at the War Office.

Despite this very strong range of legal sanctions available, the power and influence exercised by the London Press remained so great that in practice it was left to be largely self-regulating. Censorship was usually of the lightest kind, and regulations were enforced only in the very rare cases of direct confrontation or open defiance of the government, such as exhibited by the *Morning Post* over the Maurice Letter. In return, most of the London Press agreed with the historian of *The Times*, that 'their task was to sustain the morale of the nation in mortal combat', distinguishing this from 'fair criticism of the government of the day'.[26] On the fighting fronts, once the need for accredited journalists was accepted in early 1915, matters were left almost entirely in the hands of local senior commanders. The extensive provincial Press was both excluded from providing accredited war correspondents and largely ignored by the censorship regulations as simply politically unimportant.[27]

In December 1915, when Haig assumed command of the British Expeditionary Force (BEF), one newspaper ran a 'Character Sketch' which began, 'There are spots on every sun and it must be confessed that the new Commander-in-Chief does not like journalists'.[28] Throughout his career, Haig's loyalties and power base depended on the political and social elite, and he disapproved of those who sought Press and public attention. Indeed, a large part of Haig's dislike of Lloyd George was what he saw as the Welshman's obsession with the Press and publicity.[29] Shortly after Haig assumed command on the Western Front, Sassoon replied on

Haig's behalf to a letter of congratulations from Gwynne of the *Morning Post*:

> He [Haig] thinks it splendid of an editor, and one that has so many journalistic inter-
> ests like yourself, to praise him for what you call his disregard of the Press! It is that he
> feels – I am sure [inserted] – that every man should be judged by his own actions and
> merits and that it is wrong to try to influence other people's judgements. All editors, as
> you will admit, are not like yourself, nor all papers like the *Morning Post*, and for those
> who wish to steer a straight course there are too many rocks ahead without going into
> the back waters of intrigue.[30]

The idea of Sassoon, a former MP from the famous Jewish financial family,
writing to the rabidly anti-Semitic, politician-hating Gwynne, is certainly an
incongruous one. But Haig was clearly at pains to put nothing in his own hand-
writing, nor to have any idea directly attributed to himself. However, Haig was
by no means a complete Press novice. Earlier in his career he had seen Lord
Roberts' deliberate cultivation of the Press at first hand, and he had himself
played a part in publicizing the Cavalry Division in the Boer or South African
War (1899–1902) through the journalist C. S. Goldmann.[31] While at First Army
he was also kept informed of French's attempts to manipulate the Press against
Kitchener.[32] The impressive collection of newspaper cuttings kept by his wife
during the war, which form part of his papers, bears testimony to his role as
a public figure. If his own Press contacts were largely indirect, then this was a
matter of personal preference. His chief mistake on taking over at GHQ was that
both he and Charteris believed that their relationship with the Press was one over
which they could exercise complete control.

The accredited correspondents at GHQ under Haig, of which there were
usually no more than six headed by Philip Gibbs, Percival Philips of the *Daily
Express*, William Beach Thomas of the *Daily Mail*, and H. Perry Robinson of
The Times, have received much criticism, including the often-quoted judgement
of Lord Rothermere at the end of the Third Battle of Ypres (often known as
'Passchendaele') that 'They don't know the truth, they don't speak the truth, and
we know that they don't'.[33] Much of this criticism, both at the time and since,[34]
attributes to the reporters the considerable power to influence opinions in
which they and their contemporaries believed. In reality, the reporters and their

GHQ escort officers (who included the former *Manchester Guardian* journalist C. E. Montague)[35] found themselves as minor players trapped in a complicated hierarchical structure dominated by politicians, generals and newspaper owners.[36] In return for access to GHQ and to some of its secrets, they practised largely voluntary self-censorship and conformed to the military restrictions placed upon them, including pooling their reports and wearing a uniform as honorary officers. Attempts to increase their number were resisted not only by GHQ, but also by the newspaper owners themselves.

As for the truthfulness of their reports, it is a matter of record that the GHQ correspondents – and Philip Gibbs in particular – wrote, and their newspapers published, vivid accounts of the fighting experiences of individual soldiers in battle, very much in the 'New Journalism' style, but always holding out hope of victory and without criticism of the higher commanders.[37] As Gibbs put it, in an introduction to a collection of his articles which was published while the war was still being fought:

> There is no criticism in this book, no judgement of actions of men, no detailed summing up of success or failure. That is not within my liberty or duty as a correspondent with the Armies in the Field.[38]

They were also too inclined to uncritically repeat information supplied by GHQ. According to Major Arthur Lee, one of the GHQ Press Section officers (who made no effort to hide his own distaste for the Press), the purpose of the GHQ daily briefings was to tell the accredited correspondents 'as much of the military situation up to date as was considered good for them'.[39]

Still, the reporters did have some independent influence, and their advice and knowledge on events in France was sought by senior officers and politicians in Whitehall. In November 1917, when Gibbs was on leave in London, he impressed Lloyd George both with his high private opinion of Major General Charles ('Tim') Harington, Chief of Staff of Second Army,[40] and by his description, given at a dinner in his honour, of the dreadful conditions of Passchendaele.[41] According to Gibbs, he 'told the naked truth that night',[42] to Lloyd George, something that he might reveal only among fellow members of the elite. It was not that the masses did not know about the casualty lists, but that the elite were convinced that the people's faith in their leaders would be shaken if any newspaper raised wider questions about the war.

On taking over at GHQ, Haig inherited a number of Press problems, including persistent complaints from the London newspapers that daily official GHQ communiqués were dull and unhelpful, and the correspondents' reports over-censored. Much of the pressure came from the War Office, particularly from Robertson who, unlike Haig, had no choice but to deal with the Press and its owners on a daily basis. 'He who lives by the river must make friends with the crocodile', as Charteris put it.[43] On 1 June 1916, Haig had his first ever meeting with the GHQ correspondents, in one of those episodes that reveals the limitations of Haig's diary and letters as an accurate record of events. According to Haig, 'They all expressed themselves as thoroughly satisfied with the facilities given them',[44] and also 'Gibbs and Beach Thomas seem quite gentlemanly fellows'.[45] Gibbs remembered Haig's opening remarks as being something along these lines:

> I think I understand fairly well what you gentlemen want . . . You want to get hold of little stories on heroism, and so forth, and to write them up in a bright way to make good reading for Mary Anne in the kitchen, and the man in the street.[46]

Although Gibbs in particular never really forgave this insult, the correspondents gamely swallowed it. They explained their problems to Haig, who to his credit listened, agreeing to allow them greater freedom of movement and better briefings in future. Haig then briefed the reporters on the GHQ position for the forthcoming offensive, using a three-page 'Memorandum on Policy for the Press', which is one of the most important pieces of evidence on Haig's own views on the war at this stage. It began with a warning:

> A danger which the country has to face at present is that of unreasoning impatience. Military history teems with instances where sound military principles have had to be abandoned owing to the pressure of ill–informed public opinion. The [P]ress is the best means to hand to prevent the danger in the present war.

There followed pages on the progressive weakening of Germany and the increasing strength of Britain, and estimates of the losses suffered by both Germany and France since 1914, concluding:

> [T]he lessons which the people of England have to learn are patience, self-sacrifice and confidence in our ability to win in the long run. The aim for which the war is being waged is the destruction of German militarism. Three years of war and the loss of one-tenth of the manhood of the nation is not too great a price to pay in so great a cause.[47]

It is not clear if the reporters were given copies of this critical document. But even the British Army's *Official History* devotes a few pages to Haig's relaxation of censorship and improvement of Press coverage of the Western Front.[48] The quality of official communiqués was also much improved, initially by the Foreign Office loaning Charteris the novelist John Buchan,[49] who had also previously served as an official correspondent at GHQ.

All this should be seen as just one more example of Haig's thoroughness, rather than any attempt to engage with the Press himself. After this first meeting, he scarcely saw the GHQ correspondents again for the duration of the war, leaving their handling almost entirely to the Press Section staff. Even so, what the GHQ correspondents wrote for the next two years may be taken as reflecting Haig's own views and wishes very closely indeed. Haig eventually trusted Gibbs and Beach Thomas enough to ask them to compose his own weekly Commander-in-Chief's reports on the war.[50] In a little ceremony held on the Hohenzollern Bridge in Cologne on 16 December 1918, Haig gave each reporter his handshake and a small Union Jack, with the words, 'Gentlemen, you have played the game like men!'[51] which was perhaps the highest compliment in his vocabulary. The five senior reporters also later received knighthoods.

Before the 1916 Somme offensive, Haig had successfully resisted pleas from Robertson to allow 'on your invitation four or five of our big newspaper proprietors', including Northcliffe, to visit GHQ.[52] But soon afterwards, Haig received his first lesson on the real power of the Press. On 4 July, Lord Esher wrote from Paris that Repington wished to visit GHQ, but expected a personal invitation from Haig such as he had received from French, and continued to receive from the Italian and French commanders. Haig's reaction was to snub Repington, replying that he could apply through Charteris like any other correspondent. Four days later, somebody had changed Haig's mind for him. He recorded in his diary:

> Among the correspondents [visiting the front] is Repington of *The Times* ... I was
> requested from London to receive Repington for the good of the Army, so I did so at
> about 10.30 a.m .... I hated seeing such a dishonest individual, but I felt it was my duty to
> the Army to do so. Otherwise, he would have been an unfriendly critic of its actions.[53]

The meeting was a little tense, with neither Haig nor Repington quite managing
to hide their mutual dislike.[54] But despite this, Repington remained a reluctant
supporter of Haig, in keeping with his broader position of supporting the Army.
Haig sought Repington's help, for example, in June 1917, over the dispute about
manpower for the forthcoming Third Ypres offensive.[55]

On 21 July 1916, Repington's employer, Northcliffe of *The Times*, also made
the visit to GHQ at Haig's invitation. Charteris, at least, realized the critical nature
of this meeting, noting that unlike Kitchener, who had withstood attacks by the
Press, Haig had virtually no public persona or support on which to draw. 'A great
deal depends on how he and D[ouglas] H[aig] get on together', Charteris concluded, 'they have very little in common'.[56] Astonishingly, the two men got on
magnificently, with Northcliffe even attending church with Haig that Sunday.[57]
Haig gave Northcliffe complete freedom of access to information within GHQ,
and in return Northcliffe wrote frequently to Haig through Sassoon. Shortly after
this visit, Northcliffe went to the War Office and offered to put his whole Press
empire at the disposal of the General Staff (an offer he had first made tentatively
to French in 1915, but without result), apparently hoping to be placed in charge of
British propaganda, for which he believed at the time he had Haig's support.[58]

Throughout autumn 1916, Pressmen and what Charteris called the 'Press
war-lords'[59] continued to visit GHQ, only the most important being seen by
Haig himself. However, a considerable network of informal contacts also existed,
with which Haig was seldom directly involved, and which has left little record.
A rare case of such a contact becoming visible occurred in October 1916, when
Haig was visited by Major General Ivor Maxse, commanding the 18th (Eastern)
Division, whose younger brother L. J. ('Leo') Maxse was the owner-editor of the
weekly *National Review*. Haig used the opportunity to put in his diary a very clear
statement of his own official position regarding the Press:

He had heard from his brother ... that [Attorney General] F. E. Smith and others have banded together with the object of having me removed from Command of the Armies in France. Gen[eral] Maxse wished to know whether I thought he ought to urge his brother to take action in the matter. I saw him along with Gen[eral] Kiggell and I said that I had no dealings with the Press personally. That my policy had always been to give the Press as free a hand as possible. To show them everything, to allow them to talk to anyone they chose, and to write what they liked, provided no secrets were given away to the enemy. In the present case, I saw no reason to depart from this policy. If his brother chose to come to France and go round the Army and see whether F.E. Smith's statements were true or false, he was free to do so in the ordinary way. I, at any rate, could take no part in a Press campaign against anyone. All my time was taken up in thinking out how to beat the enemy of Great Britain, [I mean Germany].[60]

Nonetheless, shortly after this incident, Sassoon wrote to Gwynne congratulating him on a *Morning Post* leader attacking F. E. Smith.[61] The exact connection between the *National Review* and the rise of Ivor Maxse under Haig must remain a matter of conjecture, but Leo Maxse did visit GHQ on at least three occasions, as well as corresponding with Haig.

The main persistent problem in Press coverage of the Somme, to which there was no obvious solution, was that with so few accredited reporters at GHQ both the Canadians (who had their own propaganda organization run by Aitken, himself a Canadian by birth) and the Australians received a higher Press profile than British troops, with corresponding friction and problems in neutral countries, particularly the United States. Haig reluctantly agreed to grant interviews to overseas journalists, as 'part of the British government scheme of propaganda in neutral and other countries'.[62] This continued for just over six months, until an episode occurred that has parallels with that which befell the Kaiser nine years earlier, which again reveals Haig's close interaction with the Press, and which nearly cost Haig his career.

In early 1917, shortly after a further visit by Northcliffe, Haig finally bowed to pressure from Esher and the Foreign Office to grant interviews to some French political deputies who were also journalists.[63] These were supervised by Charteris, and by the Press Section officer responsible for liaison with the French, Major the Honourable Neville Lytton. 'He is not fluent in any language', the bilingual Lytton wrote of Haig, 'but he is not much less fluent in French than he is in English.'[64]

Haig recorded only that the Frenchmen 'seemed very pleased at my receiving them',[65] while Charteris added that 'it was intended only as a formal presentation, but D[ouglas] H[aig] took the opportunity of giving them his views that the Germans were hard hit, and that this year's big attacks should be successful'.[66]

A day or so later, the reporters submitted their pieces to Lytton for censorship, but the head of the Press Section, Colonel Arthur Hutton Wilson, required them to be cleared by Charteris, who had gone home on leave. Rather than delay the pieces, Lytton prevailed on Hutton Wilson to send them to Charteris at home in Britain, who barely glanced at them before returning them to the waiting messenger. From Charteris' description they had already been censored at the War Office, ordinarily the second tier of censorship; he later claimed that he expected them to go back to GHQ for clearance by Haig personally or by Kiggell, which was not normal procedure.[67]

No one thought anything of this matter until Charteris came back from leave on 15 February. On that day, Haig's interview appeared in several Paris newspapers, each version slightly different, and all giving long and ostensibly verbatim quotations from Haig on the critical importance of the Western Front, and the inevitability of victory there. The opinions were clearly Haig's, although the expressions were equally clearly not. Lytton felt that the problem lay in over-literal translation: what was simple rousing speech in French appeared as bombast in English.[68] To make matters worse, a translation of the version in the French newspaper l'Information also appeared in that day's The Times together with an editorial fully supporting Haig's views. Before the end of the day a Parliamentary question had been put down by the Labour MP, Philip Snowdon, and the War Office was demanding an explanation. Even King George V expressed his surprise that Haig could have given such an interview, communicating his concern through his private secretary to Lord Derby, the Secretary of State for War.[69]

At GHQ, Haig's response to these events was first to deny that he had ever given such an interview (which he had quite probably forgotten); then to argue that he had been misquoted; and then, having obtained the French reaction (which was overwhelmingly favourable), to wonder what the fuss was about.[70] Charteris also at first denied that he had ever seen the pieces, until Lytton and

Hutton Wilson produced the written evidence.[71] Repington, in London, hugely enjoyed Haig's embarrassment, spreading completely false stories over the week-end that the French were incensed at Haig's statements, and that an unknown enemy of Haig in the War Office (whom he identified as 'Z') had deliberately passed the reports in order to bring Haig down.[72]

On Monday 18 February, Robertson arrived at GHQ for lunch, and Lytton trav-elled back to London with the CIGS, briefing him on the way. The next morning, Lytton faced the War Cabinet with Robertson by his side. Neither Lloyd George, who Lytton described as 'in a towering passion',[73] nor Curzon was inclined to believe a word of Lytton's story. Bonar Law calmed the meeting down, and also spoke for the government in the Commons that afternoon. Lord Derby wrote to Lloyd George after the War Cabinet, advising him that any attempt to reprimand Haig over these interviews could well provoke his resignation.[74] Lytton briefed Northcliffe at home on the episode, as a consequence of which *The Times* and the other Northcliffe newspapers took a conciliatory line next day. According to Lytton, 'Haig would have gone' without Northcliffe's backing.[75]

Haig received letters of support from Northcliffe, and also from Aitken, (who had just accepted his peerage as Lord Beaverbrook, having hoped for a cabinet post under Lloyd George), who wrote that 'A sort of attempt has been made to take advantage of what slipped through in the Press, but this has been frustrated entirely because no decent paper would touch it'.[76] Derby's strategy for recon-ciliation, aimed simultaneously at both Haig and Lloyd George, was to blame Charteris entirely for what had happened.[77] Haig may have reacted by restrict-ing Charteris' authority, if only for a while. One of the staff officers at GHQ, Lieutenant Colonel James Edmonds (later the Army's official historian) recalled that 'Charteris was out of favour in January–February 1917 owing to a bad mis-hap over the French Press, and was not in a position to know what was going on' regarding Haig's planning for future military operations.[78] Major Lee also wrote that Lloyd George saw Charteris as the root of the supposed conspiracy, and that it was this incident which convinced Lloyd George that Charteris must be removed from Haig's side.[79]

Lytton reported to Haig on his return from London, and all assumed that the episode was closed. But the greatest damage had already been done. Lloyd George had sensed a deliberate conspiracy (although a less likely military conspirator than the aristocratic aesthete Lytton – the brother of a peer and a notable society artist – would be hard to imagine), believing that Haig was challenging his new authority as prime minister with the backing of Northcliffe and *The Times*. Without waiting to check, on the afternoon that the first stories appeared, Lloyd George had visited the War Office together with Hankey, where he suggested to a French liaison officer that the British Commander-in-Chief on the Western Front be placed under French command, the idea which became the basis of the notorious Calais Conference later that month.[80]

This Press episode was not the cause of the bad relations between Haig and Lloyd George. Given the level of heightened tension and disagreement, any small incident might have produced a confrontation. But it was the spark that lit the bonfire, leading to that confrontation taking the particular form that it did, with all the consequences for 1917 and beyond. Meanwhile, any friction between GHQ and the War Office over Press policy had largely ceased, partly through the reforms instituted by Haig, which continued through 1917, separating the Press Section from GHQ's propaganda organizations; partly through further changes in London, and the bringing of newsmen into the government propaganda organizations by Lloyd George;[81] and partly by Northcliffe being appointed in May 1917 as head of a British mission to the United States, keeping him out of the country for most of the year.

In September 1917, Gwynne of the *Morning Post* visited Haig, following this up with a letter to Charteris arguing that Haig must improve his public profile in order to oppose anti-Haig sentiments in London.[82] Charteris' resulting *cri de coeur* shows how far he had come from the belief that the Press could be controlled from GHQ:

But if we use the Press to crack up D[ouglas] H[aig] we shall have L[loyd] G[eorge] outing him at once. If we let the correspondents have an interview with him, we shall have a repetition of last February's episode. If we check Philip Gibbs writing his 'horror-mongering' stuff we shall have his paper down our throat. If we say the Boche is beaten, or even that his morale is being lowered, we shall have the W[ar] O[ffice] itself saying that we are over-optimistic and thus making it harder for Robertson to screw the necessary men and munitions out of L[loyd] [G[eorge]. All the same I have taken steps to do what I can to give some effect to Gwynne's views, for they are right and it is worth taking the risk.[83]

Newspaper owners, some editors, and even Repington, visited or wrote to Haig during Third Ypres,[84] and there is just enough evidence to suggest GHQ's complicity in a deliberate Press campaign, which Lloyd George and his associates were convinced that Haig was orchestrating through Robertson.[85] Lloyd George raised the matter with Haig directly at an angry meeting in Paris in November, although apparently stopping short of an outright accusation.[86] This does in some way explain the remarkable Press and popular reaction to the Battle of Cambrai. It was not simply a spontaneous expression of hope after the failure of Third Ypres, but a conscious attempt to boost Haig's popularity by his supporters.

It was at this critical point, at the end of 1917, that Haig lost the support of Northcliffe, who had returned to Britain. The exact circumstances may have been appropriately trivial: Northcliffe visited GHQ on 7 December, but became angry and insulted when Haig showed boredom and irritation with his reminiscences about the United States.[87] The first sign of the break was criticism in the Northcliffe Press of British generalship over the German counterattack at Cambrai. As a member of the GHQ enquiry board into the battle, Ivor Maxse (now commanding XVIII Corps), retaliated by blaming the Press for alleged false reporting, and suggested even greater military control at GHQ over the accredited correspondents – a suggestion which Haig wisely ignored.[88] However, the experience of Cambrai once more left Haig with little taste for greater involvement with the Press.

Whatever the immediate cause, the underlying motive for Northcliffe's change of allegiance was undoubtedly the prospect of political office. Northcliffe rejected Lloyd George's first tentative offer – that of the newly created Air Ministry – in the most public way imaginable, by posting his rejection in *The Times* before Lloyd George was informed of it.[89] His brother, Lord Rothermere, was given the job instead. Haig came to believe that Northcliffe's aim was nothing short of the War Office itself; a belief which formed an important part of Haig's continuing support for Lord Derby as Secretary of State for War in February 1918, when Derby was contemplating resignation.[90] It was Northcliffe's change of allegiance that led Repington to leave *The Times* for the *Morning Post*, and to his involvement in the Maurice Letter in May, the sending of which Haig utterly condemned.[91]

The neglect of the BEF's achievements in 1918 can also be traced in part to changes in Press policy both in Whitehall and GHQ at the start of the year. With Beaverbrook, Rothermere and (effectively) Northcliffe joining other Press magnates in government, newspapers increasingly reflected the Whitehall perspective that the war would last until 1919. Meanwhile, Charteris' successor as head of the Intelligence Branch, Brigadier General E. W. Cox, had no wish to deal directly with Beaverbrook or Northcliffe, who were beginning to argue for direct control of GHQ's Press and propaganda apparatus. The Press Section, renamed the Censorship and Publicity Section, was transferred to the new Staff Duties Branch of GHQ under Major General Guy Dawney, who also showed no interest in it. While the handful of GHQ correspondents remained quite inadequate in numbers, Haig did nothing to correct this, nor to win back Press support. In consequence, there was no policy or desire either in Whitehall or at GHQ to mitigate against the claims of a rout by Fifth Army in spring 1918, nor to publicize the British victories of later in the year.

In September 1918, in response to a letter of congratulation from Henry Wilson as CIGS, Haig wrote rather pointedly, 'I am not nor am I likely to be a "famous general". For that must we not have pandered to Repington and the Gutter Press?',[92] a remark which could serve as his professional epitaph. Haig's enforced interaction with the Press helped shape both his strategy and some of his battles, but his few attempts to deal with them directly were clumsy and handicapped by his limited political understanding. His preferred practice of using only indirect methods was undoubtedly correct given his own personality and limitations, but it has left a legacy of ambiguity and fragmented evidence that has prevented this important aspect of his military life being understood and valued as it deserves. The only view of events that can be positively disproved from the available record is that which Haig himself sought to promote:

that he continued the war as he began it, an apolitical soldier who engaged with the Press only when directly ordered to do so. At the other extreme, the view of Lloyd George, that Haig both initiated and directed a Press campaign to promote his own position against that of the government, remains now as it was then: a matter of opinion.

NOTES

1 Blake, R. (1952), *The Private Papers of Douglas Haig 1914–1919*. London: Eyre and Spottiswoode, Introduction, p. 64.

2 Neiberg, M. S. (2004), 'Cromwell on the bed stand: allied civil-military relations in World War I', in J. Macleod and P. Purseigle (eds), *Uncovered Fields: Perspectives in First World War Studies*. Leiden: Brill, p. 61.

3 Asquith, [H. H.] Earl of Oxford and (1928), *Memories and Reflections 1852–1927: Volume II*. London: Cassell, p. 235.

4 For a brief and interesting summary of this complex subject *see* Broks, P. (1996), *Media Science Before the Great War*. London: Macmillan, pp. 14–17.

5 National Library of Scotland: Papers of Field Marshal Earl Haig [hereafter Haig Papers] 3155.106 Diary entry 4 August 1916. Entries in the Haig Diary that appear in either of two published versions: Blake (1952) op. cit., or Sheffield, G. and Bourne, J. (eds) (2005), *Douglas Haig: War Diaries and Letters 1914–1918*. London: Weidenfeld & Nicholson, are cited from those sources for convenience.

6 *See*, for example, Riddell, [G.] Lord (1933), *Lord Riddell's War Diary 1914–1918*. London: Ivor Nicolson and Watson, especially p. 231.

7 Beaverbrook, [W. M.] Lord (1956), *Men and Power 1917–1918*. London: Collins, Introduction, p. xxii.

8 Blake (1952) op. cit., p. 189.

9 Esher [O] Viscount, (ed.) (1938), *Journals and Letters of Reginald Viscount Esher, 4 Volume 1916–1930*. London: Ivor Nicolson and Watson, p. 175.

10 Hoare, P. (1997), *Wilde's Last Stand: Decadence, Conspiracy and the First World War*. London: Duckworth, p. 211.

11 Gibbs, P. (1920), *Realities of War*. London: William Heinemann, p. 46. [US edition (1920), *Now It Can Be Told*. New York: Harper & Brothers.]

12 *See* Beckett, I. F. W. (ed.) (1986), *The Army and the Curragh Incident, 1914*. London: Army Records Society.

13 Imperial War Museum, London [hereafter IWM] Department of Documents, The Military Correspondence of H. A. Gwynne [hereafter Gwynne Papers], *passim*. Callwell, C. E. (1927), *Field Marshal Sir Henry Wilson: Volume I*. London: Cassell, p. 200 and 241; Woodward, D. R. (ed.) (1989), *The Military Correspondence of Field Marshal Sir William Robertson, Chief of the Imperial General Staff December 1915–February 1918*. London: Army Records Society, p. 56 and 115; Williams, J. (1983), *Byng of Vimy: General and Governor-General*. London: Leo Cooper, p. 55 and 85.

14 Jackson, S. (1968), *The Sassoons*. London: Heinemann, p. 166 et seq. Philip and Siegfried Sassoon are often described as 'cousins', but their relationship was not

close either in terms of blood or friendship; Philip (the third baronet) was the grandson of Siegfried's grandfather's half-brother.

15 Charteris, J. (1931), *At GHQ*. London: Cassell, p. 94.

16 IWM Department of Documents 66/121/1 *The World War I Diary of Lt. Col. Arthur Neale Lee* [hereafter Lee Papers], unpublished typescript, p. 109 for early 1917. Lee served as a major for most of the war, being promoted after its end.

17 [Anon.] (1952), *The History of The Times Volume IV. The 150th Anniversary and Beyond 1912–1948. Part I, Chapters 1–XII, 1912–1920*. London: Times Printing House, p. 274. *See also* Repington's own account: Repington, C. à C. (1920), *The First World War: Volume I*. London: Constable, London, pp. 36–9, and Bristow, A. (1995), *A Serious Disappointment: The Battle of Aubers Ridge 1915 and the Munitions Scandal*. London: Leo Cooper, pp. 147–58.

18 Repington (1920), op. cit., Volume I, p. 27.

19 Blake (1952), op. cit., p. 93.

20 Ibid, p. 93; Charteris (1931), op. cit., p. 94. *See also* Repington's 'Shell Scandal' dispatch and other newspaper reports of the battle in Bristow (1995), op. cit., pp. 152–4, together with other comments on the Press coverage of the Battle of Aubers Ridge on pp. 173–4. Repington (1920), op. cit., makes no reference to the allegation.

21 Esher (1938), op. cit., p. 166.

22 Asquith (1928), op. cit., Volume I, p. 238.

23 Charteris (1931), op. cit., p. 193.

24 *Daily Telegraph*, 28 October 1908; *see also* Massie, R. K. (1991), *Dreadnought: Britain, Germany and the Coming of the Great War*. New York: Random House, pp. 684–94; Steiner, Z. (1977), *Britain and the Origins of the First World War*. London: Macmillan, pp. 52–4; and the commentary by the two chief protagonists in the affair: Wilhelm II (ex-Kaiser) (1922), *My Memoirs 1878–1918*. London: Cassell, pp. 115–19; Bülow, Prince von, (1931), *Memoirs 1903–1909*. London: Putnam, pp. 340–50.

25 Towle, P. (1975), 'The debate on wartime censorship in Britain 1902–1914', in B. Bond and I. Roy, (eds), *War and Society, A Yearbook of Military History*. London: Croom Helm, *passim*.

26 (1952) *The History of The Times Volume IV, Part I*, p. 218.

27 This meant that it was much easier for soldiers to publish letters and photographs in their local newspapers, which are a valuable source of historical information. *See* the use made of such sources in, for example, Brown, M. (1978), *Tommy Goes To War*. London: J. M. Dent; and Bourne, J. M. (1989), *Britain and the Great War 1914–1918*. London: Edward Arnold.

28 *The Sunday Times*, 19 December 1915.

29 Jackson (1968), op. cit., p. 167; Pound, R. and Harmsworth, G. (1959), *Northcliffe*. London: Cassell, p. 506.

30 IWM Gwynne Papers, Folio 4, HAG/29, Philip Sassoon to H. A. Gwynne, 6 January 1916, marked 'Confidential and Private'.

31 *See* Goldmann, C. S. (1902), *With General French and the Cavalry in South Africa*. London: Macmillan, Preface, p. xi; Amery, L. S. (1953), *My Political Life, Volume I, England Before the Storm 1896–1914*. London: Hutchinson, pp. 128–33.

32 Blake (1952), op. cit., p. 93.

33 Quoted in Masterman, L. (1939), *C. F .C. Masterman: A Biography*. London: Nicholson and Watson, p. 296.

34 *See* Knightley, P. (1982), *The First Casualty*. London: Quartet, pp. 79–96; Farrar, M. J. (1998), *News From the Front, War Correspondents on the Western Front 1914–1918*. Thrupp: Sutton.

35 *See* Messinger, G. S. (1992), *British Propaganda and the State in the First World War*. Manchester: Manchester University Press, pp. 235–48; Sanders, M. L. and Taylor, P. M. (1982), *British Propaganda During the First World War*. London: Macmillan, *passim*.

36 Grieves, K. (1996), 'War correspondents and conducting officers on the Western Front from 1915', in H. Cecil and P. H. Liddle (eds), *Facing Armageddon, The First World War Experienced*. London: Leo Cooper, pp. 719–35.

37 Gibbs, P. (1946), *The Pageant of The Years*. London: William Heinemann, pp. 162–9, 207 and 226.

38 Gibbs, P. (1918), *From Bapaume to Passchendaele, 1917*. n.p., Introduction, p. 21; also quoted and criticized in Lloyd George, D. (1936), *The War Memoirs of David Lloyd George: Volume II*. London: Odhams Press, p. 1319.

39 IWM Lee Papers, p. 93 for July 1916.

40 Riddell (1933), op. cit., p. 300.

41 (1952) *The History of The Times, Volume IV, Part 1*, p. 345.

42 Gibbs (1946), op. cit., p. 208.

43 Charteris (1931), op. cit., pp. 153–4 citing his diary entry for 8 July 1916.

44 Haig to Robertson quoted in Woodward (1989), op. cit., p. 56.

45 Haig Papers 3155.107, Diary entry 1 June 1916.

46 Gibbs (1920), op. cit., p. 24.

47 Haig Papers 3155.107, Diary entry 26 May 1916 Appendix 'Memorandum on Policy for Press'. (The entry for 1 July gives this memorandum as apparently written on 29 May, but the difference is not significant.)

48 Edmonds, J. E. (general ed.) (various dates), *The History of the Great War based on Official Documents: Military Operations*. London: HMSO) [hereafter *Official History*] (1932), *Official History Military Operations France and Belgium 1916, Volume 1*. London: HMSO, pp. 144–8.

49 Charteris (1931), op. cit., p. 170; Haig Papers 3155.108 Diary entry 27 September 1916.

50 Gibbs (1946), op. cit., p. 168.

51 Gibbs (1920), op. cit., p. 24, and (1946) op. cit., p. 239. The ceremony was also filmed by the official cine-cameramen; *see* Smither, R. (ed.) (1994), *Imperial War Museum Film Catalogue Volume I: the First World War Archive*. Trowbridge: Flicks Books, p. 134.

52 Correspondence between Robertson and Haig quoted in Woodward (1989), op. cit., pp. 55–6.

53 Haig Papers 3155.107 Diary entry 8 July 1916.

54 Repington (1920), op. cit., Volume I, pp. 265–6; Charteris (1931), op. cit., p. 163.

55 Blake (1952), op. cit., p. 241.

56 Charteris (1931), op. cit., p. 156.

57 Haig Papers 3155.107, Dairy entries 21–2 July 1916; Charteris (1931), op. cit., pp. 156–8; Pound and Harmsworth, op. cit., pp. 502–6.

58 Pound and Harmsworth (1959), op. cit., p. 503; Esher, op. cit., p. 60.

59 Charteris (1931), op. cit., p. 225.

60 Blake (1952), op. cit., p. 170. (The last three words, given in brackets here, were added to the typewritten version by Haig at some later date.)

61 IWM Gwynne Papers Folio 4 HAG/29, Philip Sassoon to H. A. Gwynne, 8 November 1916.

62 Haig Papers 3155.107, Diary entry 29 July 1916.

63 Haig's diary mentions one interview as taking place on Thursday 1 February; Charteris, who was present and based his later account on letters home, also mentions only one interview, but places it four days earlier. Other sources refer to 'interviews'. All sources are consistent that some kind of group interview took place.

64 Lytton, N. (1920), *The Press and the General Staff*. London: Collins, p. 66.

65 Haig Papers 3155.110, Diary entry 1 February 1917.

66 Charteris (1931), op. cit., p. 192.

67 Ibid, pp. 192–4; Lytton (1920), op. cit., pp. 69–70.

68 Lytton (1920), op. cit., p. 69.

69 Liverpool Records Office, Papers of the Earl of Derby, 27/2 Stamfordham to Derby and Derby to Stamfordham, 15 February 1917.

70 Haig Papers 3155.110, Diary entries 15–18 February 1917. Other papers relating to this episode, including newspaper articles, accounts, and reports of the parliamentary debate, are appended to this section of Haig's diary. *See also* the two War Cabinet discussions of the incident: The National Archives, Kew [hereafter TNA] CAB 23/1 War Cabinet meeting 73 of 19 February 1917, and War Cabinet meeting 75 of 20 February 1917, pp. 244–9, and the account in IWM Lee Papers pp. 118–19 for February 1917.

71 IWM Lee Papers, p. 119 for February 1917.

72 Repington (1920), op. cit., Volume I, pp. 460–2.

73 Lytton (1920), op. cit., p. 70; TNA CAB 23/1 War Cabinet meeting 75 20 February 1917.

74 Liverpool Record Office, Papers of the Earl of Derby 27/2 Derby to Lloyd George 19 February 1917.

75 Lytton (1920), op. cit., p. 72.

76 Charteris (1931), op. cit., p. 194.

77 Liverpool Record Office, Papers of the Earl of Derby 27/2, Derby to Haig 20 February 1917 and House of Lords Record Office, Papers of Earl Lloyd George, F/14/4/21, Derby to Lloyd George 20 February 1917.

78 Australian War Memorial Canberra, AWM 38 Papers of Charles E. W. Bean, 3DL 7953/34, Edmonds to Bean 25 June 1930.

79 IWM Lee Papers, p. 119 for February 1917.

80 The French officer's report to his superiors is quoted as an appendix to Spears, E. L. (1939), *Prelude To Victory*. London: Jonathan Cape, p. 546. *See also* Woodward, D. R. (1983), *Lloyd George and the Generals*. London: University of Delaware Press, pp. 144–5.

81 Messinger (1992), op. cit., pp. 85–98 and 122–61; Reeves, N. (1986), *Official British Film Propaganda During the First World War*. London: Croom Helm, pp. 23–32.

82 Charteris (1931), op. cit., p. 253; Blake (1952), op. cit., p. 254.

83 Charteris (1931), op. cit., p. 254.

84 Repington (1920), op. cit., Volume II, p. 98 and 100–2; Charteris (1931), op. cit., p. 255 and 260; Blake (1952), op. cit., p. 256 and 263.

85 Lloyd George (1936), op. cit., Volume II, pp. 1318–1320; Repington (1920), op. cit., Volume II, p. 148.

86 Blake (1952), op. cit., p. 263.

87 Ibid, p. 65; Charteris (1931), op. cit., p. 273; Pound and Harmsworth (1959), op. cit., p. 598.

88 TNA WO 158/53 'Cambrai Enquiry – File No. 1', Appendix L signed by Ivor Maxse; also quoted and criticized in Lloyd George (1936) op. cit., Volume II, p. 1340. *See also* Baynes, J. (1995), *Far From a Donkey: The Life of General Sir Ivor Maxse*. London: Brassey's, p. 182.

89 Riddell (1933), op. cit., p. 291.

90 Blake (1952), op. cit., p. 287.

91 Ibid., p. 308.

89 Quoted in Terraine, J. (1963), *Douglas Haig: The Educated Soldier*. London: Hutchinson, p. 43.

3

Blackadder Goes Forth *and the 'Two Western Fronts'*
Debate 1914–1918

INTRODUCTION

It is certainly unusual, and it may well be unique, for a television light comedy series to be cited repeatedly as evidence in a major historical debate. Yet this is the case for the BBC (British Broadcasting Corporation) series *Blackadder Goes Forth*, first shown on British television in 1989, and set among British troops on the Western Front of the First World War (or 'Great War', as historians have increasingly returned to call it). Specifically, the image of the Western Front evoked by the series has been used by historians as a focus for what has become known as the 'Two Western Fronts' debate. Emerging in the 1990s as one of the more important debates in British historiography and historical education, this recognizes that in the last quarter of the twentieth century two distinct views developed of the Western Front and its experience for the British. One view, which is based chiefly on analysis of cultural artefacts and literature, tends to support the stereotype of the Western Front which was manifest in late twentieth-century popular culture, and which is also still evoked by more traditionalist British military historians.[1] The other view, which may broadly be described as revisionist, is based on extensive research into the political and military history of the Western Front in the last quarter of a century, and questions many of the assumptions of this stereotype. Although some historians have sought to move beyond the confrontation created by these two views of the Western Front, others have taken up what may truly be described as entrenched positions.[2]

As a highly successful television light comedy, *Blackadder Goes Forth* is not only an excellent example of mass popular culture, but also is set firmly in the context of the traditional stereotype, and it has become a particular target for revisionist historians. Hugh Cecil and Peter H. Liddle, the editors of the published proceedings of the landmark 1994 Leeds University conference on the First World War, which marked the emergence of the revisionist perspective as a mainstream position in British historical studies, cited the *Blackadder* series specifically as perpetuating 'myths which persist in the face of strong contrary evidence', regarding *Blackadder* and other television programmes as 'the greatest influence in moulding opinion today'.[3] Other critics of the influence of *Blackadder* on our historical understanding of the Western Front (however much they may have enjoyed it as television) include the leading revisionists Gary Sheffield and Brian Bond,[4] while Jeremy Black has taken a wider view of the series' popularity, coupled with its relentlessly cynical view of the futility of warfare, as evidence of a 'decline of deference' and late twentieth-century anti-militarism, drawing parallels with the American comedy television drama series *M*A*S*H* (1972–1983), set in a military field hospital during the Korean War.[5]

As a further example of its importance, *Blackadder Goes Forth* had, within a decade of its first transmission, become well enough established in the British popular consciousness to become part of television history. In 2000, a British television programme, *100 Great Television Moments*, presented clips based on viewers' votes for the most memorable television events of the century. The top of this poll was dominated by factual episodes (the winner was the 1969 moon landings), but the final 'over the top' scene from the last episode of *Blackadder Goes Forth* was voted in at number nine, one of only two fictional pieces to make the top ten.[6] In his 1999 BBC television series *The Western Front*, Richard Holmes, in the episode dealing with the Battle of the Somme, used in commentary a recognizable paraphrase of one of the more memorable *Blackadder* lines, 'Clearly, Field Marshal Haig is about to make another gargantuan effort to move his drinks cabinet six inches closer to Berlin',[7] on the assumption that the phrase had achieved almost proverbial status. Most interestingly of all from the perspective of the use of television as an aid to teaching history, a 1996 BBC television documentary on the revisionist view of the Western Front, *Haig: The Unknown Soldier*, used scenes from *Blackadder Goes Forth* intercut with commentary from historians in order to establish the stereotype before subjecting it to scrutiny.[8]

As a light comedy, *Blackadder Goes Forth* was naturally not created with any deep historical intentions, and it may seem strange that revisionist historians have taken it so seriously. The reason is that it provides an unusually good example of what Sellar and Yeatman's jovial classic of bad history, *1066 And All That*, called 'all the history that you can remember'[9] – a comic expression of a version of the Western Front that has become accepted in late twentieth-century culture and that is now seen by revisionists as profoundly unhistorical. As such, *Blackadder Goes Forth* contains moments of deliberate seriousness which have led to its being taken as a realistic – or at least only partly satirical – representation of the Western Front. It has evoked responses concerning the real events of the war quite unlike those of comparable British light or farcical comedies set in a historical context, such as the BBC series *Dad's Army* (1968–1977) portraying the British Army's Home Guard, and *'Allo, 'Allo* (1982–1992) ostensibly portraying the French resistance, both set during the Second World War.

By way of illustration of the issue, and as a fine example of the 'Two Western Fronts' of history and of popular culture, as part of the commemoration of the 80th anniversary of the First World War's end in November 1998, the newspaperman Max Hastings (later Sir Max) wrote for the London *Evening Standard*:

> 'Let us start with *foie gras*. And then perhaps a *piece de boeuf a l'os* . . . [We are] in that most delightful of hostelries the Château de Montreuil . . . You still do not care for champagne? The men who presided for four years over the greatest of military disasters had no such qualms. For here, between 1916 and 1918, was the headquarters of Field Marshal Sir John Haig, commander-in-chief of the British Army, who like most of his fellow generals dined nightly off china and crystal among the finest fare that Montreuil could provide.[10]

This example is chosen from many, with neither mockery nor hostile intent, but as having appeared in a major British newspaper, by an author who also enjoys no small reputation as a military historian. In fact, General Sir *Douglas* Haig (field marshal from late 1916) was Commander-in-Chief of the British Army in France from late 1915 to 1919 (the post of Commander in Chief of the British Army was abolished in 1904). His headquarters took up the entire town of Montreuil, but his own residence was a nearby simply furnished country house called the Château de Beaurepaire. This house was used as a base and to meet important visitors, otherwise Haig was at least as likely to be at a forward headquarters (or by 1918 in a headquarters train). Haig suffered from both asthma and a stomach malady, and both drank and ate sparingly, preferring water with meals. His staff could indeed provide hospitality for important guests and for rare formal occasions, (as could the staff of the American General Dwight D. Eisenhower at his headquarters in the sumptuous Palace of Versailles in late 1944, or almost any general in a comparable position throughout history). But Haig's normal regime involved a working day of about 18 hours, with both a brief lunch and dinner taken up by visitors. In this, Haig was in no way exceptional when compared to other British general officers on the Western Front, many of who suffered illnesses from overwork, including members of Haig's own staff. Also, despite positive orders (issued in October 1915) not to risk their lives in the front lines, some 78 British generals were killed in action or died on active service in the course of the war.[11]

It might be argued that such detail is only important for specialists in the field. But if, for example, a modern newspaper article had proclaimed that in 1911 the wicked King Edward IX had both practised the *droit de seigneur* and ruled without parliament, the average educated reader, without necessarily knowing about the constitutional crisis faced that year by the conventionally uxorious King George V, would nevertheless be confident that what was written was nonsense. It is hard to imagine such a divergence between the known facts and the popular image in any other aspect of twentieth-century British history than that of the Western Front, and it is trying to understand this image and its origins that has led historians to *Blackadder Goes Forth*.

THE SERIES AS TELEVISION

Since *Blackadder Goes Forth* may not be familiar to all readers, it is necessary (with due apologies) to describe the series and its origins, treating it as a television cultural artefact.[12] Altogether, four main *Blackadder* series were made for BBC television at two-year intervals from 1983 onwards, each of six 30-minute episodes. Together they represent one of the more important world-wide popular and commercial successes for British television of recent times, remaining available both in broadcast round the world and in videocassette and videodisk formats. Light, farcical comedies linked together by continuity of production, cast and style (and allegedly described by one participant as 'situation tragedy'), each series was set in a deliberately fictionalised past, featuring a cynical and scheming member of the Blackadder family and his inept servant Baldrick, in each case played by Rowan Atkinson and Tony Robinson respectively. After an initial pilot episode was filmed in 1982, but never shown on British television (although it was transmitted in the USA in the following year), the first series was transmitted in 1983 with a rewritten and recast version of the pilot as its opening episode, starring Atkinson as Prince Edmund, younger son of a fictitious late mediaeval English king, known as *The Black Adder*. The second series, *Blackadder II*, featured Lord Edmund Blackadder as a favourite at the court of Queen Elizabeth I. This was followed by *Blackadder the Third*, featuring Mister Edmund Blackadder, butler to Prince George in Regency England. The fourth series, (hence the punning title *Blackadder Goes Forth*), was also the last, and featured Captain Edmund Blackadder of the British Army. The gradual slide of the scheming and ambitious Blackadder character down the social scale through history, from prince to harassed Army captain, was part of the humour. In addition, a one-hour Dickensian parody special, *Blackadder's Christmas Carol*, was shown on television in 1987. Since then, the principal actors have appeared individually or together as *Blackadder* characters for various charity benefits, including twice on BBC television in 1998, once for the charity Comic Relief in a short sketch called *The Cavalier Years*, and once for the 50th birthday of Prince Charles in another cavalier sketch, *The King's Birthday*. In January 2000 the London

Millennium Dome exhibition included a specially made short film, *Blackadder Back and Forth*, in which the characters journey by time machine back to important moments in British history.[13] All four series have been repeatedly shown in syndication around the world, they have been released on audio and video, and the complete published scripts have appeared in book form.[14] In short, the collected *Blackadder* series and characters have taken on a much wider cultural life than the relatively small number of original episodes would suggest and, given the diversity of forms in which they are available, no estimate of a total viewing audience is possible, except to say that it is substantial.

The sixth and final episode of *Blackadder Goes Forth* was appropriately entitled *Goodbyee!*, the title being taken from a popular music hall song of the First World War, made familiar to modern audiences through its use in the 1963 stage production *Oh! What a Lovely War* by Joan Littlewood, and the 1969 Richard Attenborough film of the same name. The setting is a dugout in a British frontline trench, somewhere on the Western Front during the First World War, home to Captain Blackadder, late of the (fictitious) 19th/45th East African Rifles, and to the anonymous and seldom seen company of British soldiers that he commands. Captain Blackadder shares his dugout with two other main characters: Private S. Baldrick, late of the 'Turnip Street Workhouse Pals' (a joke at the expense of the real British 'Pals Battalions' of 1914), and Lieutenant the Honourable George Colthurst St Barleigh, played by Hugh Laurie as an typical British 'silly ass' of the Bertie Wooster type. (Laurie would later play Wooster in the television series *Jeeves and Wooster* 1990–1993, opposite Stephen Fry as Jeeves). The exact date and location are irrelevant; various (and often contradictory) references place the setting as 1917 in one of the two main British areas of fighting, Flanders or the Somme region; the company never leaves the front line, Blackadder remains in his dugout and nothing much changes. The 'Big Push' is looming in a few days, as it has been throughout the series, and Blackadder is determined not to take part in it. The two other main characters in the series do not share the life of the trenches. Ensconced at headquarters in a sumptuous chateau (at least one hundred miles to the rear) is General Sir Anthony Cecil Hogmanay Melchett, played by Stephen Fry, and Blackadder's arch-enemy, the sneering staff officer

Captain Kevin Darling, played by Tim McInnerny, whose principal ambition is to survive the war and keep wicket for the Croydon Gentlemen's cricket team. Throughout the series, the main interaction is between the front-line dugout and headquarters; no soldier of the company other than Baldrick is ever identified, and the German enemy only rarely makes an appearance.

At the end of this last episode, General Melchett orders Captain Darling to join Blackadder's company at the front, and together with Lieutenant George, Baldrick and the rest of the company they charge 'over the top' (using tactics that, as revisionists would know, were long out of date by 1917), all of them going to certain death. Despite the rest of the series, this final moment is anything but comic, with the scene of the figures moving in slow motion through the mud of no man's land slowly mixing to a green field with waving red poppies, backed by sombre music instead of the series' normal jaunty theme tune.

With its disregard of time, space and authenticity, *Blackadder Goes Forth* may be seen as the quintessential representation of the postmodernist Western Front, first described and popularized in Paul Fussell's very influential book of 1975, *The Great War and Modern Memory*,[15] which has played a major part in the teaching of the war's literature. In particular, Fussell and his followers argue that the Western Front can only be understood as a uniquely *unhistorical* event, taking place outside time. Fussell's work has since been subject to considerable criticism by revisionist historians pointing out his lack of historical rigour, and his perspective has, to some extent, been discredited.[16] But the persistence of his influence, and the basic method of approach to the First World War through literature and cultural artefacts, has contributed greatly to the existing 'Two Western Fronts'. As an expression of the Western Front as eternal, unchanging and futile, the *Blackadder* view might almost have been taken directly from Fussell. At one point Captain Blackadder describes how the war 'would be a damn sight simpler if we just stayed in England and shot 50,000 of our men a week', a more than ten-fold exaggeration of the real death rate for the war coupled with the assumption that the losses are all for nothing.[17] In a curiously gratuitous scene in the last episode, Field Marshal Haig (played by Geoffrey Palmer) is shown at his own headquarters, casually knocking over toy soldiers on a terrain model with his hand to represent his own side's casualties, and then sweeping them into a dustpan.

All four of the *Blackadder* series owed much (and much of their success) to a variety of British comedy traditions, including an acknowledged debt from *Blackadder Goes Forth* to the long running *Dad's Army*. But what was new about the series was the fusion of comic talent from two styles that appeared together in the early 1980s. One of these was a revival of 'Oxbridge' satire, a style traceable ultimately to the 1960s *Beyond the Fringe* review by undergraduates from Oxford and Cambridge Universities. Atkinson himself and fellow Oxford graduate, Richard Curtis, together scripted the first *Blackadder* series, while Hugh Laurie and Stephen Fry were products of the famous Cambridge University Footlights Dramatic Club. John Lloyd, who produced all four series, also added a strong element of continuity. The remaining three *Blackadder* series were co-scripted by Curtis with Ben Elton, a leading exponent of the rather more aggressive and politically orientated 'Alternative Comedy' style, which emerged in London in the same period. Rik Mayall, another prominent exponent of Alternative Comedy, made guest appearances in the second and fourth series as different incarnations of the flamboyant 'Lord Flashheart'. Atkinson had first come to prominence in the BBC satirical series *Not the Nine O'Clock News* (1979–1982), on which Curtis – barely out of university for a year – had also worked as a writer; this had been followed immediately by the first series of the anarchic situation comedy *The Young Ones* (1982–1984), which established Mayall and the Alternative Comedy style as viable television material.

In terms of themes and general *mise en scène*, the first series, *The Black Adder*, was to some extent the exception among the four, particularly in being set in a completely fictitious reign (the premise was that King Henry VII had managed to falsify all history books, and that one of the Princes in the Tower in fact reigned for 13 years as Richard IV, with Prince Edmund 'The Black Adder' as his younger son). Thereafter, the Curtis/Elton scripts used a broad-brush approach based on the fictional and feature film version of history. The second and third series, set in Elizabethan and Regency times, represent the earliest and latest dates respectively for a 'Romantic Age' of swashbucklers, identified by George MacDonald

Fraser as existing rather more in Hollywood than in history itself.[18] So, inevitably, *Blackadder II* includes a Sir Walter Raleigh episode with jokes about potatoes, and other episodes involving a venal clergyman and some puritans. Similarly, one episode of *Blackadder the Third* features Dr Samuel Johnson (died 1784) in conversation with Percy Shelley (born 1792), while others include the Duke of Wellington, and 'Pitt the Younger', the latter played as a precocious and squeaky-voiced adolescent.

Partly because of the success both of *Blackadder* itself, and of various cast members as their careers flourished through the 1980s, the series developed something of a repertory theatre company feel. In addition to Rik Mayall's appearances as Lord Flashheart, Miranda Richardson, who played Queen Elizabeth I as a self-obsessed teenager in *Blackadder II*, also made guest appearances in the third and fourth series. Tim McInnerny appeared regularly in the first two series as incarnations of Lord Percy, Blackadder's inept assistant, before playing Captain Darling in *Blackadder Goes Forth*. Stephen Fry played Lord Melchett, the Queen's advisor (presumably a distant ancestor of General Melchett), as a regular character in *Blackadder II*, while Hugh Laurie played Prince George the Prince Regent, again as a regular character, throughout *Blackadder the Third*. To this should be added a number of running jokes and conventions established for *Blackadder Goes Forth* from the earlier series, including one followed faithfully in every series: that the leading characters should by some contrivance die together in the last scene of the last episode.[19] By the time that *Blackadder Goes Forth* was made, the comic relationships between the characters governing it, and a certain amount of its structure, had already been established by the preceding series.

THE SERIES AS HISTORY

Many of the images and features of the stereotype Western Front lent themselves in a very natural way to the *Blackadder* treatment, especially the battle of wits between the *Blackadder* character and higher authority, and the idea that everyone should die at the end. To this existing base of established conventions and interpersonal relationships, the scriptwriters for *Blackadder Goes Forth* added some familiar clichés from the late twentieth-century popular perception of the Western Front. The first episode, 'Captain Cook', introduces the characters and their surroundings, stressing the difference between the front-line dugout and the general's chateau. The next, 'Corporal Punishment', deals with the court martial of Blackadder by General Melchett, and his consequent close escape from death by firing squad. This theme of the rigged court martial and firing squad has preoccupied recent views of the war, including the feature films *Paths of Glory* (1957) and *King and Country* (1964), and the BBC television drama series *The Monocled Mutineer* (1986). In 2006, the British government granted posthumous conditional pardons to all British soldiers shot for military offences (other than murder) during the war, the result of a long campaign of publicity and political pressure. The third episode, 'Major Star', features a concert party, with Gabrielle Glaister reprising her role from *Blackadder II* of 'Bob', the girl who has dressed up as a soldier to follow her fortune. The next two episodes, 'Private Plane' and 'General Hospital', are vehicles respectively for Rik Mayall as Squadron Commander Lord Flashheart of the Flying Corps, and for Miranda Richardson as Nurse Mary, the suspected spy. There are strong echoes here of two other BBC drama series, the 1979 dramatization *Testament of Youth*, based on Vera Brittain's experiences as a Voluntary Aid Detachment (VAD) nurse in the war, and *Wings*, the 1977 drama series about a Royal Flying Corps squadron. (The stockshots of aircraft flying that appear in 'Private Plane' were taken from the *Wings* series, at conveniently low cost to the BBC.)

In the final episode '*Goodbyee!*', Blackadder, while waiting for the final order to attack, outlines to George and Baldrick the reason for the war's outbreak:

> [T]he real reason for the whole thing was that it was just too much effort not to have a war . . . You see, Baldrick, in order to prevent a war in Europe two super blocs developed: us, the French and the Russians on one side, and the Germans and Austro-Hungary on the other. The idea was to have two vast opposing armies, each acting as the other's deterrent. That way there could never be a war . . . [But] there was one tiny flaw in the plan . . . It was b------s![20]

As should be apparent, historical authenticity is not very high on the series' order of priorities.[21] *Blackadder Goes Forth* is not the historical Western Front of the First World War, and it was never meant to be; it derives much of its humour from trading on the clichés of popular or schoolbook versions of history. But this version of the outbreak of the First World War is recognizably the 'failed deterrent' or 'war by timetable' popularized in the early 1960s by A. J. P. Taylor in Great Britain and Barbara Tuchman in the United States, drawing a parallel between the events of 1914 and the nuclear standoff of the 1960s (and made even more topical by the brief revival in Great Britain of the Campaign for Nuclear Disarmament in the early 1980s).[22] In short, this is the kind of explanation for the outbreak of the First World War that the average educated British television viewer of the 1980s might have learned at school or possibly even at university. A similar explanation for the outbreak of the war appears in the successful Tom Stoppard stage play *Travesties* (1974). Together with a liking for Alternative and Oxbridge comedy, this view of the First World War was, in Great Britain, simply part of the cultural inheritance of the early 1980s 'Yuppie'[23] generation.

FROM TRAGEDY TO FARCE

As with the previous Blackadder series, the episodes of *Blackadder Goes Forth* largely stand alone, and may be taken in almost any order. But unlike the previous series, the fact of inevitable and pointless death from the final act of attacking 'over the top' is established early in the first episode, and then features as a reference point throughout the series. In each episode the chief motivation of Atkinson's 'Captain Blackadder' character in seeking to create a concert party or join the Royal Flying Corps (and so on) is a desire to find a posting away from the front before the attack is ordered. This dark idea of waiting to die, which gives the series its underlying structure, comes directly from one of the most famous fictional versions of the Western Front: R. C. Sherriff's *Journey's End*; and both the difference between the two works, and the path from one to the other, are enlightening ones.

Journey's End first appeared in 1929 as a stage play by Sherriff, playing simultaneously in London, New York and Chicago (with touring companies taking it to 20 other countries) and a BBC radio play, followed in 1930 by a Hollywood feature film (for which Sherriff did not write the adaptation) and a novel written in collaboration with Vernon Bartlett.[24] It has been revived frequently in recent years, including London West End stage productions in the 1980s and 1990s, and a 1988 BBC television production. Indeed, taking this production of *Journey's End* together with *Wings*, *Testament of Youth* and *The Monocled Mutineer*, it is instructive just how frequently dramas related to the Western Front appeared on British television in the decade preceding *Blackadder Goes Forth*.

In contrast to the timelessness and lack of specific location for the Western Front of *Blackadder Goes Forth*, Sherriff based his play on a very specific event that was utterly familiar to many members of his original audience in 1929: a British front-line battalion on the Saint Quentin sector of Fifth Army front in the last few days before 21 March 1918, waiting not to advance but to receive a major German attack. The action is set, like *Blackadder Goes Forth*, chiefly in the officers' dugout of a company. But at the end of the play, as the Germans attack, the implication clearly exists that the officers will all die doing their duty. Although many of the front-line battalions would be overwhelmed, the German defeat in this battle was one of the major turning points in the war, leading to an Allied victory, and this was well known to contemporary audiences.

Sherriff served with the 9th East Surrey Regiment, which fought hard in this battle, although not initially in the very front line. He was not present himself, due to being wounded at Third Ypres. Nevertheless, *Journey's End* was regarded by its first audiences as highly realistic, earning Sherriff praise from Winston Churchill and a standing ovation from a specially invited audience of Victoria Cross holders, as well as support from pacifists and many others who saw the play as anti-war. In fact, Sherriff's view of the First World War, like that of many others who had served in it, was complex and ambivalent. He did not believe that it should have started, and hated the idea of fighting it; but he also believed that it had to be fought and won. Himself a public schoolboy who had been promoted from the ranks, Sherriff also meant *Journey's End* as a monument to the young men from public schools who had officered the Army at a junior level. His company commander in *Journey's End*, 'Captain Stanhope', is himself barely out of school and already holds the Military Cross, while the new addition, Lieutenant Raleigh (corresponding to the 'Lieutenant George' of *Blackadder Goes Forth*), is a naïve, newly commissioned schoolboy, but is far from being a comic figure.

As the literary historian I. F. Clarke showed in 1966,[25] for a generation before the First World War popular culture and imaginative fiction in Britain and Europe had predicted a war that would be technological in nature while being dependent on the heroic individual for its conduct. It is also a relevant fact, in the expectation of the next war being like the last one, that the experience of many British volunteers in the Boer War had also been, on the whole, quite a pleasant one, not unlike a giant scouting and riding holiday for adults. (Indeed, Colonel R. S. S. Baden-Powell had improvised a body of 'boy scouts' for his defence of Mafeking, an experience that led directly to his founding of the Boy Scout movement on his retirement from the Army in 1907.) Away from the Western Front the experiences of individuals like T. E. Lawrence ('Lawrence of Arabia') closely fitted these expectations. But on the Western Front only half the promise was delivered. The principal objection of the 'trench poets', writers such as Sassoon, Blunden, Aldington and Graves, was to the impersonal nature of mass industrialized warfare, which cramped, or removed or simply had no place for their individual humanity before it finally maimed or killed them.

In this context it is surely not a co-incidence that the first stories about Flight Commander Lionel Bigglesworth were published in 1932, in *Popular Flying*. William Earl Johns, the author of the 'Biggles' stories, was a 40-year-old former grammar-school boy and sanitary inspector, whose military flying career had been five weeks flying light DH4 bombers on the Western Front in the summer of 1918 before being shot down. But Johns, displaying the same attitudes as the ex-ranker Sherriff, unhesitatingly made his hero a teenage public-school boy and scout (fighter) pilot, promoting himself to 'Captain' Johns in the process.[26] As George Orwell noted in his classic article on 'Boys' Weeklies' in 1940, the heroes of boys' stories of the 1930s set in the First World War were either secret agents or pilots, never infantry.[27] On the Western Front only the pilot 'aces' with their single combat achieved the pre-war ideal of the heroic individual, and Sherriff's play remains one of the very rare enduring examples of the British infantry sub-altern of the First World War as hero (although also very definitely as victim). As a typical example of the continuing British television portrayal of the First World War, the BBC drama *All the King's Men* (1999), set in the Gallipoli campaign, cast David Jason as a brave but elderly and undertrained officer, whose misplaced faith in the wisdom of his superiors leads to his own death and those of his men. It is doubtful if any British play, film or television dramatization of the Western Front since perhaps 1950 has depicted something that was actually a commonplace of the war: a competent junior officer bravely and successfully leading his troops.[28] The most significant (if only partial) recent exception to this stereotyped approach to the depiction of British officers has been the drama-documentary, *The Somme: From Defeat to Victory* (2006), made for the BBC by the German-born producer Detlef Siebert, who approached the battle relatively free of any British cultural inheritance.[29]

Remarkable confirmation of the attitude already identified by Orwell among a younger generation looking at the First World War came in 1976, when a film version of the *Journey's End* story was released with the plot transferred to a Royal Flying Corps scout squadron on the Western Front as *Aces High* (starring Malcolm McDowell as 'Captain Gresham' – the 'Stanhope' figure). Additional material for the film came from Cecil Lewis' autobiographical *Sagittarius Rising*, written about his own Western Front flying experiences.[30] Whereas the action of the theatrical version of *Journey's End* remained completely within the dugout, *Aces High* enjoyed rather more freedom. In particular it includes a scene in which Gresham is invited to a 'planning lunch' at an unspecified 'headquarters', the only purpose of which appears to be to emphasize the gulf between the front-line and high command. As might have been predicted, this scene belongs very much to the Western Front described in Hastings' *Evening Standard* article quoted above. In a sumptuous chateau, a table laden with delicacies and crystal is peopled by well-fed staff officers making idle or salacious gossip, presided over by an impossibly elderly brigadier general (Ray Milland, who was 70 years old, compared to about 35–45 years old for real British brigade commanders in the war). The contrast with McDowell's gaunt and almost skeletal Gresham with his boy-like deference could not be greater.

In 1930, *Journey's End* had been a success both as a stage play and as a film. But in 1976 with *Aces High*, acceptance of the main themes of Sherriff's story by a commercial cinema audience was judged as being dependent on the film's simultaneous reinforcement of the image of the heroic pilot, chateau generalship, and other clichés of the Western Front. By the late 1980s, despite the BBC revival of the original *Journey's End*, Sherriff's portrayal of the behaviour and attitudes of officers and men in the trenches was so remote from popular cultural understanding of the Western Front that it could only be understood by a mass British television audience as the farce of *Blackadder Goes Forth*. In innocently providing entertainment for a further new young generation, *Blackadder Goes Forth* helped shape their future attitudes towards the First World War. In attracting the attention of historians of the conflict, it has also helped bring into sharp focus the nature of the debate regarding the Western Front of literature and popular culture against the Western Front of history.

NOTES

1 Although focused on the British experience, this is an international debate, and several of its contributors have been Australian, Canadian and American historians writing on the British and wider Imperial experience. *See,* for example: Eksteins, M. (1990), *Rites of Spring: The Great War and the Birth of the Modern Age.* London: Black Swan; De Groot, G. (1996), *Blighty: British Society in the Era of the Great War.* London: Longman; Travers, T. (1987), *The Killing Ground: The British Army, The Western Front, and the Emergence of Modern Warfare 1900–1918.* London: Unwin Hyman; Wilson, T. (1986), *The Myriad Faces of War: Britain and the Great War 1914–1918.* London: Polity Press; and Winter (1995), op. cit.

2 *See,* for example, Keegan, J. (1998), *The First World War.* London: Hutchinson, which rejects without debate an entire body of findings on the Western Front. For the extent to which the issue of the 'Two Western Fronts' continues to divide British historians, *see* the competing contributions by Gary Sheffield and Gavin Stamp to Howard, M. (intro.) (2008), *A Part of History: Aspects of the British Experience of the First World War.* London: Continuum.

3 Cecil, H. and Liddle, P. H. (eds) (1996), *Facing Armageddon: The First World War Experienced.* London: Leo Cooper, p. xix and fn 1.

4 Sheffield, G. (1996), '"Oh! What a futile war": Representations of the Western Front in modern British media and popular culture', in I. Stewart, and S. L. Carruthers (eds), *War, Culture and the Media.* Trowbridge: Flicks Books, pp. 54–74; Bond, B., 'A victory worse than defeat? British interpretations of the First World War', Liddell Hart Centre for Military Archives Annual Lecture, Kings College London, 20 November 1997; and Bond (2002), op. cit.

5 Black, J. (2000), *War and the World: Military Power and the Fate of Continents 1450–2000.* London: Yale University Press, p. 275.

6 *100 Great Television Moments,* first broadcast in Great Britain by Channel Four Television, April 2000.

7 This is the line as given in the published version of the *Blackadder* scripts, [Anon.] (1998), *Black-Adder: The Whole Damn Dynasty.* London: Michael Joseph, p. 350; compare with the video release version of *The Western Front* (1999), Episode 3: 'Feeding the Front'.

8 *Haig: the Unknown Soldier,* part of the BBC *Timewatch* series, first transmitted on British television July 1996; video version released May 2000.

9 Sellar, W. C. and Yeatman, R. J. (1930), *1066 and All That: A Memorable History of England.* London: Methuen, Introduction (no pagination).

10 'I do not believe our generation could have borne the martyrdom of World War One', *Evening Standard,* 2 November 1998.

11 Hussey, J. (1999), 'Portrait of a Commander in Chief', in B. Bond, and N. Cave (eds), *Haig: A Reappraisal 70 Years On*. London: Leo Cooper, pp. 12–36; Davies, F. and Maddocks, G. (1995), *Bloody Red Tabs: General Officer Casualties of the Great War 1914–1918*. London: Leo Cooper, pp. 1–44.

12 At the 18th IAMHIST Conference held at Leeds University (UK) in 1999, at which a version of this paper was first presented, it was discovered that, despite worldwide syndication of the *Blackadder* series, a contingent of distinguished American historians, deeply interested in the television and film portrayal of the Western Front, had never encountered the series before.

13 Although websites can change and update without warning, at the present time details of the *Blackadder* series and episodes may be obtained from the BBC official website www.bbc.co.uk/comedy/blackadder and from the unofficial fan website *Blackadder Hall* at www.blackadderhall.com. As may have been noticed, the designation of *Black Adder*, *Black-Adder* or *Blackadder* is to some extent arbitrary; the BBC shows a slight preference for the first version.

14 For scripts of *Blackadder Goes Forth* see (1998) *Black-Adder: The Whole Damn Dynasty*, pp. 348–438; for DVD video *see The Complete Black Adder Goes Forth*, BBC Enterprises 1992.

15 Fussell, P. (1975), *The Great War and Modern Memory*. Oxford: Oxford University Press.

16 *See*, for example, Prior, R. and Wilson, T. (1994), 'Paul Fussell at war', *War in History*, I, (1), 63–80.

17 (1998) *Black-Adder: The Whole Damn Dynasty*, p. 414. The figure for official military dead for the whole British Empire in the course of the war was 947,023, and most historians would accept a round figure of 1–1.25 million. Given that the war lasted 223 weeks, this produces a weekly average of between 4,000 and 4,500 British and Empire dead on all fronts. This is itself a horrifying figure, but quite unrelated to the *Blackadder* view of the war.

18 Fraser, G. M. (1988), *The Hollywood History of the World: From One Million Years BC to Apocalypse Now*. New York: Beech Tree Books, p. 104.

19 Strictly, at the end of *Blackadder III*, only Prince George dies and Blackadder is mistakenly accepted by mad King George III as his son and heir.

20 (1998) *Black-Adder: The Whole Damn Dynasty* p. 442.

21 The series' attitude to historical accuracy is well conveyed by Captain Darling's uniform, which mixes the red tabs of a First World War Staff officer with a Guards Brigade officer's hat and tunic of the Second World War, and which includes, entirely against the conventions of the character, both the Military Cross and George Medal for bravery.

22 Taylor, A. J. P. (1963), *The First World War: An Illustrated History*. London: Hamish

Hamilton. pp. 11–15 (note that Taylor dedicated this book to Joan Littlewood); Tuchman, B. (1962), *The Guns of August*. New York: Macmillan.

23 An acronym from 'Young Upwardly-mobile Professionals', a usage first popularized in the 1980s.

24 Kelly, A. (1997), *Cinema and the Great War*. London: Routledge, pp. 66–75.

25 Clarke, I. F. (1992), *Voices Prophesying War: Future Wars 1763–3749*. Oxford: Oxford University Press. (Originally published 1966.)

26 *See* Berrisford Ellis, P. and Schofield, J. (1993), *Biggles: The Life Story of Captain W. E. Johns*. Godmanstone: Veloce.

27 Orwell G. (1962), *Inside the Whale and Other Essays*. London: Penguin, p. 192. The essay cited, 'Boys' Weeklies', originally appeared in *Horizon* Number 3 of March 1940.

28 A related partial exception is the portrayal of the war in Australian television and cinema in the 1980s, at a time when elements within Australian politics were self-consciously attempting to create a national image independent of Great Britain. The Australian television drama series *ANZACS* (1985) follows the fortunes of Australian officers and men from Gallipoli to the end of the war on the Western Front. Even then, the hero – portrayed as a highly competent and caring officer – is killed in action. This series, like its various British equivalents, has a marked and largely unhistorical anti-British high command bias. Another Australian film of the same period, *The Lighthorsemen* (1987) portrays a competent Australian officer successfully commanding his troops in Palestine in 1917, with slightly less of an anti-British high command bias. *Gallipoli* (1981), another Australian production, is much more in the tradition of soldiers as victims, British high command as incompetent and the (unseen) British troops as not much better.

29 *The Somme: From Defeat to Victory* (2006) has been released as a BBC DVD video. *See also* the interview by Terry Payne with Detlef Siebert, 'A Bitter Lesson', *Radio Times* 1–7 July 2006. (Note that in this article Haig's name is printed as 'Hague'.)

30 Lewis, C. (1936), *Sagittarius Rising*. London: Peter Davies.

4

Cavalry and the Development of Breakthrough Doctrine 1914–1918

Whatever its other points of interest, the study of the Western Front in the First World War seldom presents the opportunity for a good laugh. But one of the few which may be almost guaranteed comes when the issue of British cavalry operations is raised. A firm consensus still exists, which grew in strength from the First World War itself and has only quite recently been challenged, that the cavalry was, in all respects, useless. Its soldiers spent their time safely in the rear, wasting rations and playing cards, or else engaged in futile mass charges in close order against machine-guns, only to be mown down and massacred. It really is a case of 'damned if you do and damned if you don't' for the cavalrymen – they are portrayed and remembered either as passive spectators to the fighting, or as its most reckless and incompetent victims.

This record of criticism is constant, from contemporary memoirs of the Western Front by infantrymen, or above all tankmen, who poured scorn on what one veteran of Cambrai called 'our medieval horse soldiers',[1] through to modern studies of the doctrines and strategy of the British Army of the First World War era, and particularly of the career of Douglas Haig, which are mostly content to take the uselessness of the cavalry for granted. To cite only a few distinguished cases, John Gooch argued in *The Plans of War* (1974) that Haig's pronouncement while Director of Staff Duties in 1909 that cavalry 'must keep close to the other arms who attack the infantry and prepare the way for the decisive action of the cavalry', (which might in other circumstances be thought a reasonably balanced judgement) shows 'an ominous faith in the effectiveness of cavalry' and therefore 'served to cement into strategic thought an outmoded doctrine'. Tim Travers' immensely influential book *The Killing Ground* (1987), which does not actually have the word 'cavalry' in its index, nevertheless describes Haig at Aldershot

Command before the war seeking to professionalize the Army by the creation of a common doctrine 'while at the same time clinging to traditional ideas about morale and cavalry'. The complete uselessness of the cavalry, and the pointlessness of Haig's plans to make use of it in battle, colours every aspect of Robin Prior and Trevor Wilson's *The Somme*, (2005) a book which otherwise goes out of its way to challenge long-accepted ideas about the battle and its conduct. In a similar fashion, while the sympathetic biography by John Terraine seeks to defend Haig by denying that he should be called a 'cavalry general', Gerald De Groot's more critical biography sees the basis for the disastrous attempts at breakthrough operations on the Somme and in the Ypres salient, as opposed to a more sensible strategy of limited offensives, in what Lloyd George called the 'ridiculous cavalry obsession' of Haig and his staff.[2] This assumption that 'cavalry generals' were *necessarily* incompetent is an exclusively British phenomenon. No such criticism has been levelled against such notable former cavalrymen as Pershing, Langle de Cary and Brusilov, or on the German side against von der Marwitz, who defended Cambrai with such effectiveness in November 1917 (possibly the only Western Front battle in which the Army commanders on both sides were cavalrymen).

The belief that Haig and his staff, like French and his staff before them, paid too much attention to the cavalry is fuelled by another consensus, that the British maintained too much of it on the Western Front, where it consumed supplies and wasted shipping. Historians from Sir Basil Liddell Hart to Norman Stone have chuckled over the absurdity that in the course of the First World War the British shipped to France a greater tonnage of horse fodder than ammunition, in the process using more shipping than was sunk by German submarines. The explanation for this, which is equally familiar, is that, as A. J. P. Taylor put it in his *The First World War*, 'most of the generals were cavalrymen'. It is common ground that what Winston Churchill in *The World Crisis* called 'large masses of cavalry' were maintained by the British on the Western Front only through 'the absurd misconceptions of the staff', in believing that they could ever be used.[3]

This conventional viewpoint, however prevalent and deeply engrained it may have become, represents, at best, a half truth. There was a role for the British cavalry on the Western Front, of a kind, and its performance was by no means a comical disaster. First, the myth that the cavalry did nothing on the Western Front, or that the life of a cavalryman was a safe billet, may be dispensed with reasonably easily. The War Office's statistics of *The Military Effort of the British Empire During the Great War*, although both incomplete and sometimes self-contradictory, give some interesting indications of what the cavalry was doing between 1914 and 1918. At its strongest, in early 1915, the British cavalry force on the Western Front numbered about 25,000 men and horses, of which some 19,000 were cavalrymen (line cavalry, yeomanry and household troops rather than supporting arms such as sappers and signallers attached to cavalry formations). According to the *Statistics*, between August 1914 and November 1918 these cavalrymen suffered 4,421 dead and 14,630 other casualties, not including officers. In fact, the cavalry had the highest proportion of killed to other casualties of all the fighting arms, with the Tank Corps having the lowest. Nor was the life of a cavalry officer a soft option. In the infantry, and in the British Army as a whole, the ratio of officer casualties to those of the 'other ranks' (the contemporary term for privates and NCOs) was broadly equal to the proportion of officers in the Army. But in the cavalry the proportion of officer casualties was more than double the average, at almost one to every nine other ranks' casualties, giving a total loss for the cavalry on the Western Front of about 21,000 over all ranks. The only fighting arm with a higher officer casualty ratio than the cavalry, and by far the most dangerous arm for officers to serve with, was (curiously) the Tank Corps again, with an officer casualty ratio of some four times the average.[4]

In absolute terms, to be sure, the life of a cavalryman in the First World War was more than twice as safe as that of a tankman, and incomparably safer than that of an infantryman. In all theatres, casualties to cavalrymen accounted for just over one per cent of all casualties suffered by the fighting arms of the British Army. But, in extreme cases, the level of casualties in cavalry regiments in battle could easily rival those of infantry battalions. By the end of the First Battle of Ypres, the 9th Lancers had lost three-quarters of their officers, the 18th Hussars had been reduced to just over a third of their strength and the 11th Hussars to just over half strength. The battles of March 1918 cost the 5th Lancers and the 3rd Hussars over a quarter of their men, while the Scots Greys lost half of theirs.[5] While casualties are not evidence of achievement, they must be taken as evidence of activity. The cavalrymen were clearly doing *something* during those four years.

A possible explanation is that the cavalry actually suffered its casualties charging machine-guns. Perhaps so, but like many other things known about the Western Front, this old cliché vanishes like smoke when attempts are made to pin down cases of it actually happening. Cavalry were certainly not bullet-proof, and Haig has been ridiculed for writing in his *Cavalry Studies* of 1907 that modern bullets had little stopping power against horses. Nevertheless, however remarkably, Haig was more accurate than his detractors have realized. Veterinary tests of the period, and combat experience both during the Boer War and the First World War, confirmed that horses do not suffer to any great extent from reaction shock. Unless the bullet was lucky enough to hit a major organ or a leg bone, it would not bring down a charging horse at anything more than almost point-blank range. Stories from the period of horses collapsing in death from wounds *after* a successful charge are surprisingly common. Like the infantry, the cavalry were far more likely to be stopped on the Western Front by artillery or barbed wire – a device invented, after all, to restrict the movement of animals – than by the machine-gun.[6]

What might be called 'the cult of the machine-gun' in relation to beliefs about the Western Front has emerged from many sources. But the idea that machine-guns rendered cavalry useless seems to owe its respectability largely to the (now slightly notorious) British Army's Official Historian, Brigadier General Sir James Edmonds. To take just one example of several, in his *Official History* of operations on the Western Front in 1918, Edmonds quotes with approval the remark of an American officer, 'you can't have a cavalry charge until you have captured the enemy's last machine-gun'. Twenty pages later in the same volume is an account of a successful charge by the Canadian Cavalry Brigade (then part of the 3rd Cavalry Division) that captured 230 prisoners, 3 artillery pieces and 40 machine-guns.[7] This achievement was in no way unique, particularly for the last year of the war; small-scale cavalry charges took place occasionally on the Western Front (although they were infrequent enough to draw comment each time) and a surprising number were both successful in their objectives, and accomplished them with relatively few casualties. On the first day of the Battle of Amiens, 8 August 1918, the 7th Cavalry Brigade (also part of the 3rd Cavalry Division) captured over 300 prisoners, including a successful charge by the 7th Dragoon Guards at the Bois de Cayeux, which took 40 prisoners, 2 artillery pieces and 10 machine-guns, at a cost to the regiment of 5 killed and 43 wounded. The total casualties for the entire Cavalry Corps over four days of battle at Amiens were 887 men and 1,800 horses, which by the standards of infantry losses on the Western Front was remarkably low.[8]

Various reasons have been advanced for Edmonds' hostility towards the cavalry, which seems to have been based, at least in part, on a personal dislike of Haig and Allenby following his experiences sharing an Army Staff College course with them. He certainly never lost an opportunity in the *Official History* to criticize the cavalry or belittle their achievements, describing the remarkable cavalry exploitation between 8 and 10 October 1918 on Fourth Army front, which netted over 500 prisoners, as something that the infantry could have done for themselves at less cost.[9] One certain contributing factor was that Edmonds, himself an officer of the Royal Engineers, believed that the adoption, at an early stage, of engineer siege techniques to the Western Front, rather than a breakthrough strategy, would have led the British to victory sooner and at less cost. While the merits of such limited 'step by step' or 'bite and hold' attacks against a strategy of breakthrough have been subject to much recent analysis, several historians have accepted almost without enquiry the fundamental idea, fostered by Edmonds, that breakthrough was impractical because of the cavalry's essential uselessness.[10]

As the often-controversial John Terraine pointed out as early as 1980, the belief that the British Army on the Western Front was handicapped by large masses of cavalry will not pass even the most straightforward test of statistics. The British began the First World War with a single cavalry division on the Western Front, expanded in October 1914 into a Cavalry Corps of three divisions. This force, together with two Indian cavalry divisions, which arrived in France in November 1914 and formed the Indian Cavalry Corps, was the BEF's main mounted component on the Western Front until March 1918, accounting at its strongest for between two and three per cent of the total BEF strength in men, and six per cent in horses. On the last day of the war, the active strength of the British cavalry in France and Belgium was 13,984 men, compared to 13,594 for the Tank Corps and 53,634 for the Machine-Gun Corps. It is quite true that the BEF consumed approximately 5.9 million tons of horse fodder during the war, compared to just over 5.4 million tons of ammunition. But the overwhelming majority of horses required by the BEF served as haulage and transport animals for the Royal Artillery, Royal Engineers, the Army Service Corps and, of course, for the infantry – a total of 449,880 horses and mules in August 1918. That Liddell Hart, who had served as an infantry officer on the Western Front, could foster such an error is surprising to say the least.[11]

The idea that cavalrymen as a group played a disproportionate role in the command of the BEF and the direction of the British war effort may also be called into question. Certainly, both the commanders of the BEF, Sir John French and Sir Douglas Haig, had either begun or served the bulk of their regimental careers in cavalry regiments, as had the CIGS from December 1915 to February 1918, Sir William Robertson. In addition, of the ten officers who at various times commanded the five British Armies on the Western Front, five were cavalrymen: Haig, Allenby, Byng, Gough and Birdwood (who had also served with the infantry and the Indian cavalry). Equally certainly, the presence of these men in high command cannot be accounted for by mere chance or statistical probability, since the proportion of cavalry in the regular British Army before 1914 was approximately eight per cent of all regular troops. But it is also hard to substantiate the view that the common denominator of having begun their careers in the cavalry either linked these very different men together, or can be held responsible for the positions to which they rose during the war. Far from their forming a united cavalry bloc, the antagonism between Haig and Allenby, or Allenby and Gough, is well known to historians. Among the more likely common factors accounting for these men holding high rank is that, like many other senior commanders who came to prominence in the First World War, they had backgrounds in socially exclusive or high status regiments, like other Army commanders including Horne (Royal Horse Artillery) and Rawlinson (Coldstream

Guards), and Robertson's replacement as CIGS, Henry Wilson (Rifle Brigade). Good social connections were required at the top of the British Army in the First World War, the most significant exception being Plumer of Second Army (from the unfashionable York and Lancaster Regiment), who was at least an Old Etonian. Once away from the very highest echelons, the number of cavalrymen holding high commands in the First World War was no greater than might have been predicted from a statistical average of the officers available, as an analysis of the *Army List* for the war years shows. By the end of the war, only one of the BEF's 19 Army Corps (not including the Australian Corps and the Canadian Corps) on the Western Front was being commanded by a pre-war cavalryman (plus, unsurprisingly, another commanding the Cavalry Corps), and two more commanding infantry divisions. Of 18 cavalrymen holding the rank of major general on the same date (of which seven were Staff College graduates and four had served in another arm during their careers), the majority were employed on staff or non-combatant duties. Even so, at the war's end the most prestigious staff grouping in the BEF, the First Echelon of Haig's General Headquarters, contained just 22 cavalrymen out of 326 officers. Away from the very highest ranks, the percentages of lieutenant generals and major generals in the Army by the end of the war who had begun their careers in the cavalry were 8.5 per cent and 7 per cent, respectively, or just about the proportion of cavalry in the pre-war Army. The only blip on the graph is the rank of temporary lieutenant general, of which 27 per cent were cavalrymen, or nine officers. Including all officers of the rank of major general or above, 31 officers were cavalrymen out of 331 in total – hardly an Army dominated by cavalrymen.[12] Admittedly, there was at least one case of promotion from major in 1914 to temporary lieutenant general by 1919, and he was a cavalryman; but this was the extraordinary G. T. M. Bridges, who had been British military attaché to four European courts before the war, who helped negotiate the American contribution to the war effort after April 1917, whose military career continued after the Armistice in such politically sensitive areas as White Russia and Ottoman Turkey, and who was in all respects a quite exceptional man. The image presented in C. S. Forester's novel *The General* of 1936, still cited in factual works on the First World War, of the typical Western

Front corps commander as a narrow-minded, pre-war regimental cavalry major promoted above his abilities, has simply no basis in fact.[13]

Even at the level of high command, it is hard to find evidence in the statistics of promotion to support the belief, held by some officers even before the First World War, in some kind of a 'cavalry conspiracy' over and above the military patronage characteristic of the late-Victorian and Edwardian Army. It is actually untrue that success in the Boer War in any way advanced the careers of cavalrymen as a group rather than those of other officers; if anything, the evidence is slightly the other way. In 1914, the only cavalrymen to hold significant positions in the BEF were French, Haig and (unsurprisingly again) Allenby as commander of the Cavalry Division. The only cavalryman to hold the rank of full general was Haig, and there were, in addition, 3 cavalrymen out of 27 lieutenant generals, and 8 out of 114 major generals, or 7 per cent again. In so far as it had any existence, the 'cavalry conspiracy' consisted of Field Marshal Sir John French and General Sir Douglas Haig, and there is little to suggest that either surrounded himself with cavalrymen in preference to other officers. In addition, while at Aldershot Command, both men had gained more experience of commanding infantry and all-arms formations than any other officer in the BEF except Sir Horace Smith-Dorrien. Since the 'cavalrymen' are often singled out among Western Front commanders for their ignorance of infantry or artillery tactics, it should be noted that Smith-Dorrien had also made his reputation as a regimental officer in commanding irregular mounted troops, as had Rawlinson, Wilson and Plumer.

However ironic it may seem, the cavalry officers of the First World War who reached high rank on the Western Front may have owed their rise largely to the simple fact of survival. Although hardly for want of trying, all the cavalry divisional and brigade commanders survived First Ypres (although one was invalided sick during the battle), so putting an effective block on promotion within the cavalry above regimental level for the next three years. Allenby, as commander of the newly formed Cavalry Corps, went on to command an Army (and later the Egyptian Expeditionary Force), as did two of his divisional commanders, while the third divisional commander and two brigade commanders went on to command Army Corps (not all of them on the Western Front). But while officers with command or staff experience were at a premium in the expanding Army of 1915, regardless of their arm of service, it was clearly not army policy to appoint cavalry lieutenant-colonels to command infantry brigades. A cavalry regimental commander who survived First Ypres would have done slightly better than average to have received any promotion at all by the end of the war, almost invariably to non-operational duties or staff-work rather than command. It was actually less likely that a lieutenant colonel commanding a cavalry regiment in 1914 would rise to command even a cavalry division than that his brigade commander would secure command of an Army Corps or his divisional commander of an Army. By 1918, in every case but one of a cavalry regimental commander being promoted, his successor was simply the senior major of the regiment or of another cavalry regiment inheriting the post by seniority.

It is highly likely that the retention of the same commanding officers, together with the *comparatively* low casualty rates, enabled the cavalry regiments to keep their pre-war character much longer than the regular infantry battalions of the BEF, something commented on by senior officers as late as 1918. However, the stagnation in promotion prospects within the cavalry also led to a steady haemorrhaging of good officers away from the cavalry to other arms, both by junior officers accepting transfers and by other ranks being commissioned, since it was common British Army practice that newly commissioned officers were moved to another regiment. It was characteristic of the Army of the period that the extent of this loss was largely determined by the attitude of individual regiments and their commanding officers. While the 11th Hussars was proud that 20 of its NCOs and privates were commissioned during the war, the 1st Life Guards managed to avoid directly commissioning a single man.[14] But despite the considerable variations between regiments, the overall trend was that, throughout the war, promotion at junior level was significantly more likely for officers transferring away from their cavalry regiments than for those who stayed behind. Contrary to the common perception, these officers did not all join the Royal Flying Corps – only about five per cent of its officers serving at the end of the war had started their careers in the cavalry. Nevertheless, by January 1918 there were 14 former cavalrymen ranking as squadron commanders, and five as wing commanders. Cavalrymen were in fact more likely to join the Tank Corps, making up 15 per cent of its officer corps by the war's end.

There remains the argument that the cavalry on the Western Front was in some way small but deadly, that despite the weakness of the British cavalry force, its very existence as an arm of exploitation led a British high command dominated by cavalry officers into planning battles around its use, in the false belief that a breakthrough on the Western Front could be achieved. This argument should be viewed sympathetically, since it contains a grain of truth – but only a grain. In order to assess its strengths it is first necessary, rather than accepting without investigation the ideas fostered by Edmonds and the cavalry's detractors, to review the actual organization and tactics of the British cavalry both before the First World war and as they evolved on the Western Front.

Largely through its experience of colonial warfare in the late-nineteenth century, and particularly the Boer War, the tactics of the British cavalry were, by 1914, years ahead of those of its continental rivals. While the French still had 12 regiments of armoured cuirassiers with breastplates, armed only with sword and pistol, and the Germans continued to practise charges of divisional size on a regular basis, the British cavalry was a very different sort of arm. In appearance, thanks to the reforms of the Haldane era, the cavalryman of the BEF closely resembled an infantryman on horseback, with a virtually identical khaki uniform, and with much the same weapons. In 1914 the cavalrymen, like the infantry, carried the Mark III SMLE rifle, and they could hold their own with it even in the legendary BEF. There were even occasional cases before the war of cavalry regiments winning regional shooting contests. Some regiments made it a point of honour to have no third-class shots, and at least one good shooting regiment, the 14th Hussars, had an actual majority of marksmen.[15] The rifle was carried in a saddle holster (indeed, the curved bolt and shortened wood-enclosed barrel of the original Mark I SMLE of 1904 had been designed with the cavalry in mind), counterbalanced on the other side of the saddle by the 1908 pattern sword. Lancer regiments carried their lances into battle, although Dragoon and Dragoon Guard regiments, which had at the end of the nineteenth century carried the lance for the front rank only, had largely discontinued the practice by 1914. Cavalry regiments, like infantry battalions, were equipped with two Vickers machine-guns. In fact, the cavalry had received these a year earlier than the infantry, in 1912, to replace the heavier Maxim gun, and the proportion of machine-guns and field guns in the British cavalry division of 1914 was higher than in the cavalry divisions of any other belligerent.[16]

In the years between the end of the Boer War and the start of the First World War the tactics of the British cavalry had been the subject of major reforms and of an intense and sometimes vitriolic dispute over the respective merits of dismounted firepower and the mounted charge. Historians have mostly interpreted this dispute as a meritorious attempt at reform under Lord Roberts as Commander-in-Chief, followed soon after by what has been described as 'a cavalry counter-reformation' under French as CIGS. An alternative explanation sees the debate not in simple terms as reform challenging reaction, but as a dispute between two rival interpretations of Roberts' period of command in South Africa during the Boer War, in which the balance of truth lay rather more with French than with Roberts. Regardless of this, the actual result was, as all commanders were agreed by 1914, not a return to outmoded tactics, but a cavalry force trained to a very high standard in both mounted and dismounted action, and in combining both. The cavalry was capable of effective dismounted skirmishing, of open order charges in troop and squadron strength against infantry and artillery, and of some quite sophisticated tactics of fire and movement, including the taking and holding of ground by 'galloping' the position – rushing it mounted and then dismounting in place – a technique that had developed in the Boer War, and of which Haig was an enthusiastic champion.[17]

The drawback to these relatively new ideas on tactics was that they were over-ambitious. They were difficult to explain to some of the more traditionally minded officers, and there were occasional (and entirely justified) complaints on exercise of cavalry trying to charge uphill against entrenched infantry. There was also an understandable and deep scepticism among officers of the infantry and artillery about the cavalry's faith in itself and its new tactics, and reluctance to use it. 'No one seemed to know what to do with it', lamented Lieutenant Colonel George Barrow (later deservedly famous for his command of the 4th Cavalry

Division in Palestine in 1918) of manoeuvres in India just before the First World War, 'and got out of the difficulty by giving it a free hand.'[18]

For scouting and protection purposes, each of the six infantry divisions of the original BEF had its own mounted contingent, consisting of a squadron of cavalry (two squadrons until spring 1914) together with a cyclist company. But the BEF's main concentration of cavalry was in the single cavalry division of four brigades, each of three regiments, plus an independent fifth brigade, which in practice tended to tag along. This cavalry division was supposed to be the main scouting force and collector of intelligence on enemy movement for the BEF in advance or retreat (although, astonishingly, it had no intelligence officer until Allenby appointed one unofficially on mobilization in 1914), as well as its decisive arm of attack in an encounter battle. But by 1914, it was accepted doctrine that, once a set-piece battle was joined, the cavalry should wait in reserve behind the main battle line for the infantry to create a break. 'This may not happen, remember', as an article in the *Cavalry Journal* put it, 'for three or four days!'[19] The cavalry, capable of acting independently with its own firepower, would then 'ride for the *G* in Gap' (an expression deriving from the British Army's 'bingo' system of map reading, replaced in 1915 by the grid system), break through, and sustain itself on a raid many miles behind the enemy lines.

The problem was that the cavalry division was simultaneously too large and too small for its conflicting roles. It was too unwieldy for effective scouting or raiding and, because there was only one of it, there was a reluctance to risk it against what were certain to be superior enemy numbers in battle. Edmonds claimed to have asked Haig before the war why four brigades were needed instead of the more usual three, and to have been told that four brigades were essential for the close order charge against another cavalry division – two brigades in the front line, one in the second line and one in reserve. Haig may indeed have said this, but only because the cavalry needed to justify their existence. John Vaughan, chief staff officer of the Cavalry Division in 1914, remembered that he and Allenby as divisional commander 'both knew from manoeuvres that three brigades were enough for a Division, but we never dared say so lest the politicos would seize the opportunity and disband three cavalry regiments.'[20] Despite requests, the Treasury would not sanction the cost of a second divisional head-quarters and supporting troops for the cavalry. In practice, during the first of the BEF's operations in August and September 1914, the cavalry functioned first as one five-brigade division (the fifth brigade being officially attached to Haig's I Corps) and then increasingly as two separate divisions, one of three and one of two brigades. This organization was made official in October 1914, when the supporting troops for the second and third cavalry divisions were created, together with the Cavalry Corps headquarters.

Paradoxically, for an arm that prided itself on aggressiveness and 'cavalry spirit', the cavalry began its career on the Western Front with a major defensive victory in covering the retreat from Mons. From the very first encounters, the British cavalry showed superiority in small-unit actions over the three divisions of the German II Cavalry Corps opposing it, including the celebrated dismounted defensive battle at Néry on 1 September. The ability of the cavalry to dominate its enemies in scouting and patrol work prevented the Germans from pressing the BEF during the retreat from Mons, and in fact made the whole manoeuvre possible. If Allenby had wrecked his cavalry in an ill-judged mass charge, he would have left the BEF vulnerable to German raiding forces, and in no state to play its decisive role in the Battle of the Marne. The one exception to days of continuous unhampered march for the BEF was Allenby's confession in the early hours of 26 August to Smith-Dorrien that he could not screen his II Corps properly, since two of his cavalry brigades under Hubert Gough had lost contact with the main force and were no longer under his command, forcing Smith-Dorrien to stand and fight at Le Cateau.[21] This was the single failure in an otherwise exceptional performance by the cavalry. If the BEF had been forced to fight a Le Cateau every day, it would have disintegrated very quickly.

The cavalry's record on information gathering was very much less impressive. It frequently found itself in front of the divisional cyclists in the retreat and behind them in the advance, while most of the crucial strategic reconnaissance for the BEF came from aircraft. Haig, who had a gift for finding fault with everyone but himself, was also unimpressed with what he felt to be the limited plans for the cavalry, positioned behind his own I Corps for the advance from the Marne, and by the apparent lack of urgency shown by its commanders.[22] Although his view has been disputed, Haig was probably right. The cavalry, like the rest of the BEF in 1914, was a perfect miniature. Its tactics and battlefield performance could hardly have been faulted, but the art of how to employ it operationally or strategically, of how to take risks with confidence with units of divisional size or greater, was missing from the high command. This is a little hard to understand from Sir John French, given his own superb handling of the Cavalry Division in South Africa in 1900. The explanation may be found in the influence of Henry Wilson, Vice-Chief of Staff of the BEF in 1914, who throughout his career had shown little faith in the cavalry or understanding of its use, and who certainly believed that during this period he was dominating French.[23]

As proof, if it were needed, of its generally high battlefield standards and professional competence, the cavalry – now reinforced to three divisions – finished 1914 at First Ypres with the one tactic for which it was theoretically untrained, by holding seven miles of improvised trenches as orthodox infantry against repeated attacks by II Bavarian Corps. This was a remarkable achievement. At full strength, a cavalry regiment of the period mustered about 600 men and horses, divided into three squadrons, each of four troops. A cavalry division was not only considerably smaller than an infantry division, but required nearly a quarter of its strength as horse-holders. Dismounted, it could muster the firepower only of an infantry brigade or about the equivalent of an under-strength infantry division for the whole Cavalry Corps – probably much less during the actual battle. 'You have done the finest thing cavalry have done in history', the survivors were told, 'as you had an Army Corps against you', leading a subaltern to record modestly that 'for a matter of fact we only did what the infantry always do, except for the fact that we had knew we had no supports or big guns'.[24] For the cavalry of even 20 years before, such an achievement would have been absolutely unthinkable. But in reality, the greatest successes of the cavalry were still in the future.

In November 1914, the British Cavalry Corps was joined by the Indian Cavalry Corps of two divisions, which remained behind on the Western Front when the Indian Corps was withdrawn at the end of 1915. The two Indian cavalry divisions were a little larger than the British divisions (with four squadrons to a regiment rather than three larger squadrons in the British pattern), and followed the normal structure of the Indian Army of one British and two Indian regiments in each brigade. Of 31 British regular cavalry regiments in 1914, 22 served with the British cavalry divisions, which were brought up to strength in November 1914 by the addition of five yeomanry regiments, and six British cavalry regiments served with the Indian cavalry divisions. The remaining three British regiments were stationed in India in 1914, of which two joined Indian cavalry brigades in Mesopotamia in the course of the war, and one (the unfashionable 21st Lancers) saw no active war service at all except for a single squadron used as divisional cavalry on the Western Front. As well as rounding out the cavalry divisions, the yeomanry also began to take over the role of divisional cavalry for some of the infantry divisions, with the squadrons being grouped together from 1915 to form corps cavalry regiments (although the squadrons often remained detached with individual divisions). This arrangement of corps cavalry regiments, three British cavalry divisions and two Indian cavalry divisions on the Western Front, remained broadly constant until March 1918, the exception being that in June 1916 one of the Indian cavalry brigades was detached for duty in Mesopotamia, and was replaced by the Canadian Cavalry Brigade. The Canadians were, in all respects, identical to British cavalry, being commanded for most of their time on the Western Front by the fire-eating J. E. B. Seely, an experienced British yeomanry officer who had been forced to resign as Secretary of State for War in May 1914 over the Curragh Incident. The only other significant change was that in November 1916 the 1st and 2nd Indian Cavalry Divisions were renamed the 4th and 5th Cavalry Divisions, respectively.

The cavalry were used once more dismounted to hold the front line during the emergency of the Second Battle of Ypres in April 1915. Otherwise, because British doctrine required a breakthrough and a defeated enemy before committing the cavalry, they did in fact spend 1915 largely sitting behind the lines waiting for the infantry to make a gap, which singularly failed to happen from Neuve Chapelle in March to Loos in September. Instead, throughout the year, corps cavalry were employed as orderlies, snipers, working parties, traffic controllers and on similar duties, while the five cavalry divisions worked to keep their horses fit and alive outdoors in all weathers – itself a full-time occupation. Also, to their disgust, as well as serving dismounted in the trenches, the cavalry were required as labour parties to actually dig them. 'No doubt this was necessary work', one officer complained, 'but nothing could have been devised to dampen the spirits of cavalrymen more'.[25] Both the morale and the standards of the cavalry declined progressively during French's period of command on the Western Front. Haig was equally disgusted, on visiting the Indian Cavalry Corps headquarters in early 1915, to find that its commander really was playing cards with his staff.[26]

Following Loos, one of French's last decisions before his replacement by Haig was that during winter, when it was hardest to keep the cavalry's horses fit out-doors, they should instead be moved to permanent indoor stables, and a single Dismounted Cavalry Division should be formed from the Cavalry Corps, to help hold the trenches along with the infantry until the better weather of the spring. Haig confirmed this decision, and the cavalry became equipped with the pano-ply of trench warfare, including bayonets, hand-grenades and, from early 1916, steel helmets and Hotchkiss automatic rifles. From then on the Dismounted Division, one division among many, shared the infantry's routine experience of the trenches each winter until the end of the war, distinguished only by the habit of many cavalry officers of wearing spurs and riding boots no matter how unsuit-able the conditions. As the better weather came each spring, the cavalrymen were reunited with their horses to take their place as part of the BEF's reserve.

Although for the British cavalry on the Western Front 1915 was largely a wasted year, it did keep its main pre-war reason for existence: the possibility of a mounted breakthrough. Most of the other major combatant nations of the First World War had rejected the idea of massed cavalry action following the experi-ence of 1914. The French attached an infantry regiment of three battalions to each of their cavalry divisions, and employed them until the end of the war as a source of mobile firepower. The Germans also, concluding as early as September 1914 that 'the dismounted cavalryman should be able to fight exactly as an infan-tryman; cavalry charges no longer play any part in warfare', reorganized their cavalry divisions as, in effect, mobile infantry brigades.[27] To this extent, the argu-ment that the British high command was guilty of a 'cavalry obsession' is valid

– of the major belligerent nations, the British alone continued after 1914 to plan as if the mounted action of the cavalry still had a part to play in war. However, the only commander on the Western Front who held consistently to this belief throughout the war was Douglas Haig himself.

Probably the first of the doubters was Henry Rawlinson, who after Neuve Chapelle, confided to his friend Henry Wilson that Haig had looked for too much. Rawlinson continued:

> [He] expects to get the cavalry through with the next push, but I very much doubt if he will succeed in doing more than kill a large number of gallant men without effecting any great triumph. I should be content with capturing another piece out of the enemy's line of trenches and waiting for the counter attack. I am not a believer in the cavalry raid, which even if it comes off will not effect very much.[28]

Rawlinson also complained about the 'cavalry generals' to Kitchener, and even indirectly to King George V. This was by no means a disinterested position, since Rawlinson had himself been heavily criticized for the losses suffered by his IV Corps at Neuve Chapelle, and excused himself by arguing that both Haig and French had insisted on continued attacks in order to get the cavalry though, the evidence for which is very slight indeed. Nevertheless, this is the first clear record of a fundamental disagreement between Rawlinson and Haig on the value of cavalry, and on breakthrough operations against 'bite and hold' tactics, which was to bedevil both their relationship as commanders and British battle planning on the Western Front to the very end of the war.

Slowly or quickly, other senior British officers on the Western Front also came to the same conclusion – that the use of cavalry on the battlefield was impractical. As early as Neuve Chapelle, French warned the commander of the Indian Cavalry Corps 'against risking his troops mounted too close to the enemy. He is not experienced at this kind of warfare and thinks he may be able to do some dashing cavalry work'.[29] Although, like Haig after him, French continued to allow in his plans for an unexpected German collapse, by Loos he seems to have largely given up any idea of a major cavalry breakthrough. Haig's own thinking by the time of Loos had advanced only as far as doubling the pre-war estimates by expecting a wearing-out fight of 'five or six days' before 'a strong Reserve of all arms' could be committed.[30] By the time of the Battle of Arras in April 1917, even Byng had rejected all belief in the offensive power of cavalry and the possibility of a breakthrough. 'We gave up that catchword some time ago', he wrote to his fellow cavalryman Philip Chetwode, who was serving in Palestine.[31] Haig's last remaining supporter among his Army commanders in seeking ways to employ the cavalry appears to have been Hubert Gough, although the planning for the first stages of Third Ypres in July 1917 suggests that he also had given up the idea of an early cavalry breakthrough by then. The same profound lack of faith in the cavalry was also exhibited by William Robertson as CIGS, who, whatever his original arm of service, was by 1916 preoccupied with sustaining a mass army in which infantry and artillery were by far the most important priorities.

In the course of the war, no new British regular cavalry or Indian cavalry regiments (of which there were 39, mostly serving in India) were created, and the only source of fresh mounted regiments for the British was the yeomanry of the Territorial Force. In 1914 there were 54 yeomanry regiments (plus two more that were formed at the start of the war, and three mounted regiments of the Special Reserve), 42 of them organized into 14 mounted brigades. Most regiments included a small number of rifle-armed cyclists who, for various reasons, could not provide their own horses. On mobilization in 1914, those yeomanry regiments which were not sent to France were consolidated into the 1st and 2nd Mounted Divisions, the former including a four-battalion cyclist brigade. The 1st Mounted Division functioned largely as a training unit, sending a brigade to Gallipoli in 1915 and two more to Egypt in 1916. The 2nd Mounted Division was sent dismounted to Gallipoli in August 1915, was progressively reinforced up to the strength of five brigades, and was then broken up in Egypt in January 1916. Two brigades were sent to Salonika, and two others to Palestine, where they helped form the Imperial Mounted Division and the ANZAC Mounted Division, alongside Australian and New Zealand troopers. In 1917, the Imperial Mounted Division was expanded to form both the Yeomanry Division and the Australian Mounted Division, and consolidated together with the ANZAC Mounted Division into the Desert Mounted Corps. The Australian cavalry, of which there were five brigades, were officially designated as Light Horse, and the single New Zealand brigade as Mounted Rifles. Although originally intended to act as dismounted skirmishers, in practice these troops were virtually identical to British cavalry in training and tactics, particularly after mostly being issued with swords in 1918, and performed some notable mounted charges. It was the yeomanry and the imperial forces, rather than the regular cavalry, who would demonstrate the continued effectiveness of cavalry in their remarkable mobile operations in Palestine in 1917 and 1918.

In Britain, the yeomanry had expanded by spring 1916 to form three divisions, although all were largely devoted to training troops for other theatres, and one was very incomplete. However, in June 1916 Robertson ordered their conversion to cyclist troops. Haig naturally protested that he was being robbed of his mounted reserve on the very eve of the Battle of the Somme, while one regiment, in a spirit of mockery and frustration, erected a tombstone 'Sacred to the Memory of Spurs'.[32] Most of the yeomanry in Britain had disappeared by November, although a few regiments escaped conversion for almost a year. In January 1917 an entire infantry division, the 74th (Yeomanry) Division – the famous 'broken spur' division – was formed in Egypt from unattached yeomanry regiments collected there, and later fought both in Palestine and on the Western Front. In the summer of 1917, those yeomanry that had survived as corps cavalry regiments also began conversion to cyclists or infantry. At the same time, Robertson adopted a policy of reducing the regular cavalry in France, each time despite Haig's protests. However, this was clearly not entirely Robertson's own decision. From early 1916, the CIGS began to come under pressure from the War Committee (later the War Cabinet) to reduce the number of cavalry in the BEF, on the general argument that they were of no value, and that the cost in shipping to transport supplies to them was too great. Perhaps predictably, the loudest demands for withdrawing the cavalry, or at least wintering them in Britain (from which they would have been unlikely to return), came from David Lloyd George. Robertson passed this pressure on to Haig, who strongly resisted either suggestion. Even King George V, on a visit to the Western Front in June 1916, was induced to raise informally with Haig the issue of whether his cavalry could be reduced in numbers or sent elsewhere.[33] As already mentioned, the result was the removal of a brigade from the 2nd Indian Cavalry Division two weeks before it was intended by Haig to play a major role in the opening of the Somme offensive.

Thereafter, Robertson's actions in seeking to reduce Haig's cavalry went far beyond any realistic saving in manpower or shipping, and suggest either a particular antagonism between Robertson and Haig on this issue, or an attempt to use the cavalry as a bargaining counter. There had already been at least one earlier event that reveals not only Robertson's attitude towards the cavalry, but also the understanding of the role of cavalry held by many civilian politicians of the time, and also the ignorance of basic military issues by politicians of which the generals of this war so often complained. On 18 May, with the Battle of the Somme about six weeks away, the War Committee chose to focus on the number of horses with the British Army on the Western Front and the supply problems that they caused, a discussion which, as it was explained to them what the role of most transport horses was, narrowed down to the cavalry. Lord Crewe (the Lord President of the Council) demanded to know 'why cavalry should be kept up, when it was never used at all', and no one present contradicted him.[34] The response from the Army Council under Robertson to this enquiry was a letter of virtual rebuke to its political superiors, insisting that they should not interfere in military matters; Haig also gave an angry response. The wider picture was that, just before the big offensive that they hoped would win the war, the War Committee had paradoxically sought to deprive Haig of his only arm of exploitation, and therefore of any chance of a major victory. The person who should have explained this to them clearly was Robertson as CIGS, but since he also had no faith in the cavalry, he failed to do so.

Thereafter the situation between Haig, Robertson and the government never improved. Perhaps the most bizarre episode occurred in July 1917, when the commander of the 4th Cavalry Division (the old 1st Indian Cavalry Division) returned from leave to find that one of his three British regiments had been ordered home without his knowledge, to be replaced by an Indian regiment.[35] By this time, all the regular cavalry regiments were noticeably below strength, and the number of reserve cavalrymen training in Britain had dropped to about 5,000 troops, or one-third of the notional reserve figure. Finally, in November 1917, Robertson stopped cavalry recruiting altogether, and it was not resumed for the rest of the war. In consequence, the number of cavalrymen and yeomen serving at home, throughout the Empire and in all theatres of war dropped from a high point of 140,452 men in July 1916 to 75,100 in November 1918.

From the very start of his command of the BEF, Haig was anxious to prove both that a breakthrough operation was possible, and that the cavalry could play a role in it, against the scepticism of many of his own Army commanders and, at best, the indifference of the CIGS. To add to his problems, the cavalry was steadily losing some of its best officers and NCOs, and was itself steadily declining both in quality and in quantity, with little prospect of making up its numbers. Placed in a position of either using his cavalry or losing them altogether, in early 1916 Haig undertook a major revision of the pre-war doctrine that the cavalry should wait behind the infantry for the line to be broken, and then exploit to a considerable distance beyond it. In January he informed his Army commanders that 'The first gap will probably not be wide enough to pass great forces through, even if they were immediately available; while small forces, however mobile, pushed through beyond supporting distance would, under the existing conditions, certainly be held up, and eventually enveloped by superior numbers'. Haig's solution was that 'The operations to be undertaken will entail both attack and defence, mounted and dismounted, and the closest co-operation between the cavalry and the other arms will be essential'.[36]

In March, as well as forming a new Fourth Army under Rawlinson for his forthcoming offensive, Haig broke up the two Cavalry Corps and disbanded their headquarters. Instead, a special force known as the Reserve Corps was formed in May under Hubert Gough, and later renamed the Reserve Army. Placed directly under GHQ control, the intended role for the Reserve Army in the forthcoming Somme offensive was to be held back when Rawlinson's Fourth Army attacked, but to be close enough to the front to fight its way forward, rather than wait for a perfect gap. As Haig instructed Rawlinson in April, 'Opportunities to use cavalry, supported by guns, machine-guns etc., and infantry should be sought for, both during the early stages of the attack and subsequently'.[37] If this method of attack worked, GHQ's most optimistic forecast called for the cavalry to advance only as far as Bapaume before turning back to attack the enemy trenches from the rear – an advance of just 10 miles and a far cry from the plans for deep cavalry raids of earlier years. Haig impressed on Gough the need to improve the standard of the cavalry for this operation. 'Above all', Haig wrote, 'he is to spread the "doctrine" and get cavalry officers to believe in the power of their arm when acting in co-operation with guns and infantry.'[38]

What exactly this meant in terms of organization and training, and how radical a departure Gough's force represented from pre-war cavalry and infantry tactics is, at this distance, hard to assess. Edmonds's *Official History* is quite silent on the subject, hardly giving the Reserve Army a mention before the start of the battle. Gough's own account in his memoirs is thoroughly confused, stating at one point that the object was 'to create a striking force of all arms – with cavalry predominating' and, at another, that his orders were 'to advance through the centre and raid Bapaume'.[39] There does not seem to have been any clear written doctrinal statement from Haig to Gough. The issue is further complicated by the fact that the command, structure and nature of Gough's force became the subject of a serious dispute between Rawlinson and Haig. What is known is that from April 1916, after Gough's additional appointment by Haig as Temporary Inspector General of Training of Cavalry Divisions, the cavalry divisions began to take the mounted troops (the divisional cavalry, cyclists and, in some cases, armoured cars) of infantry divisions for special training courses lasting about two weeks. The cavalry divisions themselves also undertook special training in how to cross trench lines rapidly with regimental or brigade-sized forces. No combined training appears to have taken place below divisional level, and the co-operation that Gough envisaged was entirely among divisions. In June, an infantry division that had been already earmarked for the Reserve Army, the 25th Division, spent two weeks training in mounting an attack on the enemy's third line of trenches after the first two lines had been captured and breaking out into open country, culminating in a rehearsal exercise watched over by Gough. (Interestingly, it was also at this time that the 25th Division adopted a horseshoe as its divisional sign.) By 16 June, plans existed to attach II Corps of three infantry divisions to the Reserve Army, which then consisted only of the 1st and 3rd Cavalry Divisions and the 2nd Indian Cavalry Division. This training and structure clearly suggest that the embryo Reserve Army plan was for the 25th Division to exploit any success by Fourth Army, closely followed by two or more of the cavalry divisions (probably with the 2nd Indian Cavalry Division in front) and then by the infantry of II Corps following up.[40]

In one sense, Gough's Reserve Army harked back to the Napoleonic concept of a General Reserve which Haig had learned at the Staff College, while 'the intelligent co-operation of the three arms' had become an Army cliché long before the First World War. But in another sense, Haig's concept of an all-arms striking force clearly pointed the way to the future of mobile warfare. However, the idea was also very ambitious. A cavalry division on the Western Front occupied nearly ten miles of road space, and needed to be held at least that distance behind the front to be safe from enemy artillery before the initial attack. Bringing these reserve forces through the chaos of the rear areas and destruction of the battle-field demanded techniques of staff-work, traffic control and an understanding of large-unit warfare which the British Army in 1916 was only just beginning to grasp.

The main reason that the exact nature of Haig's plan for the Reserve Army is hard to discern is that it was thoroughly sabotaged by Rawlinson as commander of Fourth Army. On 21 June, after repeated attempts, Rawlinson at last secured Haig's agreement that Gough's force should come under Fourth Army rather than GHQ. Next day, II Corps was taken away from Reserve Army, leaving it with only the three cavalry divisions, while Rawlinson explained to his corps commanders that, although Haig insisted on the presence of the cavalry in the attack plan, he did not expect them to be used. For the day of the attack, two of the three cavalry divisions would be assembled about five miles behind the British front, but they were only to advance through the centre in the wake of two reserve infantry divisions if the German front collapsed completely.[41] When the battle began on 1 July, Rawlinson quite simply ignored the Reserve Army, leaving it without orders. At midday, despite having just been informed of the successful capture of Montauban by XIII Corps, Rawlinson decided that there was no chance of an exploitation and stood the Reserve Army down, refusing even to commit XIII Corps's reserve division. Gough, together with his chief of staff, waited all day at Fourth Army headquarters in ignorance of what was happening, not prepared to interfere.[42]

At almost exactly the time that Rawlinson was deciding not to use the cavalry, the chance for exploitation was there, on the British right near Montauban and Mametz, where, in contrast to the rest of the front, the attack had met with some success. This was where Rawlinson least expected the advance to succeed, and where he believed the German line to be strongest, setting the first day's initial objective for the infantry attack (the 'Green Line') as the German second line of trenches, rather than the third line as in the centre and on the left. Gough also appears to have expected the breakthrough to come in the centre. What would have happened had Rawlinson used the Reserve Army as Haig intended, and exploited his limited success on the right, must be a matter of speculation. But as it happened, the reserve division for XIII Corps was one of the best divisions in the Army, the 9th (Scottish) Division. Reviewing the map of the Somme battlefield or the ground as it exists today, and taking into account the situation as it was known at Fourth Army headquarters by about midday on 1 July 1916, it does not strain credulity to suggest that if held close to the original Fourth Army front and moved forward promptly, the 25th Division and 2nd Indian Cavalry Division might between them have gained another mile or two in company with the 9th (Scottish) Division, past such places of later horror as Delville Wood and High Wood to the British third objective (the 'Purple Line') which was the greatest advance expected that day. Only three or four German battalions would have stood in their way at the time; in the actual battle, when on 3 July two battalions of the 9th (Scottish) Division attacked Bernafay Wood, about 1,000 yards east of Montauban, they found it virtually undefended and secured it for the loss of only six casualties. The next two or three days' fighting might even have taken the fresh troops of the Reserve Army (which by then would have numbered at least three cavalry and four infantry divisions) perhaps two more miles, a distance which it would ultimately take the British Army on the Somme until 20 November to cover, with staggering losses. Those who agree with Rawlinson that the cavalry was valueless would regard this speculation as ludicrously optimistic. Whether the Reserve Army concept of an all-arms force would have succeeded in July 1916 remains one of the great 'what if's' of the British Army's experience on the Western Front.

Following the bloody fiasco of 1 July, a different tone appeared in Rawlinson's diary, when he portrayed himself as anxious to use the cavalry but doubtful of the chances of doing so, possibly as a result of his discussions with Haig. But the assault by Fourth Army on High Wood which followed on 14 July only showed the staff-work difficulties of bringing the cavalry forward once the attack had started. Following the success of his night attack, Rawlinson called at 7.40 a.m. for the 2nd Indian Cavalry Division to exploit forward. The division began to move from its assembly area at 8.20 a.m., but by midday the German artillery, which was its main target, had already begun to withdraw. 'Oh! If we could get the cavalry through to charge them!' Rawlinson lamented.[43] In fact two regiments of the leading Secunderabad Cavalry Brigade had been in position for some time, and it is not at all clear why orders to advance took so long to reach them. It was not until nearly 7.00 p.m. that they crossed the British front line and went into action. In a fine piece of co-operation, while two infantry battalions charged into High Wood itself and captured its southern corner, squadrons of two cavalry regiments, the 7th Dragoon Guards and 20th Deccan Horse, delivered a simultaneous charge south of the wood, which broke into the unfinished German Switch Line defences, killing or capturing over 60 of the enemy. Finally, driven back a short distance to a defensible position, the cavalry dismounted and dug in. Failing to receive infantry support during the night, they pulled back with their prisoners in the early hours of the morning, having taken around 100 casualties.[44]

Two things are noteworthy about this charge, other than the fact of its success. The first is that with only two regiments advancing in line it was too weak to maintain momentum. The second is that the cavalrymen were not so much shot down as pinned down after their initial charge had spent itself, being able to keep the ground that they had already gained but unable to push on further. It did not take much military imagination to realize that if troopers from two regiments could charge successfully for 1,000 yards into unprepared German defences, a further two brigades committed early enough in the day could have continued the charge by a further 1,500 yards to the east, so taking the German positions at Longueval and Delville Wood in the rear and obviating the need for a further month's hard fighting. The problem of using the cavalry effectively in the conditions of 1916 was not one of tactics or its vulnerability to machine-guns, but of staff-work and of how to get a large enough force of cavalry through early enough to make a difference before the night fell, at a time when communications beyond the front line depended on nothing better than dispatch riders, aeroplanes, kite balloons and homing pigeons, together with the ubiquitous flag Morse and runners.

Delays on the approach, resulting in the cavalry arriving too little and too late, would be the pattern for the next two years, making a vicious circle that with every failure there was less reason for the other arms to expect the cavalry to achieve anything next time. There was even a strong suspicion that the infantry could have taken High Wood themselves during the day, but had been forced to wait for the cavalry at Rawlinson's insistence, resulting in a further bloodbath before the wood was finally taken two months later.

On 7 September the Cavalry Corps was reformed under Lieutenant General Sir Charles Kavanagh, including all five cavalry divisions. Four days later, Kavanagh met Rawlinson to discuss the employment of the cavalry in the forthcoming battle of Flers-Courcelette, and a solution to the problem of getting the cavalry up in time. Rawlinson records that they agreed that 'the leading regiment must settle the moment for the cavalry to go through', a significant advance in doctrine. But Rawlinson's own views, recorded on the day before the attack, reveal that, although he was prepared to entertain the idea of the cavalry being of some use after the experience of 14 July, he had either not grasped Haig's all-arms concept, or had rejected it. 'I think that there is a fair chance of getting the cavalry through', Rawlinson wrote, 'but I am a little anxious lest Kavanagh should act prematurely and thus compromise the action of the other arms, particularly the artillery which would have to cease fire'.[45] Once more, the cavalry received no orders from Fourth Army on the day of the attack.

An ironic footnote to the discussion of the cavalry's role on the Somme comes from Siegfried Sassoon's *Memoirs of an Infantry Officer*, describing a march past

Rawlinson as Army Commander before the battle. 'He had taken the salute from four hundred officers and NCOs of his Army', Sassoon wrote with some bitterness. 'How many had been killed since then, and how deeply was he responsible for their deaths? Did he know what he was doing, or was he merely a successful old *cavalryman* whose peace-time popularity had pushed him up to his present perch?'[46] (emphasis added). By 1916, the belief that all the Army's ills were the fault of the cavalry and of cavalry generals was so well established that Sassoon could take it for granted. The error of calling Rawlinson a cavalryman remains surprisingly common among otherwise careful modern historians of the war.

The year of Arras and Passchendaele went by, leaving the cavalry with little to show except a steady deterioration both in their numbers and in the quality of their junior leadership. Meanwhile, both Robertson and the War Cabinet continued to press Haig to reduce his cavalry force in the light of the German unrestricted submarine warfare campaign, begun in February 1917. Haig's sensitivity towards the deteriorating quality of his cavalry force, his anxiety to justify its existence in battle and the increasing impossibility of replacing its losses are all reflected in the manifestly contradictory orders that he gave the Cavalry Corps for its role in Arras. 'They should be carefully handled so that their value may remain unimpaired', Haig ordered, 'it is essential that the Cavalry Corps should be in a condition to deliver an effective blow against the enemy in battle; this moment has not yet arrived'.[47] To order the cavalry to attack and at the same time not to take casualties was simply not possible.

For Arras, two of the cavalry divisions were held in reserve with First Army and Fifth Army. The Cavalry Corps, consisting of two cavalry divisions, one infantry division and the remaining cavalry division in corps reserve (a structure similar to that planned by Gough for the Reserve Army before the Somme, but without the additional infantry corps), was placed under Third Army command, and the orders issued by Allenby as commander of Third Army show that he had a much better understanding of how to use the cavalry than Rawlinson. For the first day's attack on 9 April, Kavanagh's two leading cavalry divisions were drawn up in positions north-west and south of Arras respectively, with the heads of their columns less than 4,000 yards from the British front line. Allenby's orders were that if his main attack by VI Corps succeeded in breaking through the German defences, a distance of about 5,000 yards to the Green Line, the Cavalry Corps could then exploit for a further 5,000 yards to the line of the River Sensée, which it would hold until relieved by the infantry, and then advance for a further bound of 5,000 yards in the direction of Cambrai to complete an all-arms advance of some eight miles. The main drawback to the plan was that, because of the shallowness of the British front before Arras, the cavalry divisional columns would have to pass through the town before coming into action. Also, in the light of Haig's orders, Allenby made it clear that the cavalry was not to be used unless the first infantry attacks achieved total success. 'The enemy may bring up his reserves and show a strong battle front about the Green Line or in front of it', Allenby predicted with unsurprising accuracy. 'In this case the Cavalry Corps will not advance'.[48] With the strong German resistance to Third Army's initial attack, and the driving sleet and snow in which the battle was fought, it was not until the third day that the cavalry got a chance to come properly into action. Two brigades of the 3rd Cavalry Division were put through in support of an infantry attack, enabling three of their regiments to capture the village of Monchy-Le-Preux from the Germans in a surprise 'gallop' attack. It was an enterprising piece of work but, although soon reinforced by the infantry, the two brigades sustained over 600 casualties in holding the village against German counterattacks. Byng, who commanded the Canadian Corps at Arras, confessed that 'it seems rather a pity to lose all these chaps who were perfect cavalrymen for the sake of a village which is a complete shell trap for the British side'.[49]

For Third Ypres even Haig gave up the idea of a cavalry exploitation on the first day – at least temporarily – in his anxiety to husband the cavalry for their decisive advance later in the battle. The cavalry was intended to take part only after its first phase, the seizing of the Staden-Passchendaele ridge, which ultimately occupied the whole of the autumn. In preparation for the second phase, the cavalry began in September, on Haig's orders, to train in co-operation with tanks as well as infantry, but the chance to use the two arms together never came. Once again, the cavalry were left waiting around behind the lines.

The cavalry's next opportunity came in the Battle of Cambrai in November

1917, a battle that is still surrounded by controversy, particularly as to why the British attack was launched so late in the year and what it was supposed to achieve. What is clear is that in terms of staff-work and all-arms co-operation the battle was a shambles on the British side. On its first day, 20 November, four separate corps headquarters, III Corps, IV Corps, the Cavalry Corps and the Tank Corps (the last unofficially), all issued contradictory orders to the leading cavalry and infantry brigades. The Tank Corps version of co-operation was reduced to 'we go straight in and sit on the Germans until the cavalry come'.[50] Haig recommended to Byng, now commanding Third Army, the employment of 'detachments of all arms, lightly equipped' to lead the attack, a revival of his ideas from before the Somme, but Byng ignored the suggestion.[51] The result was almost a case-study in an unco-ordinated battle plan, which thoroughly deserved to fail. It is a reflection of the poor planning for Cambrai that on the right of the battlefield the attack was launched in front of one of the few obstacles on the Western Front that was genuinely impassable for cavalry, the St Quentin-Escaut Canal. 'Horses can cross almost anything', Brigadier General Seely, commanding the Canadian Cavalry Brigade, pointed out, 'they can even swim broad rivers, as they have often done in war. But the one thing they cannot get over, unless they can bridge it, is a canal with sheer-sided banks. They can get in but they can't get out'.[52] Incredibly, Byng's orders called for III Corps, led by the tanks, to seize the crossings over the canal south of Masnières with the intention of passing the whole Cavalry Corps – less the 1st Cavalry Division, which was to cover its inner flank by moving between Marcoing and Fontaine – through this tiny series of bottlenecks, and ride in a giant arc clean around Cambrai from south-east to north-west to regain the British line. It was a comparatively simple matter for the Germans defending the canal to destroy the bridges as the tanks approached with the infantry and cavalry behind them.

The result was an unmitigated and frustrating failure for the cavalry. One of Seely's Canadian regiments, the Fort Garry Horse, found an undefended footbridge and got elements of one squadron, estimated at 133 troopers, across with half an hour of daylight left, only to have the commander of the 2nd Cavalry Division (apparently on the advice of an infantry brigade commander) refuse permission for any further reinforcement to follow. Cut off behind enemy lines, the squadron charged through the German rear areas before stampeding their horses with nightfall. Only 46 men re-crossed the canal that night. Further north, between Marcoing and Masnières, the 7th Dragoon Guards also got a squadron across one bridge, but had to fall back under enemy fire. In the centre, the failure of IV Corps to clear Flesquières resulted in the 1st Cavalry Division also getting just one squadron into action. Belonging to the 4th Dragoon Guards, this delivered a successful charge near Cantaing, retiring with over 70 prisoners for the loss of 7 men and 15 horses. But that was all. The commander of IV Corps was convinced that a gap had been there and that the cavalry had missed it, and entered a formal complaint against the 1st Cavalry Division after the battle. The cavalrymen were deeply humiliated. In confidential reports to Haig, officers blamed the failure partly on poor co-operation with the other arms, but chiefly on the promotion block, which had forced good officers out of the cavalry, and on their generally poor morale and lack of faith in themselves.[53]

In the German counter-attack which followed Cambrai, the cavalry was used once more in its familiar emergency role, as dismounted firepower to plug the British line. But on 1 December a dreadful incident took place, born of the immense frustration felt by senior cavalry officers at their failure a few days earlier. The Mhow Cavalry Brigade, fighting dismounted in support of the 1st Guards Brigade, was ordered to make a mounted attack against the German positions, apparently at Kavanagh's personal insistence and over the protests of its divisional and brigade commanders. This was an exercise in futility to rival the worst experience of the infantry on the Western Front. After a charge by the 2nd Lancers (Gardner's Horse) had been pinned down after achieving some success, the 6th Inniskilling Dragoons sent an unsupported squadron forward into uncut wire in an attempt to gallop the Villers Guislain ridge. Blasted by artillery, machine-gun and rifle fire, the squadron was virtually wiped out, losing 112 men and 187 horses for no result.[54]

The cavalry's failure at Cambrai also brought the question of its continued presence on the Western Front to a head. By this stage of the war the cavalry issue had become, for Lloyd George in particular, little more than another weapon

with which to attack Haig; and Robertson, who was struggling to survive politically as CIGS and was finally replaced by Wilson in February 1918, gave Haig no
support at all. Haig's desperation at the prospect of losing his cavalry is reflected
in the arguments with which he defended them in front of the War Cabinet
on 7 January, stressing their value in defensive operations and even describing
the cavalry as 'resembling highly trained mobile infantry rather than the old
cavalry arm', something which would have been anathema to him before the
war.[55] Rejecting this special pleading by Haig, the War Cabinet ordered a major
cavalry redeployment with the stated aim of reinforcing the cavalry in Palestine
and reducing the amount of shipping needed to supply the Western Front. In a
complicated juggling act of troop movements, the two Indian cavalry divisions in
France were broken up, and their Indian regiments, together with one divisional
headquarters, were sent to Palestine, where they were reformed by breaking up
the Yeomanry Division to provide the British troops and a second divisional
headquarters. In return, nine yeomanry regiments in Egypt and Palestine were
formed into five machine-gun battalions and sent to the Western Front, where
the three Household Cavalry regiments, together with six yeomanry regiments
(including two of corps cavalry that had somehow survived so far) were marked
for conversion to cyclist or machine-gun battalions. The three British cavalry
divisions were reorganized, with the Canadian Cavalry Brigade joining the
3rd Cavalry Division. (Perhaps significantly, the only yeomanry regiment to
survive with the cavalry was also the most socially prestigious, the 1st Queen's
Own Oxfordshire Hussars as part of the 2nd Cavalry Division.) The net result
was 19 fewer regiments of cavalry in France for two more in Palestine – hardly
the substantial reinforcement for the Egyptian Expeditionary Force that Lloyd
George claimed in his memoirs. This redeployment deprived Haig of almost
half of his mobile reserve for the forthcoming German offensive of March 1918,
while so much shipping was needed to bring it about that no net saving on ships
was made.

The Household Cavalry and yeomanry had already surrendered their horses,
and the Indian cavalry had embarked at Marseilles, when the German offensive
began on 21 March – a fact for which Gough never forgave Robertson. In the

emergency, the yeomanry regiments (with one exception) reclaimed their horses and joined in with the regular cavalry, providing an effective mobile defence for the retreating Third and Fifth Armies based on small dismounted fire teams together with occasional mounted charges of troop or squadron strength. The most famous mounted attack of the battle (perhaps largely because of Seely's skill as a self-publicist) was delivered by a squadron of Lord Strathcona's Horse of the Canadian Cavalry Brigade, which charged to help secure Moreil Ridge in front of Amiens from the Germans on 30 March.[56] To argue whether such a small cavalry force played a significant role in halting the German offensive is to miss the point that the essence of the British defence was all-arms co-operation, in which the cavalry played a vital part by providing mobile firepower and occasional shock charges. Haig and Gough were certainly convinced that a principal reason for the German defeat was their failure to employ their own cavalry as an arm of exploitation. There were cases of British battalions retreating in virtual panic at totally unfounded rumours of German cavalry attacking.

For the remainder of the war, the Household Cavalry, as lorry-borne machine-gunners, provided the fire support for cavalry divisions, which had regained something of their prestige and their confidence since the dark days of Cambrai. Haig worked to revitalize the cavalry, breaking the promotion jam by removing two divisional and six brigade commanders, and only narrowly rejected the idea of removing Kavanagh himself as Cavalry Corps commander. Haig also stressed the training of the cavalry troop under its leader as the basic tactical unit, and on leadership from the front in the attack. This planning paid off in the Battle of Amiens, before which Haig insisted that Rawlinson find a major role for the Cavalry Corps. Rawlinson's solution was to draw partly on Haig's improvements to the cavalry, partly on the experience of Arras and later battles, and partly on his own previous experience of commanding mounted troops before the war. For the first day of the battle, 8 August 1918, the cavalry divisions were drawn up in their assembly areas as dispersed brigades rather than in divisional columns, with each brigade area about 8,000 yards behind the front, and the difficult staff-work problems of bringing them up and passing them through the infantry early enough were finally solved. An hour after the first infantry attack, the cavalry brigades were in position only 2,000 yards behind the original front and ready to go through.

The first objective for the cavalry was set as the old Amiens outer defence line, which ran from Le Quesnel northwards to the River Somme at Bray, a distance of at most five miles from the original British line. Edmonds, in the *Official History*, criticized the cavalry for advancing only as far as this objective, and not attempting to press on a further four miles south-west to its second objective at Chaulnes until late afternoon, by which time the strengthening German defences had made the advance impractical. However, the Fourth Army account, which is confirmed by the cavalry divisional war diaries, makes it clear that the cavalry were only obeying their orders: they were to advance through the infantry to secure the Amiens outer defences, but then hold them until the arrival of the infantry before pushing on once more.[57] This use of mounted troops to 'gallop' a position and secure it was familiar from previous battles and had been part of Allenby's plan at Arras, but had never been attempted before on such a scale. It was also highly reminiscent of similar mounted 'gallops' by British mounted troops against defended positions in the Boer War, including those under-taken by the 8th Mounted Infantry under (the then) Lieutenant Colonel Henry Rawlinson. In effect, Rawlinson had integrated the cavalry into his usual 'bite and hold' scheme in order to double the size of the 'bite' from 5,000 to 10,000 yards, enough to take it through the German defences.

The cavalry's success on 8 August put its value on the Western Front beyond dispute. All the first line of objectives had been taken by early afternoon, together with 1,300 prisoners. Successful mounted charges were delivered by the 5th Dragoon Guards of the 1st Cavalry Brigade (one against a train-load of surprised Germans) and the 7th Dragoon Guards of the 7th Cavalry Brigade, although an attempt by the Canadian Cavalry Brigade to 'gallop' Beaucourt Wood, defended by three German infantry battalions, was unsuccessful. Even Rawlinson admitted that the cavalry had done 'splendid work', while Fourth Army's war diary pays tribute to 'the cavalry and infantry co-operating admirably'.[58]

The only significant criticism of the cavalry after the battle came from the tankmen, resulting from the failure of co-operation between the cavalry and the

new Medium A Whippet tanks, which had otherwise also had a very successful day. The problem was that the Whippets could not keep up with the cavalry
in the advance, but tended to surge ahead on their own when under fire. This
reflected more a lack of faith on both sides, and the difficulties of co-ordinating
an all-arms battle, rather than any inherent weakness of the cavalry or its tactics.
Indeed, the difficulty of how to co-ordinate other arms with armour became
one of the great military problems of the twentieth century, one that was never
solved with complete satisfaction.

From Amiens onwards, a major problem for Haig was trying to convince his
sceptical Army commanders that this time he was right and the war could be
won quickly. On finding that, for the Third Army's attack on 21 August, Byng had
planned to use only a brigade of cavalry, Haig told him that 'the Cavalry Corps
is now 100 per cent better than it was at Cambrai. He must use the cavalry to the
fullest extent possible'. Haig also instructed his Corps commanders to 'reinforce
where we are winning, not where we are held up!' – the classic catchphrase of successful exploitation tactics.[59] Even corps cavalry were temporarily reintroduced
by a regiment being given to each corps involved in the attack, while a brigade
of infantry in buses was added to the lorried machine-guns of the Household
Cavalry to turn the Cavalry Corps into a true all-arms formation. But by this date
the cavalry was a steadily wasting asset, and on 1 September the Cavalry Corps
was pulled back into reserve to keep it up to strength in case the German front
should collapse altogether. With the malice characteristic of someone who, in
his own eyes, was never wrong, Haig wrote to Henry Wilson as CIGS that 'our
shortage of cavalry is daily becoming more noticeable, and there is no doubt
that your predecessor committed a serious error in sending off to Palestine two
cavalry divisions last February. I hear that they are doing little or nothing there'.[60]
This remark was almost ludicrously untrue, as Haig would find out a few days
later when Allenby's thunderbolt of mobile warfare shattered the Turkish forces
in Palestine.

Major exercises were mounted for the Cavalry Corps in September to test its
co-operation tactics, including the use of overflying aircraft machine-gunning
the ground only a few yards ahead of the charging cavalry – something for which

Haig had high hopes, and which later became standard practice for British airmen co-operating with White Russian cavalry in the War of Intervention. The Cavalry Corps was used once more, on 8 October on the Fourth Army front in its final successful breakthrough near Le Cateau, before being withdrawn to rest two days later. Thereafter, individual regiments and brigades were used across the front to spearhead the British advance through to the Armistice. But by this date the entire Cavalry Corps, at fewer than 14,000 men and horses, was not very much stronger than the original Cavalry Division of 1914. In fact, the War Cabinet had only narrowly decided in June not to reinforce Haig by sending the Australian Mounted Division from Palestine to France. The final irony about the cavalry on the Western Front was not that there was too much of it, but that at the end of the war there was actually not enough.

In summing up, it is clearly a mistaken judgement to describe the cavalry on the Western Front as a failure. The last doctrinal pamphlet for infantry divisions issued by the British Army in France, *SS135 The Division in Attack* of November 1918, included a section on cavalry which summarized what the Army had learned in four years of fighting: 'Cavalry will be used to complete the enemy's defeat after he has been driven out of his last organized defensive system, *or whenever a favourable opportunity may arise*', (emphasis added), the pamphlet read, adding that 'the moral[e] effect of cavalry, combined with the fire of its horse artillery and machine-guns, must be exploited to the full', and that 'all supporting cavalry must be kept close behind the leading troops ready to take advantage of any opportunities which may arise'.[61] But although the cavalry played a greater part in victory than is usually realized, its success was of a middling sort. Its two greatest achievements were defensive operations covering retreats, and its tactical innovations and contribution to the last great offensives of 1918 fade into insignificance compared with those of the artillery, infantry or engineers.

Nevertheless, it is certainly wrong, given the success of cavalry operations in Palestine and Mesopotamia, and also in Poland and Russia in the years immediately following the First World War, to argue that those who continued to believe in the value of the cavalry after 1918 were either misguided or short-sighted.

A true replacement for the cavalry, in the form of a practical genuinely fast tank, did not exist in the First World War or for some years thereafter. Horsed cavalry became obsolete only when mechanical armoured vehicles, which were less vulnerable to fire, became as manoeuvrable over all terrain, easier to maintain and cheaper to keep. This was far more a long-term technological and even social phenomenon than an issue of military tactics. It happened in Western Europe in the inter-war period, but not in Eastern Europe until after the Second World War, and in some parts or the world it has not actually happened yet.

Finally, there is the interesting problem of the alternative past. What would have happened if Haig had asserted his authority over Rawlinson before July 1916, as he did before August 1918, and the Reserve Army had been used as he intended? In September 1944, it was considered worthwhile to risk three airborne divisions in Operation Market-Garden to end the Second World War before Christmas. The result was the disaster at Arnhem, the notorious 'bridge too far' in which the leading division was virtually wiped out. But what would have happened if the cavalry divisions of the Reserve Army, organized and positioned as Haig had intended, had been risked by Rawlinson on the late morning of 1 July 1916? Would the British Army have been spared the rest of the Somme – perhaps even Passchendaele too? We shall never know.

THE BRITISH CAVALRY DIVISIONS OF THE FIRST WORLD WAR

AUGUST 1914

THE WESTERN FRONT

The Cavalry Division
1st Cavalry Brigade
2nd Cavalry Brigade
3rd Cavalry Brigade

4th Cavalry Brigade (including the composite Household Regiment)

5th Cavalry Brigade (independent)

November 1914

The Cavalry Corps

1st Cavalry Division

1st Cavalry Brigade

2nd Cavalry Brigade

9th Cavalry Brigade (from April 1915 – including one yeomanry
  regiment)

2nd Cavalry Division

3rd Cavalry Brigade

4th Cavalry Brigade (including one yeomanry regiment)

5th Cavalry Brigade

3rd Cavalry Division

6th Cavalry Brigade (including one yeomanry regiment)

7th Cavalry Brigade (including one yeomanry regiment)

8th Cavalry Brigade (including one yeomanry regiment)

The Indian Cavalry Corps

1st Indian Cavalry Division

Mhow Cavalry Brigade (including one British line regiment)

Lucknow Cavalry Brigade (including one British line regiment)

Sialkot Cavalry Brigade (including one British line regiment)

2nd Indian Cavalry Division

Ambala Cavalry Brigade (including one British line regiment)

Secunderabad Cavalry Brigade (including one British line regiment)

Meerut Cavalry Brigade (including one British line regiment)[*]

---

[*] This brigade left the division in June 1916.

September 1916

The Cavalry Corps

1st Cavalry Division
1st Cavalry Brigade
2nd Cavalry Brigade
9th Cavalry Brigade (including one yeomanry regiment)

2nd Cavalry Division
3rd Cavalry Brigade
4th Cavalry Brigade (including one yeomanry regiment)
5th Cavalry Brigade

3rd Cavalry Division
6th Cavalry Brigade (including one yeomanry regiment)
7th Cavalry Brigade (including one yeomanry regiment)
8th Cavalry Brigade (including one yeomanry regiment)

4th Cavalry Division
Mhow Cavalry Brigade (including one British line regiment)
Lucknow Cavalry Brigade (including one British line regiment)[*]
Sialkot Cavalry Brigade (including one British line regiment)

5th Cavalry Division
Ambala Cavalry Brigade (including one British line regiment)
Secunderabad Cavalry Brigade (including one British line regiment)
Canadian Cavalry Brigade

March 1918

The Cavalry Corps

1st Cavalry Division
1st Cavalry Brigade
2nd Cavalry Brigade
9th Cavalry Brigade

---

[*] The British line regiment with this brigade was sent to India in 1917.

2nd Cavalry Division
3rd Cavalry Brigade
4th Cavalry Brigade (including one yeomanry regiment)
5th Cavalry Brigade

3rd Cavalry Division
6th Cavalry Brigade
7th Cavalry Brigade
Canadian Cavalry Brigade

A Household Cavalry Composite Brigade of motorised machine-gunners formed the Cavalry Corps reserve.

APRIL 1917

EGYPT AND PALESTINE

The Desert Column
The ANZAC Mounted Division
22nd Mounted Brigade
1st ALH Brigade
2nd ALH Brigade
NZ Mounted Brigade

The Imperial Mounted Division
2nd Mounted Brigade
6th Mounted Brigade
3rd ALH Brigade

All 'Mounted' brigades are British yeomanry, except for the New Zealand Mounted Brigade. ALH brigades are Australian Light Horse. The composition of both divisions seems to have changed frequently.

JULY 1917

The Desert Mounted Corps
The ANZAC Mounted Division
1st ALH Brigade
2nd ALH Brigade
NZ Mounted Brigade

The Yeomanry Division
6th Mounted Brigade
8th Mounted Brigade
22nd Mounted Brigade

The Australian Mounted Division
3rd ALH Brigade
4th ALH Brigade
5th Mounted Brigade

The 7th Mounted Brigade and the Imperial Camel Corps Brigade were independent as part of the Desert Mounted Corps reserve at this date.

MARCH 1918

The Desert Mounted Corps
The ANZAC Mounted Division
1st ALH Brigade
2nd ALH Brigade
NZ Mounted Brigade

The Australian Mounted Division
3rd ALH Brigade
4th ALH Brigade
5th ALH Brigade

4th Cavalry Division
10th Cavalry Brigade
11th Cavalry Brigade
12th Cavalry Brigade

5th Cavalry Division
13th Cavalry Brigade
14th Cavalry Brigade
15th (Imperial Service) Cavalry Brigade

The cavalry brigades were all composed of one yeomanry regiment (from breaking up the Yeomanry Division and the mounted brigades) and two Indian cavalry regiments (sent from France), except the 15th, which was composed of three Indian regiments maintained by the ruling princes of their respective states.

August 1915

GALLIPOLI

2nd Mounted Division
1st Mounted Brigade
2nd Mounted Brigade
3rd Mounted Brigade
4th Mounted Brigade
5th Mounted Brigade

September 1915

2nd Mounted Division
1st Composite Brigade
2nd Composite Brigade
1st Scottish Horse Mounted Brigade
1st Highland Mounted Brigade

In December 1915, this division was withdrawn to Cairo and reorganized back to its original structure. In January 1916 it was broken up as follows:

1st Mounted Brigade – renumbered 22nd Mounted Brigade, served with the ANZAC Mounted Division and the Yeomanry Division, renumbered 12th Cavalry Brigade and reorganized, served with 4th Cavalry Division.

2nd Mounted Brigade – renumbered 6th Mounted Brigade, served with the Imperial Mounted Division, the Yeomanry Mounted Division, renumbered 14th Cavalry Brigade and reorganized, served with 5th Cavalry Division

3rd Mounted Brigade – renumbered 7th Mounted Brigade, served in Salonika (independent), returned to Egypt June 1917, renumbered 10th Mounted Brigade and reorganized, served with 4th Cavalry Division.

4th Mounted Brigade – renumbered 8th Mounted Brigade, served Western Egypt and with the Yeomanry Division, renumbered 11th Cavalry Brigade and reorganized, served with 4th Cavalry Division.

5th Mounted Brigade – served Western Egypt, renumbered 13th Cavalry Brigade and reorganized, served with 5th Cavalry Division.

NOVEMBER 1918

MESOPOTAMIA

6th Indian Cavalry Brigade (including one British line regiment)
7th Indian Cavalry Brigade (including one British line regiment)
11th Indian Cavalry Brigade (including one British line regiment)

August 1914

THE HOME FRONT

1st Mounted Division
Eastern Mounted Brigade
1st South Midlands Mounted Brigade
2nd South Midlands Mounted Brigade
Notts and Derby Mounted Brigade

September 1914

1st Mounted Division
Eastern Mounted Brigade
South Wales Mounted Brigade
Welsh Border Mounted Brigade
North Midlands Mounted Brigade
Cyclist Brigade (four battalions from Territorial Force infantry regiments)

2nd Mounted Division
1st South Midlands Mounted Brigade
2nd South Midlands Mounted Brigade
Notts and Derby Mounted Brigade
London Mounted Brigade

May 1915

1st Mounted Division
1st South Wales Mounted Brigade
Welsh Border Mounted Brigade
2/1st South Wales Mounted Brigade
2/1st North Midlands Mounted Brigade

2nd Mounted Division
1st Mounted Brigade
2nd Mounted Brigade
3rd Mounted Brigade
4th Mounted Brigade

This division was sent to Gallipoli in August 1915.

2/2nd Mounted Division
2/1st Notts and Derby Mounted Brigade
2/1st South Midlands Mounted Brigade
2/2nd South Midlands Mounted Brigade
2/1st London Mounted Brigade

APRIL 1916

1st Mounted Division
1st Mounted Brigade
2nd Mounted Brigade
3rd Mounted Brigade
4th Mounted Brigade

These have no relationship to the brigades of the same number that fought with 2nd Mounted Division at Gallipoli and were renumbered later in Egypt. In July 1916, the division was converted to cyclist troops and renamed **1st Cyclist Division,** and in November 1916 this division was broken up.

3rd Mounted Division
2/1st Notts and Derby Mounted Brigade
2/1st South Midlands Mounted Brigade
2/2nd South Midlands Mounted Brigade
2/1st London Mounted Brigade

This division was previously 2/2nd Mounted Division. In July 1916 (after 1st Mounted Division had become 1st Cyclist Division) it was renamed **1st Mounted Division**. In September 1916 it was converted to cyclist troops and renamed **The Cyclist Division**.

4th Mounted Division
13th Mounted Brigade
14th Mounted Brigade
15th Mounted Brigade
16th Mounted Brigade

This division was created in March 1916; in July 1916 it was converted to cyclist troops and renamed **2nd Cyclist Division**; it was broken up in November 1916.

JANUARY 1917

The Cyclist Division
1st Cyclist Brigade
2nd Cyclist Brigade
3rd Cyclist Brigade
4th Cyclist Brigade

This was the old 2/2nd Mounted Division/3rd Mounted Division/1st Mounted Division. It served at home until the end of the war.

NOTES

1 Major Philip Hammond, 'F' Battalion, Tank Corps, quoted in Woolcombe, R. (1967), *The First Tank Battle: Cambrai 1917.* London: Arthur Barker, p. 85.

2 Gooch, J. (1974), *The Plans of War: The General Staff and British Military Strategy c.1900–1916.* London: Routledge & Kegan Paul, p. 117; Travers, (1987) op. cit., p. 5; Prior, R. and Wilson, T. (2005), *The Somme.* New Haven, CT: Yale University Press, p. 51; Terraine (1963) op. cit., p. 21; De Groot, G. (1988), *Douglas Haig 1861–1928.* London: Unwin Hyman, p. 234; Lloyd George (1936) op. cit., Volume II, p. 2038. Criticisms and correctives of this view have only appeared recently and can be seen, in particular, in Philips, G. (2007), 'Scapegoat arm: twentieth century cavalry in anglophone military historiography', *The Journal of Military History*, 70, (1), 37–74; and Badsey, S. (2008), *Doctrine and Reform in the British Cavalry 1880–1918.* London: Ashgate.

3 Taylor (1963), op. cit., p. 20; Liddell Hart, B. H. (1972), *History of the First World War.* London: Pan Edition, p. 35; Stone, N. (1975), *The Eastern Front 1914–1917.* London: Hodder & Stoughton, p. 49; Churchill, W. S. (1960), *The World Crisis 1911–1918.* London: 4-Square Edition, p. 583.

4 [Anon] His Majesty's Stationery Office (1922), *Statistics of the Military Effort of the British Empire During the Great War 1914–1920.* London: HMSO, pp. 65–6, 207–8, and 245–6 (hereafter *Statistics of the Military Effort*).

5 Sheppard, E. W. (1939), *The Ninth Queen's Royal Lancers 1715–1936.* London: Gale & Polden, p. 255; Burnett, C. (1926), *The Memoirs of the 18th (Queen Mary's Own) Royal Hussars 1906–1922.* Winchester: Warren & Son, p. 74; Lumley, L. R. (1936), *History of the 11th Hussars (Prince Albert's Own) 1908–1934.* London: RUSI, p. 188; Pomeroy, R. L. (1938), *History of the Scots Greys (The Second Dragoons) August 1914–March 1919.* London: privately printed, p. 149; Harvey, J. R. and Cape, H. A. (1923), *The History of the 5th (Royal Irish) Regiment of Dragoons from 1689 to 1797 and Afterwards The Fifth Royal Irish Lancers from 1858 to 1921.* London: Gale & Polden, p. 410; Willcox, W. T. (1925), *The 3rd (King's Own) Hussars in the Great War (1914–1919).* London: John Murray, p. 257.

6 *See* Haig (1907) op. cit., p. 8, and the criticisms by J. F. C. Fuller in his introduction to Wolff, L. (1958), *In Flanders Fields.* London: Longman & Green, p. xiii, Marshall-Cornwall, J. (1973), *Haig as Military Commander.* London: B. T. Batsford, p. 65 and Collier, B. (1961), *Brasshat: A Biography of Field Marshal Sir Henry Wilson.* London: Secker & Warburg, p. 96. For contemporary evidence *see* TNA WO 33/463 'Reports on experiments with various bullets against animals' (1908); Smith, F. (1898), 'The effects of the Lee-Metford bullet on the bones of horses', *Journal of the Royal United Services Institute*, 38, 41–50; Denison, G. T. (1868), *Modern Cavalry.* London:

Thomas Bosworth, p. 182; and Preston, R. M. P. (1921), *The Desert Mounted Corps*. London: Constable, pp. 80–4.

7   Edmonds (1947), *Official History, France and Belgium 1918, Volume V*, p. 196 and p. 216; *see also* Ellis, J. (1975), *The Social History of the Machine-Gun*. London: Crosset, pp. 111–48; and Terraine, J. (1992), *The Smoke and the Fire: Myths and Anti-Myths of War*. London: Leo Cooper, pp. 130–42. For Edmonds, *see* Bond, B. (1972), *The Victorian Army and the Staff College 1854–1914*. London: Eyre Methuen, pp. 158–69; Green, A. (2004), *Writing the Great War: Sir James Edmonds and the Official Histories, 1915–1948*. London: Routledge; and Travers, op. cit., pp. 10–11.

8   Montgomery, A. (1919), *The Story of the Fourth Army in the Battles of the Hundred Days, August 8th to November 11th 1918*. London: Hodder & Stoughton, pp. 44–6; Edmonds (1947), *Official History France and Belgium 1918, Volume IV*, p. 53 and p. 158; Brereton, J. M. (1982), *A History of the 4th/7th Royal Dragoon Guards 1685–1980*, Catterick: privately printed, pp. 338–9; Pomeroy, R. L. (1924), *The Story of a Regiment of Horse: Being the Regimental History from 1685 to 1922 of the 5th Princess Charlotte of Wales's Dragoon Guards*, Volume I. Edinburgh: Blackwood, pp. 325–8.

9   Edmonds (1947), *Official History France and Belgium 1918, Volume V*, p. 235; Montgomery (1919), op. cit., p. 200.

10 *See*, for example, Travers, T. (1992), *How the War Was Won: Command and Technology in the British Army on the Western Front 1917–1918*. London: Routledge; Prior, R. and Wilson, T. (1992), *Command on the Western Front: The Military Career of Sir Henry Rawlinson 1914–1918*. Oxford: Blackwell; and most recently, Harris, J. P. (2008), *Douglas Haig and the First World War*. Cambridge: Cambridge University Press.

11 Figures taken from (1922) *Statistics of the Military Effort*, pp. 65–6, 207–8, 249, 400, 484–5 and 521; Terraine, (1922) op. cit., pp. 161–6.

12 These figures are taken from an analysis of the British Army's monthly *Army List* (London: HMSO) between January 1915 and January 1918; *see also* Haig Papers 3155.220j, 'Composition of the British Armies in France, 1 February 1919'.

13 Forester, C. S. (1936), *The General*. London: Penguin; Dixon, N. (1976), *On the Psychology of Military Incompetence*. London: Jonathan Cape, p. 307; Messenger, C. (1976), *The Art of Blitzkrieg*. London: Ian Allen, p. 11; Cohen, E. A. and Gooch, J. (1990), *Military Misfortunes: The Anatomy of Failure in War*. New York: The Free Press, p. 305. *See also* Bridges, T. (1938), *Alarms and Excursions*. London: Longmans.

14 Brett-Smith, R. (1969), *The 11th Hussars (Prince Albert's Own)*. London: Leo Cooper, p. 232; and Lloyd, R. A. (1938), *A Trooper in the Tins*. London: Hurst & Blackett, p. 75.

15 Brown J. G. and Bridges, E. J. (1932), *Historical Records of the 14th (King's) Hussars*,

Volume II 1900–1922. London: RUSI, p. 251 and 272; Spears, E. L. (1967), *The Picnic Basket*. London: Secker and Warburg, p. 77; Lumley (1936), op cit., p. 10.

16 Charrington, H. V. S. (1927), *Where Cavalry Stands Today*. London: Gale and Polden, p. 25.

17 For differing views *see* De Groot (1988), op. cit., p. 94; Spiers, E. M. (1977), 'The British Cavalry 1902–1914', *Journal of the Society for Army Historical Research*, 57, (230), 71–9; Bidwell, S. and Graham, D. (1982), *Fire-Power: British Army Weapons and Theories of War 1904–1945*. London: Allen & Unwin, pp. 32–4; Phillips, G. (2002), 'The obsolescence of the *Arme Blanche* and technological determinism in British military history', *War in History*, 9, (1), 39–59; Badsey, S. (2007), 'The Boer War (1899–1902) and British cavalry doctrine: a re-evaluation', *The Journal of Military History*, 71, (1), 75–97.

18 Barrow, G. de S. (1941), *The Fire of Life*. London: Hutchinson, p. 130.

19 'Eques' (pseudonym) (1908), 'Cavalry on the battlefield', *The Cavalry Journal*, 3, (10), p. 143.

20 Edmonds quoted in Gardner, B. (1965), *Allenby*. London: Cassell, p. 75; Steiner (1977) op. cit., p. 194; Vaughan, J. (1954), *Cavalry and Sporting Memories*. Bala: The Bala Press, p. 161; TNA WO 163/18 'Army Council Decisions 1913 Number 734'.

21 Liddell Hart Centre for Military Archives, Kings College London University: Papers of Field Marshal Viscount Allenby: 6/VI/26 Philip Chetwode to Archibald Wavell 20 June 1938 and 6/VI/10 George Barrow to Archibald Wavell; Wavell, A. (1940), *Allenby: a Study in Greatness*. London: Harrap, pp. 136–8.

22 Haig Papers 3155.98, Diary entries 7 and 9 September 1914.

23 IWM: Diary of Field Marshal Sir Henry Wilson [hereafter Wilson Diary] entries for August and September 1914, e.g. 22 September 'of course he [French] has no brains at all'.

24 National Army Museum London: 7511–7580 Papers of Captain J. Arthur Talbot-Rice, Talbot-Rice to his parents, 4 November 1914.

25 Lumley (1936), op. cit., p. 258.

26 Haig Papers 3155.101, Diary entry 18 April 1915.

27 Colonel General Erich von Falkenhayn, Minister for War, quoted in the 'Editor's Notes' of the *United Service Magazine*, Volume LI New Series (1914) p. 226.

28 Churchill Archive Centre, Churchill College Cambridge University, Papers of General Lord Rawlinson [hereafter Rawlinson Papers], Diary entry, 14 March 1915; *see also* IWM Wilson Diary entry 15 March 1915 and TNA PRO 30/57 WB17–18 Papers of Field Marshal Lord Kitchener, Rawlinson to Kitchener, 23 March and 1 April 1915.

29 Quoted in Holmes, R. (1981), *The Little Field Marshal: Sir John French*. London: Jonathan Cape, pp. 273–4.

30 Haig Papers 3155.101, Diary entry, 9 July 1915, Travers (1987) op. cit., p. 127.

31 IWM Papers of General Sir Philip Chetwode [hereafter Chetwode Papers] Folder 3, Julian Byng to Philip Chetwode, 30 May 1917.

32 Rogers, H. C. B. (1959), *The Mounted Troops of the British Army 1066–1945*. London: Seely Service, p. 233.

33 Haig Papers 3155.106 Diary entry 7 June 1916, Robertson to Haig, 19 May 1916, Haig to Robertson 20 May 1916 and Haig to Robertson, 20 May 1916. *See also* TNA CAB 22/65 'Minutes of the War Committee Meeting 9 November 1916, Statement of the Secretary of State for War', pp. 4–5.

34 The War Committee deliberations may be found in TNA CAB 42 'Minutes of the War Committee Meeting 18 May 1916'; this episode is discussed at length in Prior and Wilson (2005), *The Somme*, pp. 12–14.

35 [Anon] (1929), *A Short History of the 1st King's Dragoon Guards*. Aldershot: Gale & Polden, p. 38.

36 Haig Papers 3155.104 Diary entries for 8 and 18 January 1916 and Paper 32(b) p. 31.

37 Haig Papers 3155.105 Haig Diary secret memorandum to Rawlinson 13 April 1916; *see also* Prior and Wilson (1992) op. cit., pp. 147–50.

38 Haig Papers 3155.105 Diary entry 9 April 1916.

39 Edmonds (1932), *Official History France and Belgium 1916 Volume I*, p. 193 and p. 267; Gough, H. (1931), *The Fifth Army*. London: Hodder & Stoughton, pp. 132–7.

40 TNA WO 95/518 'Fifth Army General Staff War Diary April–December 1916', entries for 13–28 June; WO 95/523 'Reserve Army AA&QMG War Diary April-December 1916', note from Fourth Army showing composition of Reserve Army, 19 June 1916, and note from Fourth Army cancelling the above note, 23 June 1916; WO 95/1823 12th Division General Staff War Diary January–August 1916, entries April–June; WO 95/2221, '25th Division General Staff War Diary, March July 1916', entries May–July, particularly training exercise 13 June; WO 95/1141 '3rd Cavalry Division General Staff War Diary October 1914–May 1919', entries March–July 1916; WO 95/1097 1st Cavalry Division General Staff War Diary January 1915–September 1919', entries April–July 1916.

41 TNA WO 95/518 'Fifth Army General Staff War Diary April–December 1916', entries for 23 and 28 June, and Fourth Army order to Reserve Army, 22 June 1916; Edmonds (1932), *Official History France and Belgium 1916 Volume I*, Appendices, p. 89 and 150; Prior and Wilson (1992) op. cit., pp. 150–5.

42 Rawlinson Papers, Diary entry 1 July 1916; Gough, op. cit., p. 137.

43 Rawlinson Papers, Diary entry 14 July 1916; *see also* Haig Papers 3155.107 Diary entry 13 July 1916.

44 Holmes, R. (2004), *Tommy: The British Soldier on the Western Front 1914–1918*. London: HarperCollins, pp. 440–2; Brereton, op cit., pp. 326–7; Tennant, E. (1939), *The Royal Deccan Horse in the Great War*. Aldershot: Gale & Polden, pp. 476–50; Norman, T. (1984), *The Hell They Called High Wood*. London: William Kimber, pp. 99–112.

45 Rawlinson Papers, Diary entries for 11, 14 and 15 September 1916; *see also* Haig Papers 3155. 108 Diary entry 14 September 1916.

46 Sassoon, S. (1930), *Memoirs of an Infantry Officer*. London: Faber & Faber, p. 163.

47 Haig Papers 3155.111 Diary entry 20 March 1917, note 337; *see also* TNA CAB 22/73 'Minutes of War Cabinet Meetings, Memorandum on Cavalry by Lord Curzon14 November 1916', p. 5; Haig Papers 3155.214h Diary entry 23 November 1916 'Memoranda on Cavalry'.

48 Quoted in Falls [Edmonds] (1940), *Official History France and Belgium 1917 Volume I*, Appendices, pp. 100–4.

49 IWM Chetwode Papers, Folder Three, Byng to Chetwode 30 May 1917; Oats, L. B. (1966), *I Serve: The Regimental History of the 3rd Carabineers*. Norwich: Jarold & Son, pp. 223–5.

50 Miles [Edmonds] (1948), *Official History France and Belgium 1917 Volume III* p. 29; *see also* Williams (1983) op. cit., pp. 171–212; Hammond, B. (2008), *Cambrai 1917: The Myth of the First Great Tank Battle*. London: Weidenfeld & Nicholson.

51 Haig Papers 3155.119 Haig to Byng 3 November 1917 Note 6.

52 Seely, J. E. B. (1930), *Adventure*. London: Heinemann, p. 213; *see also* Miles [Edmonds] (1948), *Official History France and Belgium 1917, Volume III*, pp. 307–9.

53 Haig Papers 3155.119 November 1917 Notes 111 and 115; Woolcombe (1967), op. cit., pp. 136–7; Seely, op. cit., pp. 274–7.

54 Hammond (2008) op. cit., pp. 396–401; Evans R. (1951), *The Story of the Fifth Royal Inniskilling Dragoon Guards*. Aldershot: Gale & Polden, p. 149; Moore, W. (1988), *A Wood Called Bourlon: The Cover-Up After Cambrai 1917*. London: Leo Cooper, pp. 156–7.

55 TNA CAB 23/13 'Minutes of War Cabinet Meetings, Evidence of Field Marshal Sir Douglas Haig, 7 January 1918'; *see also* CAB 23/14 'Minutes of War Cabinet Committee on Manpower Meetings, 4th Meeting, December 1917'.

56 Seely (1930) op. cit., p. 303; Grodzinski, J. R. and McNorgan, M. R. (2000), '"It's a Charge, Boys, It's a Charge!" Cavalry Action at Moreil Wood, 30 March 1918', in D. E. Graves (ed.), *Fighting For Canada: Seven Battles 1758–1945*. Toronto: Robin Brass Studio, pp. 260–5.

57 Haig Papers 3155.130 Diary entry 1 August 1918; Montgomery (1919) op. cit., pp. 23–4; Edmonds (1947), *Official History France and Belgium 1918 Volume IV*, p. 55; TNA WO 95/1097 1st Cavalry Division General Staff War Diary January

1915–September 1919, 'Narrative of Operations 1st Cavalry Division 8th to 11th August 1918'.

58 Rawlinson Papers, Diary entry 8 August 1918; TNA WO 95/437 Fourth Army General Staff War Diary July–August 1918, 'Summary of Operations 8 August'; Brereton (1982) op. cit., pp. 338–9; Pomeroy (1924) op. cit., pp. 325–8.

59 Haig Papers 3155.130 Diary entries 19 and 21 August 1918.

60 Haig Papers 3155.131, Diary entry, Haig to Wilson 1 September 1918.

61 A transcript of this pamphlet has been published as Beach, J. (intro.) (2008), *The Division in Attack 1918 SS 135 T/1635 40/WO/7036*, Strategic and Combat Studies Institute Occasional Paper No 53. Shrivenham: SCSI.

5

The Battle of The Somme *(1916):*
The Film of the Battle

If the average person on a British street was asked what was the most widely watched, most historically significant and for its time the biggest money-making film ever made in the United Kingdom, the chances are very great that they would give the wrong answer. If they were told that it was a black-and-white, silent, official documentary film released in 1916 and called *The Battle of the Somme*, most people would probably deny having ever heard of it. But show them a few scenes from the film, and there is a much better chance that they would recognize images of the Western Front that they had seen more than once on television, and which had given them much of their insight into the First World War. Unfortunately, through indifference, ignorance or simple laziness on the part of the makers of television documentaries and newscasts about the war, this has included in recent times the frequent use of scenes from *The Battle of the Somme* out of context or inappropriately, helping to foster a popular image of the Western Front that is far from historically accurate. This repeated misuse of what is both a classic film and a critically important piece of historical evidence can be traced back at least to the BBC television documentary series *The Great War* (1964), and shows no sign of abating yet.

In July 2005 *The Battle of the Somme* was included in the United Nations Educational, Scientific and Cultural Organization (UNESCO) Memory of the World Register of cultural artefacts of global importance, the first British contribution (and one of the very few films) to be included in the Register, joining such cultural landmarks as Beethoven's 9th Symphony, the Gutenberg Bible, and the Bayeux Tapestry. To quote from the UNESCO citation:

> The 1916 film *The Battle of the Somme* is uniquely significant both as the compelling documentary record of one of the key battles of the First World War (and indeed one

which has come to typify many aspects of this landmark in twentieth century history) and as the first feature-length documentary film record of combat produced anywhere in the world. In the latter role, the film played a major part in establishing the methodology of documentary and propaganda film, and initiated debate on a number of issues relating to the ethical treatment of 'factual' film which continue to be relevant to this day. Seen by many millions of British civilians within the first month of distribution, *The Battle of the Somme* was recognized at the time as a phenomenon that allowed the civilian home-front audience to share the experiences of the front-line soldier, thus helping both to create and to reflect the concept of Total War. Seen later by mass audiences in allied and neutral countries, including Russia and the United States, it coloured the way in which the war and British participation in it were perceived around the world at the time and subsequently, and it is the source a number of iconic images of combat on the Western Front in the First World War which remain in almost daily use ninety years later.[1]

In the history of the First World War, *The Battle of the Somme* remains what it always has been since its first appearance, the absolutely essential starting place for any discussion of how the British people at home understood the Western Front during the war, and how the British Army in the First World War has been understood around the world ever since.

Just before 11.30 a.m. on 10 August 1916, an audience of newspapermen, officials of the Foreign Office, members of the cinema trade and officers of the Army's General Staff assembled at the Scala Motion Picture Theatre in the West End of London. This oddly mixed group was there at the invitation of the proprietor, Dr E. Distin Maddick, to watch the first screening of *The Battle of the Somme*, the documentary film of over an hour in length shot chiefly on the first day of the Somme offensive, which had opened so disastrously for the British on 1 July with the loss of over 57,000 casualties in a day – nearly one third of them dead.[2] Before its start the audience was read a letter from the recently appointed Secretary of State for War, David Lloyd George:

> You are invited here to witness by far the most important and imposing picture of the war that our staff has yet procured. The Battle of the Somme, furious and desperate as it has been, is a first and most important phase in what is an historical struggle, unique in its scope and world-wide significance. I am convinced that when you have seen this wonderful picture, every heart will beat in sympathy with its purpose, which is no other than that everyone of us at home and abroad shall see what our men at the Front are doing and suffering for us, and how their achievements have been made possible by the

sacrifices made at home. Now, gentlemen, be up and doing also! See that this picture, which is in itself an epic of self-sacrifice and gallantry, reaches everyone. Herald the deeds of our brave men to the ends of the earth. This is your duty. Ladies, I feel that no word is necessary to urge upon you the importance of throwing in the whole ardour and strength of your invaluable aid. Mothers, wives, sisters and affianced ones, your hearts will beat, your voices speak in honour and glory of the living and the dead. You are great and powerful. This is your mission.[3]

Although there is no mention of the film in Lloyd George's writings on the war and he had in fact contributed nothing to its making, his letter provides a clear statement of the interpretation placed on *The Battle of the Somme* by the British government at its highest level. It certainly impressed its first audience. 'If anything were needed to justify the existence of the cinematograph', wrote a reporter for *The Times*, 'it is to be found in [this] wonderful series of films'. *The Bioscope*, the leading cinema trade journal, declared that 'no written description by an eyewitness, however graphic his pen; no illustration by any artist, no matter how facile his pencil; no verbal description by the most interested participator in the event, could hope to convey to the man at home the reality of modern warfare with the force and conviction shown in this marvellous series of pictures'. Even those responsible for *The Battle of the Somme* seemed over-awed by it. 'It makes other films look very small', observed its producer, William F. Jury, while the secret propaganda organization run by the Liberal MP Charles Masterman from Wellington House in London (often, if unofficially, known as the War Propaganda Bureau or WPB) noted that 'the general opinion of trade experts of this film is that it is the most remarkable film ever made in this country'.[4] In the following month, *The Battle of the Somme* would be seen in cinemas packed to capacity throughout Britain. It would be exported to more than 18 other countries. Coming at a time when the value of film as propaganda was unproven, its success set film on the way to becoming one of the key elements in the British propaganda war. The control of all British film secured by the Canadian-born Conservative MP and millionaire Sir [William] 'Max' Aitken (later Lord Beaverbrook) shortly after the great success of *The Battle of the Somme* provided a valuable lever in his struggles over the next two years to bring British propaganda under one organization. The Ministry of Information, formed in February 1918, marked only a partial success for Beaverbrook; crucial elements such as the Directorate of Enemy Propaganda and the National War Aims Committee remained outside his control as minister. But it is improbable that even so much would have been achieved without the enormously strong position given Beaverbrook as effective controller of British film propaganda, a control that in large measure he owed to *The Battle of the Somme*.

From at least the time of the Crimean War of 1853–1856, in which the steamship and the telegraph had made rapid reporting of British military operations over long distances feasible for the first time, relations between the British Army and the press had been generally marked by mutual antipathy, coupled with a reluctant acceptance that some form of co-operation between them was inevitable and essential for both sides. In the most recent British major war, the Boer War of 1899–1902, the British commanders, particularly Lord Kitchener, blamed what they saw as sensationalism and irresponsible criticism of the Army by the domestic press for encouraging the enemy and lengthening the war. In the closely studied Russo-Japanese War of 1904–1905 they saw the Japanese, who enforced rigid censorship and control of the press, enjoy a clear advantage over the Russians, who did not.[5] This military predisposition for censorship extended to still photographs, which it was feared might aid the enemy as much as careless words – a fear which largely proved groundless in the course of the First World War, although as for all other twentieth-century wars the overwhelming bulk of military information did come from open sources such as newspapers.[6] As the newly appointed Secretary of State for War, Lord Kitchener took steps in September 1914 to expel all newsmen and photographers from the Western Front, partly in accordance with agreed security procedures and partly in accordance with his personal inclinations. At the same time a new subsection was created in MO5, the War Office Intelligence section, designated MO5(h) and intended to watch over publicity and censorship.[7] But in contrast to a deep suspicion of the press camera, the official attitude to the cinema was one of indifference. 'The cinema', so a report for the War Cabinet in 1917 ran, was at the start of the war 'almost universally regarded as an instrument for the entertainment of the masses; the educated classes thought of "the pictures" as responsible for

1. A still from the film *The Battle of the Somme* (*see* page 126) showing the moment of the infantry attack on 1 July 1916, now believed to be one of the few outright fakes in the film. Photograph Q70168, courtesy of the Imperial War Museum, London.

2. The posed official photograph of Field Marshal Sir Douglas Haig taken on 12 September 1917 (*see* page 168) while

3. The official photograph of British stretcher-bearers in the Third Battle of Ypres taken by John Warwick Brooke on 1 August (*see* page 177) and published in the *Daily Mirror* on 6 September 1917. Photograph Q5935, courtesy of the Imperial War Museum, London.

4. The first of the sequence of aerial photographs taken by Lieutenant John Webster of the trench raid by 9th Durham Light Infantry on 15 September 1917 (*see* page 150). Narrow Trench runs across the lower part of the frame, intersected by a sunken lane on the left (compare with the map on pages 144–5) and running British infantry are just visible in no-man's land towards the top of the frame. Photograph Q58653, courtesy

turning romantic schoolboys into juvenile highwaymen, as a sort of moving edition of the "penny dreadful".[8] Despite initial fears that the entertainment industry would contract with the war, the cinema actually experienced a boom, attributed to the increased wealth and demand for entertainment from workers employed on munitions or other aspects of war production. Apart from the need for entertainment as a relief from the war, it was also, with the developing notions of a Home Front, vaguely treasonable to be downhearted. Although a very new form of entertainment, the cinema had supplanted the music hall even before the war. As might be expected, the typical cinema-goers were more likely than average to be young and working class, consisting mainly of working-class family groups with children. By 1916 there were about 5,400 cinemas in Britain with seats between them for a million people, and over 20 million cinema attendances a week from a total population of 43 million, with many people attending two or three times a week. With the average ticket costing four pence, the introduction of a one-penny Entertainments Tax in May 1916 caused attendances to fall to about 15 million a week by 1918, but even this represented by far the largest single form of working-class entertainment in the country.[9]

For the first two months of the war, before Kitchener's ban became effective, cinema cameramen, like other reporters, had considerable freedom in the battle zones of Western Europe. As one example, the Topical Film Company anticipated the German invasion of Belgium by sending out their cameraman, F. V. Engholm, in late July 1914, who managed to film 11 short newsreels up to the fall of Antwerp (two years later he was to be appointed as the only cameraman permanently employed by the Royal Navy).[10] But although a number of cameramen later told many interesting stories of their exploits in 1914, disappointingly little film has survived to substantiate their claims. Thereafter, as Kitchener made his ban effective, cameramen vanished from the Western Front. This required no positive legislation: permission was simply refused them to film the Army in the war zone. According to J. Brooke Wilkinson, acting as Secretary to the British Board of Film Censors, the War Office was at the start of 1915 only narrowly talked out of banning the export of newsreels from Britain altogether on security grounds. As a compromise the Board itself assumed responsibility for censorship of these films.[11] In their struggle with their own governments over censorship in the First World War (and indeed in later wars), it was a standard ploy for the media of all countries to claim that the enemy was gaining a propaganda advantage through a more enlightened policy towards media access. Even so, in this case the British cinema companies had a point: the German government had at the war's start created a special film trust to co-ordinate film manufacture, while the French government permitted filming of its own armed forces in May 1915, although not in the very front lines.[12] Great Britain began the war with a professional Army, tiny in comparison with those of France and Germany, and despite increasing dissatisfaction with the results, control of events on the Western Front was for much of the first two years of the war felt to be the responsibility of the professional soldiers, not least by those soldiers themselves. But it was also during this period that the notion of a Home Front developed, marking the acceptance by the civilian population of their share in the war's suffering, and their share of the responsibility for winning it. Implicit in this political and social bargain between government, military and people was a demand for information on the success of their efforts, and reassurance that their sacrifice was worthwhile. At first a military propaganda apparatus that was over-concerned with security failed to provide either, and certainly remained indifferent to the potential of the popular cinema.

The first cameraman working from Great Britain to circumvent the ban was the wonderfully named Canadian, Hilton de Witt Girdwood, who, working from entirely commercial motives, obtained permission from the India Office to film Indian troops on the Western Front in July 1915, although by disputing copyright the War Office blocked the screening of his film *With the Empire's Fighters* in cinemas until September 1916.[13] In the absence of genuine British newsreels, there was a boom in fictional war dramas and French official films of the war being shown in British cinemas. In May and June 1916, a suitably edited version of a German war newsreel was shown at the Scala, so beating the first major War Office production by a little over two months.[14]

Charles Masterman's propaganda organization at Wellington House had been created in September 1914 to influence opinion in Britain and neutral countries.

Its main overseas target was the United States of America, and its first efforts were aimed at the intelligentsia through books and pamphlets.[15] Almost at once, Wellington House felt the lack of good photographs to improve its material, and throughout 1915 it became increasingly frustrated with the military obsession with security, which had limited photographs of the Western Front to occasional releases from the two regular Army officers (neither of them a trained press cameraman) taking pictures for GHQ Intelligence.[16] When it proved impossible to reach agreement with the London newspaper magnates of Fleet Street on the conditions under which news photographers might operate in the war zone, Wellington House turned instead to the less powerful cinema newsreel firms.[17] In August 1915, Sir Hedley LeBas, a senior member of Masterman's organization, approached J. Brooke Wilkinson with the offer of a permanent official newsreel organization based at Wellington House itself. Brooke Wilkinson had previously been active in this direction, and unknown to Wellington House he was already negotiating with the War Office for a similar organization. On 25 March 1915 he had attended a meeting of the Topical Committee of the Film Manufacturers' Association, which as its name suggests was composed of the heads of the leading British newsreel companies: Barker, British & Colonial, Eclair, Gaumont, Jury's Imperial Pictures and the Topical Film Company. Its chairman, T. A. Welsh, the Secretary of Gaumont, authorized Brooke Wilkinson to approach the War Office (with which he already had some standing through his censorship work) to negotiate the newsreel filming of British forces on the Western Front. As Brooke Wilkinson later remembered, he was told after two months that the idea had been approved by the Army Council.[18] Strictly, this cannot have been true. The Army Council met only once in 1915, in November, and neither on that occasion nor in its seven further meetings before July 1916 did it discuss film. However, the full Army Council included the financial members from the Treasury, whose main peacetime function was control of the Army Estimates. On the outbreak of the war the Army received vastly increased credit, and in typical Kitchener fashion the military members took to holding informal meetings without their Treasury colleagues, and with no written record, until pounced upon by an irate Treasury in April 1916.[19] It was presumably at one of these meetings that Brooke

Wilkinson's proposal was approved. The driving force at the War Office behind the idea of newsreel film was almost certainly then, as later, the Permanent Secretary Sir Reginald Brade. What Lord Kitchener thought of the matter, and how his initial objections were finally overcome, is not known.

By 20 July 1915 a working plan had emerged for the film project. The Topical Committee would pay, insure and equip two cameramen to produce short films of immediate news value and some permanent historical worth. The Army would lodge and transport them while on the Western Front, where they would come under the control of the grandly titled Military Director of Cinematograph Operations, Captain (later Lieutenant Colonel) J. H. C. Faunthorpe. They would be part of the Press Section at GHQ, sharing facilities with the news reporters who had themselves been granted similar official status by the Army. Since there had been no military plans for British propaganda in peacetime, this Press Section actually fitted, rather uneasily, into the GHQ Intelligence Branch as I(d), commanded then and for most of the war by Colonel Arthur Hutton Wilson. Dr Maddick at the Scala provided liaison between the cameramen and the War Office when they were in London. The hiring charge to the cinema trade of any films produced was 4½d a foot, of which the War Office claimed a penny in royalties, along with copyright on the films and the right of censorship.[20] The censoring body, M05(h) in London, also provided the inter-titles (captions inserted between the shots) for these silent films, apparently by agreement with the censors of GHQ Intelligence. When all this was satisfied, the Topical Committee had the right to film British forces anywhere in France and Belgium (and, optimistically, Germany), and to exhibit the resulting film anywhere in Britain and the Empire except India, Egypt, and the Dominions of Australia, Canada, New Zealand and South Africa. The War Office also ruled that only monochrome film was to be used, although a primitive colour system was available, possibly on grounds of taste as the colours often appeared lurid. The final terms were agreed, after another round of negotiations, on 25 October 1915, whereupon the Topical Committee invited Charles Urban of Kineto Films (a well-known producer who already had some standing with the military) to join it, and Brooke Wilkinson to be its Secretary, and renamed itself the British Topical Committee for War Films.[21]

These protracted negotiations were drawing to a successful conclusion when Brooke Wilkinson was approached by LeBas on behalf of Wellington House with their ideas for film. Rather than further complicate the position by letting the secret organization approach the War Office, Brooke Wilkinson suggested instead a separate cinema committee, composed of himself, William Jury, Charles Urban and T. A. Welsh, to work for Wellington House on their film project. As Masterman's wife later remembered him telling her, the last two members were meant to represent agents and renters respectively.[22] This committee produced a short and successful propaganda film, *Once Upon A Time*, for Wellington House. This was followed by a major project, formalized on 23 September 1915 by an agreement between Charles Urban and Sir Claud Schuster, Clerk of the Crown and Masterman's honorary advisor. The agreement was for the filming 'of certain portions of the British Fleet and British Army in the United Kingdom', the Western Front being in the jurisdiction of the War Office alone. Despite opposition from the Royal Navy, which proved even more negative than the Army in its obsession with security, Urban's cameramen filmed the Grand Fleet and Army camps at Aldershot, and some previously shot film was supplied by the Vickers munitions works, together making up a full-length documentary called *Britain Prepared*. Opening in London at the Empire Theatre on 29 December 1915, this was the first major British official documentary film of the war, and the only major film made entirely by Wellington House. At its first performance, Arthur Balfour as First Lord of the Admiralty provided the official view of this film by telling the invited audience of his conviction that 'such representations as you are about to see, which I have done my individual best to further, will do much in this, as in other countries, to put the great operations of the war that are now going on in their true perspective. The world has yet to know, and it does not yet know, how much it owes to the British Fleet'. After six successful weeks in London the film toured the provinces, and Wellington House arranged for its export. On 8 August 1916, Welsh resigned from his various British commitments in order to supervise the distribution of British films in France for Wellington House. His place as Chairman of the Topical Committee was taken by William Jury. Meanwhile A. C. Bromhead, the Managing Director of Gaumont, took *Britain*

Prepared to Russia to play before the Czar. Bromhead reported that he had also shown the film to Russian troops in the front lines, at least close enough to draw German fire. Dwelling heavily on the role of the Royal Navy, the film went some way towards explaining the apparent lack of British military effort in 1915 to the hard-pressed Russians. Charles Urban also took his creation to the United States. However, cinema men there found the film dull, or, as they politely told Urban, 'too intellectual' for American tastes. Undaunted, Urban re-edited the film into a new American version, and the owner of the Patriot Film Company, William J. Robinson, a British citizen resident in New York, organized a syndicate that rather reluctantly bought this new version from Urban for $25,000.[23]

The arrival of newsreel cinema as a propaganda vehicle in Britain, along with the increasing importance of propaganda to total war, brought with it a corresponding increase in the number and authority of government institutions dedicated to its control. Following a War Office conference in January 1916, the old censorship subsection MO5(h) expanded to become a new section as MO7. In April it was transferred under Colonel Warburton-Davies to the new Directorate of Military Intelligence as MI7, the Directorate of Special Intelligence (its old parent organization became MI5, the British Counterintelligence department, or the Security Service, as it has become widely known).[24]

Therefore, as things stood in early 1916, an obsession with secrecy in film propaganda at the expense of efficiency and accessibility in British thinking had produced duplication, maladministration and confusion. A War Office department too secret to exist officially was censoring all British official 'information' films. These films were being sponsored by two committees, one based at Wellington House (itself doing work too sensitive for it to exist officially) and the other from the War Office. These committees, with virtually identical membership, consisted of representatives of prominent newsreel firms. However, only the War Office committee had the right to film troops on the Western Front. In November 1915, this position was regularized slightly by agreements between the Topical Committee and Wellington House, but there was no official contact between Masterman and the War Office.[25] In July 1916, yet another organization added to the confusion: the Canadian War Records Office, the creation of Sir Max

Aitken, who was granted the rank of lieutenant colonel by the Canadian government for the purpose. This would not have affected British arrangements but for
the close ties between Aitken and Sir Reginald Brade at the War Office. In his
own specialized vocabulary of political friendships, Aitken was 'intimate with' the
Permanent Secretary, who in turn was 'devoted to' the Canadian millionaire. In
July 1916, having already despatched the first Canadian still photographer to the
Western Front, Aitken concluded agreements with both the Topical Committee
and Wellington House, giving the Canadian government access to their films
and the right to hire their cameramen. From that time onwards Aitken and the
Canadians were a constant and major factor in British propaganda development. The disadvantages of so many competing organizations was singled out
for particular criticism in the investigation conducted into British propaganda by
Robert Donald for Lloyd George in January 1917 (one of his first acts on becoming prime minister), which led to the creation a month later of the Department
of Information as part of the Foreign Office, given full status as the Ministry of
Information a year later, with Aitken – now Beaverbrook – as minister.[26]

Beaverbrook, like Lloyd George, actually contributed nothing to the making of *The Battle of the Somme*, but in capitalizing on its success took his first
steps on the way to controlling British propaganda. The Topical Committee
had never intended, in any case, to make such a major documentary. Its two
cameramen, Geoffrey H. Malins of Gaumont and E. G. ('Teddy') Tong of Jury's
Imperial Pictures, left for France on 2 November 1915 (four months before the
War Office finally reached agreement with the newspapers over the employment
of the first official still photographer, Second Lieutenant Ernest 'Baby' Brooks)
with the intention of making short newsreels. The first series, consisting of brief
information films on what life was like for the various branches of the Army in
or near to the front lines, was 'trade-shown' to potential distributors at the West
End Theatre, Coventry Street, London, on 4 January 1916. Thereafter, the two
cameramen produced a further five series of similar films at monthly intervals
until the start of June, when Tong was invalided home with some form of illness.
A member of the Topical Committee, J. B. (John Benjamin) McDowell, head of
British & Colonial, volunteered to replace him and left for the Western Front on

28 June. These first films were generally well received, but contained scenes that had clearly been taken in training camps or even deliberately staged to masquerade as the front lines. Although glad enough to have them after two years of effort, the cinema trade itself found them both suspect and dull, and pressed for a more honest and dramatic record of the war.[27]

Until July 1918, when honorary ranks were made compulsory for them, the official cameramen on the Western Front wore officer's uniform without rank or unit badges, or even the distinctive green armband of the Press Section. Malins accepted an honorary rank as a lieutenant; McDowell preferred to remain a civilian. Both were dependent on the generosity of GHQ for chauffeured cars to transport their equipment, but these were available on average for only three days each week.[28] On arrival near the trenches, the luckless chauffeur was often pressed into service carrying most of the equipment. Nevertheless, festooned with about 70 pounds of highly inflammable nitrate-based film, a camera and a tripod, the official cinematographers were both handicapped and vulnerable, and tended to film from locations close to roads. A camera filming from a trench was sometimes mistaken for a machine-gun and attracted hostile fire, without even the ability to fire back. Remarkably, no British cameraman was ever killed on the Western Front, although there were some injuries, and in 1918 McDowell (who had been required to take a military commission as a lieutenant) was awarded both the Military Cross for bravery and the OBE. Unless mounted on a car or railway truck the cameras could not 'track' to provide a moving shot, changes of focus or camera-angle were difficult, zoom lenses were unknown and second chances impossible. The technical limitations of the hand-cranked cameras ruled out filming in the open during an attack or crossing no man's land to film the enemy. Filming British soldiers behind cover in the front trenches was dangerous, but possible. Unfortunately a panorama of the battlefield taken at considerable risk from the front line produced only the most unsatisfactory results: a blur of movement in the distance against the washed-out greys of the monochrome sky. Far better quality material could be taken in the rear areas, where there was both the time and safety to film properly. Heavy artillery presented several advantages for the cameraman: since the loading and firing of a big gun followed an unvarying routine, it was comparatively easy to film several firings from different angles, editing them together into a single all-round sequence.

Just as much as the nature of the war, it was these limitations of the camera that produced a Western Front film record of monstrous guns and strange landscapes, the sinister 'empty battlefield' of twentieth-century industrialized warfare, and in an unusually exaggerated form. What the cameras showed, both to the British public for the first time in 1916 and to historians ever since, was a war in which men suffered but achieved nothing. Soldiers were pictured marching, often in high spirits, to the front-line trenches. There, as the moment of the attack came, they waited, faces strained with tension. Then they vanished out of the camera's sight until it found them again collapsing with pain at a dressing station or fatigue at a rest camp. The bewilderment felt by the common soldier in a major battle, stemming largely from his inability to see its overall shape, was certainly not exclusive to the First World War, and even less so to film as a means of recording war. But in this particular case, the technical limitations of the film record reinforced impressions of the shapelessness of war, and the helplessness of individuals in war, far beyond the point of objectivity, with the novelty of the film only serving to increase the impact. It was even more unfortunate that the first battle the British public would see presented in this confused and confusing manner had also been a genuine disaster, marked by heavy losses and lack of overall control. The central paradox of filming the war was that only deliberate deception, the use of faked material, could restore the whole truth to the films. Actual combat, the climax and heroism of war as it was traditionally understood, was beyond the power of the film-makers to record.

On 25 June, Malins was sent to the British Fourth Army that was holding positions north of the River Somme, to film the opening of the new offensive, being joined by McDowell soon after his arrival at GHQ on 28 June. Malins did his best, both at the time and in his memoirs, to suggest that McDowell was his subordinate and assistant, and for the filming of *The Battle of the Somme* he did not mention either McDowell or the still photographer, Ernest Brooks, with whom he worked in partnership. Fortunately the available evidence, above all the film itself, has allowed their respective roles to be reconstructed, and locations for many of the film's scenes identified with a great degree of certainty.[29] Malins was assigned to 29th Division at the northern end of the Fourth Army near Beaumont Hamel, where the attempted attack would produce one of the greatest disasters of the day. In contrast, McDowell was with the 7th Division opposite Mametz, nearly at the other end of the British line and not far from the point where the attack would meet with relative success. On the day of Malins' arrival, the starting day for the offensive was put back to 1 July, since a longer preliminary bombardment was needed. With a tight schedule, the two cameramen motored separately along the areas just behind the front lines, filming the preparations for the battle, including the heavy guns in action and the infantry battalions being marched up through the small villages to their final positions before the attack. They also filmed a few scenes of troops preparing to go into action that would later be represented in *The Battle of the Somme* as taking place on the day of the attack itself. On the morning of 1 July, Malins followed the men of the 1st Lancashire Fusiliers through the approach trenches to their final position in a sunken lane, then filmed a famous sequence of the explosion of a giant British mine under the German strongpoint at Hawthorn Redoubt. He did film some soldiers advancing across no man's land, but only from a distance, followed by scenes of the dead and wounded, and German prisoners coming in. At about noon, as it became clear that no advance would be made, Malins probably motored down to join McDowell at the Minden Post dressing station behind the 7th Division's front positions, where they filmed the wounded of both sides. Either on the same day or shortly afterwards, the cameramen went forward from this position and filmed the German trenches captured by the division's advance. Finally they filmed the troops who had attacked on 1 July coming out of the line to rest. It is not known precisely when they left the battlefield, but the first rushes of their material were shown to the Topical Committee in London on 12 July.[30]

On seeing these rushes, the committee realized that by luck, skill or accident its two men had produced a haunting masterpiece, far too valuable to break into short features. Jury in particular felt that 'the subject would appeal to every man, woman and child in the country', and volunteered to set his own business aside in order to make a full-length documentary of the battle. This involved some rapid re-negotiation with the War Office, ending in Brade settling for 40 per cent of the film's profits, at least £2,000 being guaranteed – a modest enough sum, and evidence of the comparatively low expectations the War Office still had of the result. In no sense does *The Battle of the Somme* represent the deliberate manufacture of a propaganda film with mass appeal in order to offset the disaster of 1 July. The ultimate destination of the money, and of all the receipts taken by the War Office for its films, was a charitable fund for disabled soldiers and the dependents of those killed in the war.

Malins claimed in his memoirs that he was responsible for editing those parts of *The Battle of the Somme* that he had filmed. Charles Urban also claimed that his own role in making the film was under-rated, and he is usually credited as one of its editors; whether McDowell took part in the editing is not known. But as the evidence stands there can be no doubt that *The Battle of the Somme* was Jury's creation. Censorship was carried out by the subsection of MI7 known as MI7(a), and the completed film returned to France for a double-check. One of the censors at GHQ, Major Arthur Lee, later recorded that he helped censor *The Battle of the Somme* on 25 August, which, given its release date, was presumably his misreading for 25 July.[31] It is certain that the whole film was completed less than a month from the Topical Committee's decision to make it, and first previewed at the Scala on 10 August as described.[32]

After the impression the film had made on its first audience, trade demand for *The Battle of the Somme* exceeded even their expectations. It opened in London on 21 August at 34 different cinemas, and appeared in the major provincial cities a week later. In order to maximize its availability, there were no exclusive rights, and Jury as booking director dropped the hiring fees progressively from £40 in the first week by £5 a week; after 2 months he introduced a scheme for the film to be booked for three nights for £6, deliberately putting it within the price range of the village hall. At the end of the first week, advance bookings for the film neared the 1,000 mark and the final total has been estimated at more than 2,000 cinemas taking the film, with profits of more than £30,000 (about six times as great as the initial War Office estimate). The film was still being booked by British cinemas 15 months after it opened in London. Distin Maddick at the

Scala felt able to present Brade with an extra donation of 200 guineas (£210) as ten per cent of his first week's takings.[33]

The number of people in the United Kingdom who saw *The Battle of the Somme* during the first year or so from its release cannot be known with certainty, but it has been estimated with some degree of accuracy, based on the bookings recorded in the ledgers, the average cost of a cinema ticket when compared with money received, and contemporary newspaper accounts. *The Times* reported that 'hundreds of thousands' of people saw the film in its opening week, with more being turned away at the cinema doors. At the Scala and other cinemas there were queues all day booking tickets, and the film was widely reported as break-ing box office records wherever it was shown. Several cinema owners cancelled films booked months in advance to take *The Battle of the Somme*, in some cases for a full week rather than the usual few days. The risk was justified; by the most modest calculations in its first six weeks there were at least 20 million ticket sales for *The Battle of the Somme*, the equivalent of almost half the country's popu-lation. It was particularly noted that middle-class people who would normally never visit the cinema were coming to see the film in unprecedented numbers.[34] In Glasgow the film drew 'tremendous crowds', and both there and in Edinburgh cinemas were packed from 11 a.m. to 10.30 p.m. – an experience repeated in other cities, seaside towns and industrial centres of the north. One Leeds proprietor advertised a visit to *The Battle of the Somme* as 'a duty you owe to the Imperial Government'; another quoted Lloyd George, 'If the exhibition of this picture all over the world does not end War, God help civilisation!'[35] The view that seeing the film was an Imperial duty received a form of official endorsement when on 2 September the Royal Family was given a private showing of the film at Windsor, following which King George V was quoted as saying that, 'the public should see these pictures that they may have some idea of what the Army is doing, and what it means'. Two days later there was another private viewing at the Scala, this time for senior officials of the War Office, Ministry of Munitions and Board of Inventions, presumably trying to acquaint themselves with the phenomenon that had occurred. One Glasgow cinema owner gave a free show to wounded soldiers back from the war; and, like troops shown the film in France, they seem to have been favourably impressed. Over the next year, if Jury's declared intention of bringing *The Battle of the Somme* to every man, woman and child in the country was missed, it was not through lack of capacity within the cinema industry, or lack of effort on both sides.

This was a major opportunity not simply for a documentary record but for British propaganda. However, it is clear that no attempt was made to direct the film overtly to the aid of the British war effort; the chance was simply missed. Through haste and poor control the British propaganda organizations had combined to produce something that cannot be reasonably described as a propaganda film, except by the most relaxed definition. *The Battle of the Somme* was assembled at short notice from material never intended to provide a continuous narrative. As a result, the battle, as interpreted by the film, has no logic and no direction. There are no scenes of planning or higher commanders; neither Haig as General Officer Commanding-in-Chief nor Rawlinson as General Officer Commanding Fourth Army is mentioned by name or implication. The only general to be filmed is an anonymous figure on horseback. Significantly, the cameramen did come forward to film this general in detailed close-up, identifying him, and the scene survives in another film. But it was either discarded or censored out of *The Battle of the Somme*.[36] It would be nearly a year before the official films began to show that the Army's leaders did not merely inspect troops and entertain visitors, but actually planned and fought battles. The need to smooth out the violent contrast between the failure at Beaumont Hamel and the success east of Mametz as the film crosses between the work of the two cameramen and so from one end of the British line to the other, produces a battle that is patternless and at last bewildering – a world of events without cause or reason. Finally, the film has no enemy. Because film was taken entirely from the British side, Germans appear on it only as prisoners, often wounded, or as the dead. The completed film itself stressed the humanitarian behaviour of British soldiers towards German prisoners, in contrast to the supposed barbarity of their enemies, who appeared in it as unarmed, tired, harmless and often in pain, in marked contrast to the 'barbarous Hun' of much British propaganda.[37] The limitations on film composition were added to the technical limitations of the cameras to produce not a historical record but a film version of a Western Front battle stereotype, foreshadowing the spate of post-war trench memoirs that did much to establish the modern cultural interpretation of the war, and which were often highly unrepresentative of the real trench experience.[38] The image of the Battle of the Somme created and established in the public consciousness by this film was as much a product of the film technology and cinema industry of the time as of any other factor.

Probably in an attempt to exploit regional feelings, based on the old county system of British infantry regiments, the censors of MI7 allowed official films to list the regiments shown by name, removing the battalion number to prevent precise identification. In *The Battle of the Somme* altogether 18 regiments were mentioned by name, stretching across Britain from Highlanders to Cornishmen, although most of the film seems to have been taken up with the activities of just three battalions. Malins appears to have gone out of his way to film kilted soldiers, a decision vindicated in the demands received by *The Bioscope* for bagpipers to play accompaniment to the film. Otherwise the inter-titles provided by MI7(a), of which at least one member of the GHQ Press Section had a low opinion, were no more than bald statements of fact and place, or else the crudest possible attempts to influence opinion. Again the British propaganda organizations failed through the military pre-occupation with security. By making the writing of the film's inter-titles an aspect of censorship and divorcing it from the making of the film itself, they either failed to provide positive statements to counter the depressing evidence of the film images, or through inexperience made an effort so crass that it was counter-productive. 'Along the entire front the munitions "dumps" are receiving vast supplies of shells', ran one example, 'thanks to British munitions workers', which was almost certainly a reference to increased production since the 'Shell Scandal' of 1915. In reality, the inefficiency of shell production, particularly in quality control, was a major factor in the British disaster on 1 July.[39] It would have been better propaganda to turn this failure into an appeal to munitions workers for greater efforts; a subtlety of which the British film-makers were capable by 1918, but not when they made *The Battle of the Somme*.

The reviewer of *The Times*, loyally sharing Lloyd George's official view of the film, suggested that it gave 'a glimpse not merely of the horrors of war but also of its glories'.[40] But the noiseless songs of the happy, brisk figures, silent like their own pale ghosts as they marched to war, evoked a very different response from most audiences. Some even interpreted the film, in contrast to the War Office view but in keeping with the remark claimed for Lloyd George as its political head, as a plea for pacifism, arguing that 'no better means could be found of making English men and women determined to stop a repetition of such a war as the present one'. A few viewers simply objected to film as a medium for presenting the war. The outraged Dean of Durham led a small protest against 'an entertainment which wounds the heart and violates the very sanctity of bereavement', and there were other complaints of the film being trivialized by being shown in company with fictional dramas or even comedies, and of the cinema trade profiting from the dead. But as far as can be told these objections came from a tiny minority; most of those who saw the film were not only deeply impressed, but also deeply moved. It is an indicator of the popularity of *The Battle of the Somme* that a cinema owner who objected to the film could find no other way to protest but by displaying a sign that his cinema alone would not be showing it.[41] By far the most common reaction, even from what the trade press described as the 'educated classes', or middle and upper class, was neither bellicose patriotism nor outraged revulsion, but simply pity and horror, and it was the scenes of wreckage and death that were remembered. According to Malins, this was part of the film-makers' intentions: 'The film takes you to the grave', he later wrote, 'but it must not leave you there'.[42] But in *The Battle of the Somme*, there was nowhere else to go. There had been no breakthrough, no great victory, no celebration; only the wounded and dead with Lloyd George's promise of more to come and a hope that no such war would happen again. A singularly unconvincing scene of yet another column of marching troops, happily waving their helmets at the camera as they marched to battle 'seeking further laurels' (and very probably filmed before the battle) was the only ending offered. Nor, since its creators had been taken so much by surprise by its popularity, did the film have any planned sequel. Malins and McDowell may both have been involved in editing *The Battle of the Somme* in July; Malins and probably McDowell spent early August filming King George V's visit to the Western Front for the film that became *The King Visits*

His Armies in the Great Advance, then Malins appears to have been loaned temporarily to the Canadians.[43] The following year, another full-length documentary appeared, ponderously titled *The Battle of the Ancre and the Advance of the Tanks*, composed of footage shot by Malins and McDowell in the Somme area between September and November 1916. Although this was almost as popular and well received as *The Battle of the Somme*, as its name suggests its main selling point was the first appearance on film of the new invention of the tank, used by the British for the first time in war in September. In contrast to an entire film devoted to the disastrous first day, the remainder of the Somme offensive, nearly five months of fighting, has no coherent film coverage. The distortions in British cultural interpretations of the Western Front, which lasted through most of the twentieth century, can be seen to start with the film *The Battle of the Somme*, through a mixture of accident, technical limitations and official unpreparedness.

For contemporary audiences, *The Battle of the Somme*'s most dramatic moment was the actual infantry attack. As a group of soldiers scrambles out of a trench, two men fall back apparently dead; and as they clear the wire into the distance a further two fall. Malins laid claim to having filmed this striking episode, and a counter-claim was made on behalf of McDowell. *The Bioscope*'s music critic recommended the jaunty *Light Cavalry Overture* by Franz von Suppé to support this scene, and the first invited audience at the Scala actually cheered the men over the top. But most viewers of *The Battle of the Somme* saw only the falling bodies. *The Times*'s critic found this the film's most pathetic scene, while in one West End cinema a woman's cry of 'Oh God, they're dead!' marked the moment.[44] Even that most experienced chronicler of the heroism of violence, the 60-year-old Henry Rider Haggard, found this the film's most impressive scene. 'There is something appalling', he wrote, 'about the instantaneous change from fierce activity to supine death. Indeed the whole horrible business is appalling. War has always been dreadful, but never, I suppose, more dreadful than today'.[45] Lloyd George's secretary and mistress Frances Stevenson, who had lost a brother on the Western Front, wrote after a private viewing of *The Battle of the Somme* that, 'I have often tried to imagine what he went through, but now I *know*, and I shall never forget'.[46] Not only did unprecedented numbers of people watch *The

Battle of the Somme, but with a few exceptions people welcomed the film and saw it as an authentic portrayal of the Western Front.

Geoffrey Malins' memoirs provide an account of his filming these famous sequences, portraying the infantry attack as coming immediately after the blowing of the Hawthorne Redoubt mine rather than (as in fact) ten minutes later:

> The earth was down [from the explosion]. I swung my camera round onto our own parapets. The engineers were swarming over the top, and streaming along the sky line ... Then another signal rang out, and from the trenches immediately in front of me, our wonderful troops went over the top. What a picture it was! They went over as one man. I could see while I was exposing [the film], that numbers were shot down before they reached the top of the parapet; others just the other side.[47]

It is therefore of some significance that the two shots of British troops going over the top have been convincingly identified as fakes. Although suspicion was always attached to these shots, the claim of fakery was made most strongly in 1979 by another British official cameraman, Bertram 'Billy' Brooks-Carrington, who served on the Western Front in 1917. According to Brooks-Carrington, the film was shot by Malins at the St Pol trench mortar school behind the lines, and in 1917 he had talked to the men involved, including one of the 'dead' men. But at the same time, Malins did not lie completely in his memoirs, but rather embellished the truth. The two sequences that he described appear in reverse order in *The Battle of the Somme*, first the staged 'over the top' sequence, then a genuine sequence filmed by panning his camera across no man's land from the same position as the Hawthorn Redoubt mine explosion, which does indeed show small and almost indistinguishable figures of men running across no man's land and falling dead. This was the paradox – even the irony – of filming an attack on the Western Front: technological and practical limitations meant that a genuine shot of the attack taken at considerable risk conveyed almost nothing to the public, and in order to reveal the truth it was necessary to resort to fakery. Despite later claims that *The Battle of the Somme* was a faked propaganda film, this sequence is also one of the few outright fakes in it, as distinct from scenes taken out of context, or misleading inter-titles.[48] Its use represented an attempt to provide the elements of human involvement and heroism missing in the film. The attempt backfired disastrously and was never repeated: no other British wartime film shows, or pretends to show, the moment of death in a real battle. It was doubly unfortunate for the film as propaganda that its makers did not go on to provide the missing leadership, enemy and pattern that the Somme offensive possessed and that *The Battle of the Somme* does not.

Making use of the contacts it had established for *Britain Prepared*, Wellington House added *The Battle of the Somme* to its export lists. Welsh handled the film with some success in France, and Gilbert Frankau took it to Italy in October 1916 with equal success. In various forms, the two major films, or scenes from them, found their way into the Netherlands, Switzerland, Denmark, Greece, Romania, China, Iceland, Peru and many other countries round the globe. By one account a copy reached German cinemas, so reversing the position of less than a year before. But in the United States, Urban found trouble. Robinson's syndicate, which had lost $30,000 on *Britain Prepared*, was reluctant to take the new film. Rescue appeared to come from the International Film Service with an offer to take scenes from both films, provided that Urban surrendered distribution rights. In terms of an end product, the fragile distinction between the Wellington House cinema committee and the Topical Committee had collapsed. But this episode itself nearly produced a scandal. International Film Service was part of the press empire of William Randolph Hearst, regarded by the British as the leading pro-German propagandist in the United States for his anti-British and isolationist stance. Robinson warned Urban that if Hearst gained control of the film he would suppress it, and on this basis persuaded his syndicate to take *The Battle of the Somme* for itself. Robinson even felt it necessary to issue a sworn affidavit clearing Urban of any treachery in dealing with Hearst.[49] It is a reflection on the maladministration of British propaganda at the time that such a strange situation could have come about in the first place. Indeed the same International Film Service was one of the four main outlets in the United States for British official war photographs. Moreover, to the alarm of the Foreign Office, from April 1917 the sole British official cameraman for the whole of the Mesopotamia theatre of war was an American employee of International called Ariel Varges, working under contract for the British.[50]

Luckily for the reputations of the British propaganda organizations the Germans either failed to discover these absurdities, or else refused to exploit them. Viewed in terms of Wellington House's main overseas target, the United States, *The Battle of the Somme* must be judged a failure. It came too late to have any real influence on American opinion before that country entered the war, and seems to some extent irrelevant to the major issues of trade and finance, which were central to the United States' decision to do so. None of the detailed investigations conducted between the wars by Americans into the British propaganda assault on their neutrality even mention film. Searching for clues as to how their country had entered one war and might avoid another, the investigators ignored or dismissed this particular form of propaganda as a factor in the decision.

The main problems that had delayed the first agreements on filming the Western Front had been copyright and finance, and both were still extremely grey legal areas for the film industry. Sir Reginald Brade at the War Office believed that, as the law stood, he had no more inherent right to a share in the profits from films of the Western Front than in the profits of newspapers for articles written by their war correspondents. Further, as a government institution, the War Office could not create a monopoly on filming without its profits becoming technically forfeit to the Treasury. All Brade felt able to do was to appeal to the patriotism of the Topical Committee in order to extract payment. By the end of 1916, despite all the careful agreements and the massive success of *The Battle of the Somme*, he had still received nothing for his charities. He pressed the Topical Committee to renegotiate its contract in the light of the film's success, and when this produced no response he authorized Aitken to try again for him. After meetings in October between Aitken and the Committee members failed to produce any result, the original agreement with the War Office was dissolved by mutual consent. The body which replaced the Topical Committee, and at once assumed responsibility both for the exploitation of *The Battle of the Somme* and control of the Western Front cameramen, was a considerably more simple affair. Known as the War Office Cinema Committee, it was composed of just three men: Aitken as Chairman, Brade as Secretary, and William F. Jury as film expert. Already holding the key card in that it controlled filming on the Western Front, this committee was able to extend its authority until by April 1917 it controlled all British official filming in all theatres of war, including the British Home Front and the war at sea. Sir Graham Greene, Brade's counterpart at the Admiralty, joined the committee in recognition of this, but never found it necessary to attend its meetings.[51] To avoid the Treasury's claim of a monopoly, it was necessary for both Aitken and Jury to work without payment, and the latter made a substantial loss on his own business as a result. Compensation was made for this after the war, when Jury was granted exclusive control over all British official wartime film for his own company for three years and given a knighthood at Aitken's (now Beaverbrook's) insistence.[52] It was a fine and, in some ways, happy ending to the process which had begun with his decision to make *The Battle of the Somme*. Aitken also received his reward for supporting film: after (to use his own phrase) his relegation to the peerage as Lord Beaverbrook ended his greatest British political ambitions, it was his control of film, the new arm of propaganda, which guaranteed his success in the long fight to win control of the British propaganda machine. On his appointment as Minister of Information in February 1918 he made Jury the head of the Ministry's Cinema Department.

The Battle of the Ancre and the Advance of the Tanks was a great commercial and popular success, and in some ways as remarkable a film as *The Battle of the Somme*. But the alchemy and co-incidence of circumstances that had made *The Battle of the Somme* such an achievement could not be re-created. After the third of the major British 'battle' films, *The German Retreat and the Battle of Arras*, appeared in June 1917, Beaverbrook ordered a change in propaganda film policy, which led to the bulk of the film taken being released twice weekly as the *War Office Official Topical Budget* newsreel. No major film on the scale of *The Battle of the Somme* was made again for the rest of the war, and the great British victories of the 'Hundred Days' August to November 1918, the greatest victory ever won by the British Army (at least in terms of scale), has no film record to compare with that of the disaster on the first day of the Somme offensive.

Over the winter of 1916–1917 Malins wrote and attempted to publish his memoirs, which were promptly blocked by Brigadier General Charteris as ridiculous exaggerations and had to wait until after the war for publication. He worked intermittently for both the British and the Canadians on the Western Front through failing health, until being discharged in June 1918.[53] McDowell stayed on until the end of the war, to become the doyen of a team of cameramen that never numbered more than three at any one time, trying its best to film a British Army of more than 70 divisions. But despite the limitations imposed by their cameras, the indifference of the military authorities who maintained them, and the sometimes confused organizations that supplied and supported them, these men made an impact out of all proportion to their numbers. Their ghostly soldiers and monstrous guns are by far the most familiar image of the First World War today. Scarcely a week goes by without a scene from *The Battle of the Somme* appearing in a television programme somewhere in the world. The most surprising aspect in the sometimes bizarre story of the making of this remarkable film is the manner in which crucial decisions on its nature, matters fit for ministers to decide, were taken by comparatively junior officers, civil servants and businessmen, for pragmatic reasons of convenience or for no apparent reason at all. It was from this strange course of events that the dominant image of the British Army on the Western Front was established in 1916, and has remained until the present day.

NOTES

1 UNESCO Memory of the World Register www.portal.unesco.org/ci/en/ev.php-URL_ID=23174&URL_DO=DO_TOPIC&URL_SECTION=201.html The inclusion of *The Battle of the Somme* on this Register was largely the achievement of Roger B. N. Smither, who, at the time, was Keeper of the Film and Video Archive of the Imperial War Museum, London.

2 The print described in this paper is Imperial War Museum Film and Video Archive film catalogue number IWM 191 *The Battle of the Somme* (1916, produced by William F. Jury). Viewing copies of *The Battle of the Somme* on film have been in circulation since the Imperial War Museum inherited the British official film collection in 1919. VHS video copies were released by the Imperial War Museum commercially in association with DD Video in 1987, and in 2000 as a joint release *The Battles of the Somme and the Ancre*, each with a booklet of viewing notes to which the present author contributed. In 2008, a digitally restored version of *The Battle of the Somme* was released on DVD by the Imperial War Museum in association with Dragon Digital, also with an accompanying booklet from which some information in this essay has been taken. In addition, the Imperial War Museum holds two collections of papers related to the production and distribution of the film and the institutions responsible. One collection is held by the Film and Video Archive and referred to here as the IWM (Film) Papers; the other is held by the Department of Photographs and refereed to here as the IWM (Photo) Papers. *See also* Smither (1994) op. cit, with an introduction by the present author.

3 Quoted in the *Bioscope*, 17 August 1916, p. 576. An invitation to the original screening is preserved in the IWM (Film) Papers. For the events of the first day of the Somme offensive the classic account is still Middlebrook, M. (1971), *The First Day on the Somme*. London: Allen Lane, although some of its judgements have been superseded by Prior and Wilson (2005) op. cit.

4 *The Times* 11 August 1916 3d; the *Bioscope* 10 August 1916 p. 476 and 17 August 1916 p. 577; IWM Department of Printed Books, 'Third Report of the Work Conducted for the Government at Wellington House', p. 101.

5 Towle (1975) op. cit., pp. 103–16.

6 Lytton (1920) op. cit., p. 118; Carmichael, J. (1989), *First World War Photographers*. London: Routledge.

7 TNA WO 32/9304 'Military Press Control: History of the Work of MI7, 1917–1919' and WO 32/9303 'Summary of the Work Done by MI7b in 1917'.

8 TNA INF 4/6 Department of Information memorandum to the War Cabinet (not dated) 1917.

9 TNA INF 4/2 J. Brooke Wilkinson, 'Note on Film Publicity During the War

Years', p. 280; Hiley, N. (1995), 'The British cinema auditorium', in Dibbets, K. and B. Hogenkamp (eds), *Film and the First World War*. Amsterdam: Amsterdam University Press, pp. 160–70; Reeves, N. (1996), 'Through the eye of the camera: contemporary cinema audiences and their experience of war in the film "Battle of the Somme"', in Cecil and Liddle, op. cit., pp. 780–800; Low, R. (1950), *A History of British Film Volume IV 1914–1918*. London: George Allen & Unwin, pp. 25–33.

10 IWM (Film) Box 'General Files' File 'MoI Papers', Engholm to Foxen Cooper, 30 January 1925; McKernan, L. (1992), *Topical Budget: The Great British News Film*. London: BFI Publishing, pp. 22–4.

11 TNA INF 4/2 Brooke Wilkinson op. cit., pp. 286–7.

12 TNA INF 4/2 Department of Information memorandum to War Cabinet (not dated) 1917; Malins, G. (1920), *How I Filmed the War*. London: Herbert Jenkins, pp. 40–8; Renne, J., *et* Ford, C. (1961), *Le Cinema et la Presse 1895–1960*. Paris: Armande Colin, pp. 199–204.

13 Hiley, N. (1993), 'Hilton de Witt Girdwood and the Origins of British Official Filming', in *The Historical Journal of Film, Radio and Television*, 13, (2), 129–48.

14 IWM (Film) Box 'General Files', file 'Topical Film Company Papers', Wile to Jeapes, 30 January 1916, 5 April 1916 and 19 June 1916.

15 Sanders, M. L. (1975), 'Wellington House and British Propaganda During the First World War', *The Historical Journal*, XVIII, (I), 119–46; Masterman (1939) op. cit., pp. 272–308.

16 TNA HO 139/31/124 'Brooks Western Front Official Photographs', C. D. M. Campbell to F. H. Mitchell, 1 August 1916 and F. H. Mitchell to C. D. M. Campbell, 3 August 1916.

17 IWM (Photo) Box One, File 2, memorandum by E. A. Gowers, undated, 1916.

18 TNA INF 4/2 Brooke Wilkinson, op. cit., pp. 292–301.

19 TNA WO 163/21 'Army Council Proceedings 1915 and 1916', and WO 33/750 'Interim Report of a Committee on War Office Expenditure 1916'.

20 These British systems of money and measuring may be unfamiliar to some readers. A pound Sterling was represented by the sign £ (a crossed 'L' for *librum*, the Latin for pound), and was divided into 20 shillings, represented by the sign 's' (for shilling), each of which was divided into 12 pence, represented by the sign 'd' (for *denarius*, a Roman coin); for example, a sum of four pounds, three shillings, two and a half pence would be written £4 3s 2½d. Film lengths were measured in feet, at 12 inches to the foot, 3 feet to a yard, and 1,760 yards to a mile (roughly 1.6 kilometres).

21 TNA INF 4/2 Brooke Wilkinson, op. cit., pp. 292–301; *The Times*, 5 September 1916, 6d; Lytton, op. cit., pp. 116–19; Farrar (1998) op. cit, pp. 66–79.

22 Masterman (1939), op. cit., p. 283.

23 IWM (Film) Box 'Contractual Arrangements' agreement between Schuster and Urban, 23 September 1915 and affidavit by Robinson; TNA INF 4/2 Brooke Wilkinson, op. cit., 298–305; Masterman (1939) op. cit., pp. 283–4; Brownrigg, D. (1920), *Indiscretions of the Naval Censor*. London: Cassell; IWM Department of Documents 'Third Report on the Work Conducted for the Government at Wellington House, September 1916', pp. 101–7.

24 TNA WO 32/9304 'Histories of MI7 and Subsections', p. 8.

25 IWM (Film) Box 'Contractual Arrangements', Withers to Masterman, 7 November 1916.

26 Beaverbrook (1956) op. cit., p. 44; Robertson, P. (1978), 'Canadian photojournalism in the First World War', *History of Photography*, 2, (1), 37–52; IWM (Film) Box 'Contractual Arrangements', agreement between Aitken and Wellington House, 12 July 1916.

27 TNA INF 4/2 Brooke Wilkinson, op. cit., pp. 296–7; Malins (1920) op. cit., p. 51; *Bioscope*, 17 August 1916, p. 577. For the films themselves *see* Smither (1994) op. cit.

28 IWM (Film) Box 'General Correspondence' Till to Sofer Whitburn, 13 September 1920; House of Lords Record Office, Papers of Lord Beaverbrook, Beaverbrook to Brade, 30 March 1917.

29 The most recent and most complete account of the filming process for *The Battle of the Somme* is Fraser, A. H., Robertshaw, A. and Roberts, S. (2009), *Ghosts on the Somme: Filming the Great Battle, July 1916*. London: Pen & Sword. For the most recent interpretation of the film from a cultural (rather than factually historical) perspective, *see* Hodgkins, J. (2008), 'Hearts and minds and bodies: reconsidering the cinematic language of The Battle of the Somme', in *Film and History*, (38), (1).

30 *The Times*, 5 September 1916, 6d; Malins (1920) op. cit., pp. 121–82; IWM (Film) Box 'General Files 1919–1939', File 'MoI Papers', Nicholas to Foxen Cooper, 2 November 1916. The Imperial War Museum Film and Video Archive holds a list of the sequences in *The Battle of the Somme*, colloquially, if inaccurately, known as a 'dopesheet', apparently compiled in the early 1920s, which attempts to identify the scenes in the film; however, it has been shown to be not always accurate.

31 IWM Department of Documents, Lee Papers, p. 95 for August 1916.

32 TNA INF 4/2 Brooke Wilkinson, op. cit., pp. 296–9; Malins (1920) op. cit., pp. 178–82; Brownlow, K. (1979), *The War, The West, and the Wilderness*. London: Secker & Warburg, p. 54.

33 *The Times*, 22 August 1916, 3e, 1 September 1916, 9f and 5 September 1916, 6d; Low, op. cit., p. 29.

34 *The Times*, 29 August 1916, 5d and 5 September 1916, 6e. Ledgers held at the Film and Video Archive of the Imperial War Museum show that the last recorded

wartime booking of *The Battle of the Somme* in Great Britain was 3 November 1917, 15 months after its first release. The original calculations of the size of the film's audience were made by Nicholas Hiley. *See also* Reeves (1996) op. cit., pp. 784–5.

35 *The Times*, 29 August 1916, 3e, 29 August 1916, 5d, and 5 September 1916, 6e; *Bioscope*, 24 August 1916, p. 751, 31 August 1916, p. 809, 7 September 1916, p. 943, 14 September 1916, p. ii, 21 September 1916, p. xiii; *see also* Beckett, I. F. W. (2006), *Home Front 1914–1918: How Britain Survived the Great War*. Kew: The National Archives, p. 174; Reeves (1996) op. cit, p. 785.

36 The officer in question, identified in the film as 'a divisional general', was Major General Sir Henry de Beauvoir de Lisle commanding the 29th Division, filmed by Malins. The film including the close-up sequence is in the Imperial War Museum Film and Video Archive as film IWM 440–06 *Our Empire's Fight For Freedom – Reel 6; see* Smither (1994) op. cit.

37 For examples of this propaganda, not all of which was officially produced or sanctioned, *see* Haste, C. (1977), *Keep the Home Fires Burning: Propaganda in the First World War*. London: Allen Lane, pp. 79–107.

38 Barnett, C. (1972), *The Collapse of British Power*. London: Eyre Methuen, pp. 424–35; *see also* Fussell (1975) op. cit. and Todman (2005) op. cit.

39 The inter-title reference is *The Battle of the Somme* inter-title 8; *see also Bioscope* 17 August 1916, p. 627; Lytton (1920) op. cit., 119; Middlebrook (1971) op. cit. and Keegan, J. (1976), *The Face of Battle*. London: Jonathan Cape, pp. 234–7.

40 *The Times*, 11 August 1916, 3d.

41 *The Times*, 2 September 1916, 3b, letter from James Cooper, 25 August 1916, 7d; letter from 'HMS', 31 August 1916, 9c; letter from 'Ubique', 1 September 1916, 7d; letter from H. Henley Henson, Dean of Durham, 4 September 1916; letter from E. Roy Lankester; *Bioscope*, 10 August 1916, p. 476; Reeves (1996) op. cit.

42 Malins (1920), op. cit., p. 181; *The Times*, 2 September 1916, 3b; letters from '46' and 'Orbatus', 4 September 1916, 11d; letter from A. Conan Doyle, 6 September 1916; letter from Lucy Clifford, 7 September 1916; letter from Ernest Myers.

43 Malins (1920), op. cit., p. 163; *The Times*, 5 September 1916, 6d.

44 *Bioscope*, 17 August 1916, p. 627 and 24 August 1916, p. 751; *The Times*, 11 August 1916, 3d; *Daily Mirror*, 11 August 1916, p. 10.

45 Higgins, D. S. (ed.) (1980), *The Private Diaries of Sir Henry Rider Haggard*. London: Cassell, p. 84.

46 Quoted in Reeves (1996) op. cit., p. 790.

47 Malins (1920), op. cit., p. 163; *see also* Brownlow (1979), op. cit., p. 65.

48 Smither, R. (1993), '"A wonderful idea of the fighting": the question of fakes in *The Battle of the Somme', The Historical Journal of Film, Radio and Television*. 13, (2), 149–68.

49 TNA INF 4/2 Brooke Wilkinson, op. cit., pp. 310–12; IWM (Film) Box 'Contractual Arrangements', affidavit by Robinson; IWM Department of Documents 'Third Report on the Work Conducted for the British Government at Wellington House, September 1916', pp. 101–7; Masterman (1939) op. cit., p. 287.

50 IWM (Photo) Box One, File 2, minute by E. A. Gowers, 26 March 1917.

51 House of Lords Record Office, Papers of Lord Beaverbrook, Brade to Wood 3 December 1916, Brade to Aitken 21 December 1916, and Brade to Barstow 22 September 1917; Beaverbrook to Greene, 11 December 1917, Green to Beaverbrook, 12 December 1917, and Beaverbrook to Scott, 21 December 1917.

52 House of Lords Record Office, Papers of Lord Beaverbrook, Brade to Barstow, 15 August 1917, Beaverbrook to Brade, 7 July 1917.

53 Several errors and misconceptions about Malins' life and career have been cleared up by the work of Nicholas Hiley; *see* his introduction to the 1993 Imperial War Museum facsimile reprint of Malins (1920) op. cit., for what is presently the most accurate account of Malins' career.

6

The Raid on Narrow Trench 1917

The First World War was fought, and came to be seen as fought, by entire countries and empires; a war on a scale never before seen in history. On the Western Front, battles were fought by generals, but in another sense they were also fought by armies, each over a million strong. It became a commonplace that a Western Front battle was, unlike any previous battle in history, far too large an event for any one person to see or to comprehend anything but a small fraction of events. Writing the history of the First World War suffers from the same problem: historians can either consider very large issues about the war, asking political, social or cultural questions on a scale that makes any definite answer effectively impossible; or they can write about military events, including strategy and battles, knowing that one narrative cannot possibly cover everything; or they can look at a smaller scale, at what Peter Simkins has called the 'building blocks' of Western Front history, from which a more complex structure may eventually be discerned.[1]

Trench raids are a valuable example of this sort of 'building block' history. Raids were carried out by all sides from very early on in the war, involving any number of men from a handful to over a battalion. Their main underlying purpose was to maintain a sense of enmity between troops in the opposing trenches, in order to prevent what the military authorities perceived as any lack of aggression on the part of the troops. Additional reasons for raiding included the idea that it would wear down the enemy, and promote a sense of superiority over them that would be valuable when a major attack came, plus other more tangible benefits such as identifying enemy troops opposite and taking prisoners for interrogation. A big raid was seen as training for a larger attack, and as a way for soldiers to demonstrate to their enemies and to themselves what good fighters they were. Raiding was also seen as a way of assisting a major offensive taking place elsewhere on the Western Front, by keeping the enemy aware that other parts of the front needed to be defended, by denying him any 'rest sectors' in which his troops could recover and as part of a general strategy of attrition.[2]

The raid on the German positions in Narrow Trench (the name given on British trench maps of the time) took place on Saturday 15 September 1917, in the British Third Army sector near Arras, itself the scene of the major British offensive in April that year. Narrow Trench was the front line of the German trench system defending the village of Chérisy, about 10 miles south-east of Arras. It was a big raid, undertaken in three phases by the equivalent of a reinforced British battalion, and it was one of 19 raids undertaken that month by the Third Army in general support of Third Ypres, which was being fought further to the northwest. It provides an impressive demonstration of British trench-fighting tactics by the middle of 1917. It is also unusual in that, starting at 4.00 p.m. (British time), in daylight, it is believed to be the only trench raid to be photographed from the air while it was actually taking place.[3]

The raid had its origins five months previously in the Battle of Arras, in which the British attack eastwards produced a salient at the village of Monchy-le-Preux. Although the battle itself was deemed to be effectively over within a few days, the British, needing to straighten out their line to protect Monchy, made a slow, grinding advance eastwards to the south of the village, in what became officially known as the Second Battle of the Scarpe. The German response was to build and strengthen new defences in the standard defence pattern of this stage of the war, a three-fold trench system with a front-line trench, a second-line trench immediately behind it, and a reserve position some distance to the rear, in this case incorporating Chérisy village. Both this reserve trench complex and the second line were properly completed, but for some unexplained reason, possibly the speed of the British advance, construction of the front-line trench was botched. Narrow Trench ran for most of its length absolutely straight and perpendicular to the front, with none of the curves and bays that protected properly built trenches. Meanwhile the British advance had taken them to within 250 yards of Narrow Trench, where they gave their front-line trenches opposite the Germans the names Bulfinch Trench and Ibis Trench. Due to a slight curve in the ridge that ran across no man's land, neither side could see the other except at special observation posts; any trench built further out into no man's land would have been a death trap silhouetted on top of the ridge. The ground behind the German positions at Narrow Trench and Narrow Support dropped away quite steeply to the reserve line and Chérisy, reached by a communication trench called Neva Lane by the British, who named their own main communication trench back from Bulfinch Trench and Bulfinch Support as Foster Avenue. For a time there was stalemate; but in terms of trench warfare the Germans were in a difficult position. If they abandoned Narrow Trench and made the ruins of Chérisy village their front line, they would be completely overlooked by the British from on top of the slope. But even so, their decision to hold Narrow Trench was still an obvious mistake, for which they would eventually have to pay.

The troops who would make the raid on Narrow Trench came from the British 50th (Northumbrian) Division, part of VI Corps in Third Army (this use of different numbering styles for the military hierarchy was meant to minimize confusion between units, so that in an order or on a map a brigade could not be confused with a division, etc.). The 50th Division had a pre-war existence as the Northumbrian Division of the Territorial Force, and it had been fighting on the Western Front since April 1915. Its divisional commander was Major General Sir Percival S. Wilkinson KCMG CB, a very typical British 'dug out' officer of the period, meaning one who was over-age and near the end of his career when summoned back to command by the outbreak of the war. Wilkinson had joined the Royal Northumberland Fusiliers in 1883 at the age of 18, but had spent most of his career in West Africa commanding native troops. In 1914 he was already a major general, but had been passed over and was commanding a brigade of Indian infantry. The war had revitalized Wilkinson's career, and exactly a year after its start he took command of the 50th (Northumbrian) Division in France. In June 1916 he received as his GSO1 (General Staff Officer 1st Grade, or chief staff officer) Lieutenant Colonel Henry Karslake, a 37-year-old career gunner who had won the DSO in the Boer War in 1902. The First World War had halted Karslake's studies at the Army Staff College Camberley, and he had gone to France as a captain with his battery. Thereafter a steady rise had culminated in his posting as the chief staff officer of a fighting division.

Troops from two battalions of the 50th (Northumbrian) Division would be involved in the raid on Narrow Trench, both from 151 Infantry Brigade under Brigadier General Neville J. G. Cameron. A true Cameron of the Cameron Highlanders, his lifelong ambition was to command the regiment's 1st Battalion, in which he had started his career. Now 43 years old, Cameron had already been wounded twice since 1914, and each time had returned to the front. His brigade, like its parent division, had a pre-war existence as the Durham Brigade of the Territorial Force, and in an army that rarely combined battalions from the same regiment in the same brigade it was unusual, in that all four of its battalions were Territorials of the Durham Light Infantry.

If Wilkinson, Karslake and Cameron appear as typical of the pre-war Army, the two battalion commanders involved in the raid were far removed from the traditional image of a British lieutenant colonel. The 8th Durham Light Infantry ('Durhams' or 'DLI'), recruited chiefly from Durham city and its surrounding area, were commanded by what Army humour called a 'temporary gentleman', promoted from the ranks. Lieutenant Colonel James Hall Martin had joined the Army as a private in 1898 and gone to war in 1914 as a sergeant major. Commissioned in 1915, he held the substantive rank of lieutenant, promoted to acting lieutenant colonel to command his battalion at 46 years old in June 1917. Commissioning from the ranks in this way had become a very common Army practice by the second half of the war.[4]

The other battalion involved in the raid, 9th Durhams, recruited chiefly from Gateshead, was commanded by a man who was already an Army legend. A holder of the Victoria Cross, in 1917 Lieutenant Colonel Roland Boys Bradford was 25 years old. The youngest of four sons of a middle-class family resident at Milbank House in Darlington, his youth and unusual middle name often led to others calling him 'Boy' Bradford. Prior to the war, his eldest brother George had been commissioned in the Royal Navy, while his two middle brothers had joined the Territorial Force or its predecessors, being mobilized with their units in 1914. Roland also joined the Territorial Force in 1910, and transferred to the Regular Army in 1912, being commissioned into the 2nd Durhams. In 1914 he also went to war with his battalion, leaving only his sister, the family's your home. All the Bradford brothers were decorated for heroism in th᷉ war; in 1916 Thomas Bradford had been given a training post in Ireland, po᷉ sibly because of wounds, and in May 1917 James Bradford had died of wounds on the Western Front. Roland, although also only a substantive lieutenant, was promoted to acting lieutenant colonel to command the 9th Durhams in August 1916; he had won his Victoria Cross on the Somme in October, by taking tempo- rary command of a neighbouring battalion as well as his own in order to secure a critical objective. By all accounts he was an outstanding leader and tactician, and worshipped by his men. After the Battle of Arras, in which 50th (Northumbrian) Division had fought, Roland introduced to his battalion the hymn 'Abide With Me', to be adopted as a distinctive symbol of their faith in God, in their cause, and in each other – a practice that the battalion took to its heart. In June 1917 he took home leave for his Victoria Cross investiture, then came back to resume command of his battalion.[5]

The men who would defend Narrow Trench against the Durhams came chiefly from the city of Hamburg. In the German Army, the three battalions of a regi- ment served together as a brigade-sized unit, and 76th Reserve (2nd Hanseatic) Infantry Regiment was one of three regiments forming 17th Reserve Division. The regiment had suffered a bad summer, holding trenches only knee- or waist- deep against the British positions before Arras. On 14 August a surprise British bombardment had obliterated a 250-yard stretch of trench, and most of one company with it. On the last day of the month the regiment was finally taken out of line, only to be shifted southward to the badly sited position at Chérisy with Narrow Trench as its front line.[6]

The 50th (Northumbrian) Division had come back into line opposite Chérisy on 15 June. In the British system, only two brigades held the divisional front of 3,000 yards, with the third brigade in reserve. The four battalions of each bri- gade moved between front line, support line, brigade reserve and rest, seldom spending more than four days in each position. Within the battalions also, companies were rotated between front-line duty and rest, so that the ordinary soldier was unlikely to spend more than a night or two in a front-line trench,

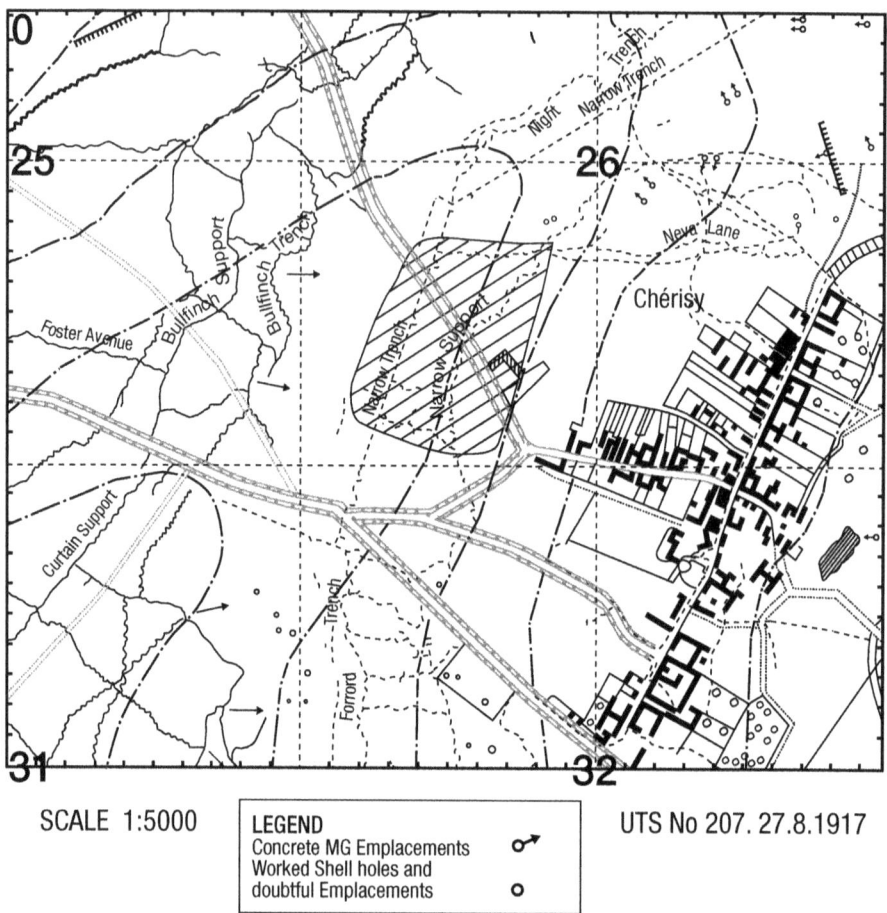

SCALE 1:5000

LEGEND
Concrete MG Emplacements   o⃗
Worked Shell holes and
doubtful Emplacements   o

UTS No 207. 27.8.1917

The map reproduced here is based on an original from the 50th (Northumbrian) Division War Diary showing the plan for the raid on Narrow Trench. The map shows pre-war sunken lanes or cart-tracks running across the battlefield and into Chérisy village, and both the British and German trench systems in September 1917. On the original map (opposite), British trenches were printed in black, German trenches (with their British codenames) were printed in red, and the shaded area showing the target of the raid has been marked in blue wax pencil (TNA WO 95/2810).

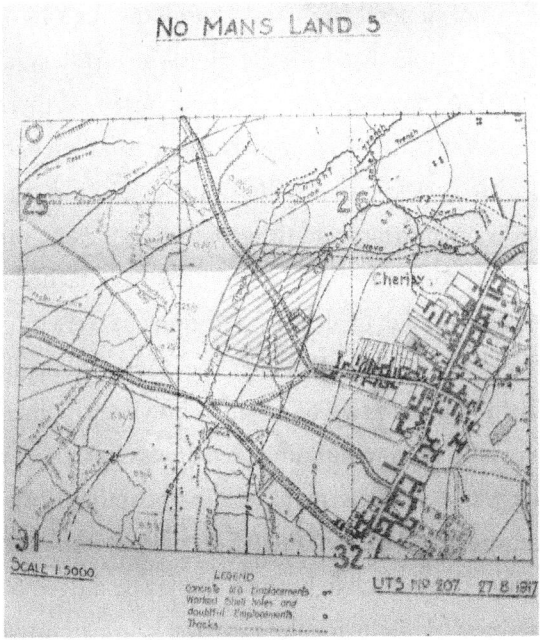

except in unusual circumstances. During August, 9th Durham spent altogether 12 days holding the front line, for the loss – in what was judged a quiet sector – of 3 men dead and 11 wounded, the everyday 'wastage' of the Western Front. On 1 September, having watched 76th Reserve Infantry come into the line opposite them, they moved into brigade reserve.

It is not known who first suggested the raid on Narrow Trench, but with a new, unidentified, enemy unit in the area it was only a matter of time before one was planned. The raid could be said to have started only two days after 9th Durhams went into reserve, when on 3 September, 50th (Northumbrian) Division's Commander Royal Artillery (CRA) issued new wire-cutting orders to his medium mortar crews. For a raid involving two battalions, Brigadier General Cameron of 151 Infantry Brigade would be the officer in charge, although the plan would be drawn up by the divisional staff under Lieutenant Colonel Karslake, subject to Major General Wilkinson's approval. Much of the success or failure of the raid would depend on the artillery plan at Corps level, put together by the staff of Brigadier General Herbert de T. Phillips, the VI Corps Commander Heavy Artillery (CHA), together with the divisional artillery, although Phillips himself was actually on leave when the planning began. At this date, in a British infantry division, each infantry brigade had an attached light battery of six 3-inch Stokes mortars, with a reserve under divisional command consisting of a battery of 9.45-inch heavy mortars and three batteries of 2-inch medium mortars (which fired an iron rod of that diameter to which was attached a 'plum pudding' or 'toffee apple' sphere of high explosive). The mortars were to 'cut' German wire by simply blasting it away. Four days later the divisional artillery, six batteries of 18-pounder field guns and two of 4.5-inch howitzers, joined in the fire plan by shelling Chérisy and the surrounding area. It was not a heavy bombardment, which might have warned the Germans of a forthcoming British attack, but the light, intermittent shellfire typical of the Western Front on a quiet sector. Even so, the scale of what was considered light shelling may be judged from the fact that, by day and sometimes by night for the next week, apparently by co-incidence, 1,950 shells fell on the German positions near Chérisy.[7]

On 5 September, Roland Bradford's 9th Durhams were relieved from brigade reserve and marched back to their rest area south of Arras. On the following morning the officers were briefed on Karslake's written orders for the raid. Karslake followed the practice of circulating questionnaires to various officers following engagements, and his orders for the raid reflected what had been learned from previous experiences. The plan listed four objectives for the raid:

to obtain an identification

to kill as many Germans as possible

to destroy all dugouts

to bring back or destroy German machine-guns and trench mortars.

The raid would be in three phases, the third of which was still being finalized. The first phase would involve A, B and C Companies of the 9th Durhams, the second would involve only C Company of the 8th Durhams, and the third would depend on Special Brigade Royal Engineers, the Army's experts on chemical warfare.[8] Borrowing an ordinary farm plough, the 9th Durhams dug a replica of the

German trenches and spent an afternoon practising over it. On the following day, the 151 Infantry Brigade came back into divisional reserve, and the divisional artillery fire plan for the raid started.

The next morning, Lieutenant Colonel Martin reviewed his C Company, under Captain Bennett M. Williams, a 33-year-old qualified barrister who had joined the Army as a volunteer in 1915. Like most fighting formations, C Company was notably under strength, and Martin detached ten men from each of his other companies to bring it up to five officers and 110 other ranks. C Company then had its first attempt over the replica trenches provided by the 9th Durhams. Meanwhile the divisional Commander Royal Engineers (CRE), Lieutenant Colonel Harold E. F. Rathbone, visited each of his three field companies. Early next day, the 7th Field Company was ordered to prepare a detachment for the raid. In the Army jargon of the time, the officer commanding this detachment would have been described as 'scraping the bottom of the barrel', as suitable men became harder to obtain for the demands of the Western Front in the second half of the war. Conscripted in March 1916 and commissioned exactly a year later, Second Lieutenant William Henry Rebbeck was just 25 years old (the same age as Bradford) but only 5 feet 6 inches tall and 9 stones in weight; he needed glasses, and was married. Given four corporals and eight sappers, and after experimenting with gun cotton and Stokes mortar bomb charges on the abandoned dugouts of the Hindenburg Line, Rebbeck produced 17 improvised explosive packages for the raid. Aerial photographs showed only eight dugouts in Narrow Support, immediately behind Narrow Trench. But the most recent reconnaissance also showed a machine-gun nest built in a small sap projecting forward from Narrow Trench, just at the point where A Company of the 9th Durhams was planning to attack.[9]

For the next two days the raiders continued to train. On Monday the divisional artillery switched to targeting Narrow Trench alone, leaving the mortars to continue wire cutting. On Tuesday 11 September the final preliminaries of the raid were set in motion. The heavy artillery of VI Corps joined in shelling Narrow Trench, together with Night Trench, which was just further north. Brigadier General Phillips' staff arranged for supporting fire during the raid from two neighbouring divisions, and contacted Number 12 Squadron, the VI Corps reconnaissance squadron, for spotter aircraft. A day later, Phillips returned from leave and approved the plan. Lieutenant Colonel Rathbone made another routine visit to his Royal Engineer companies, checking out some special equipment for the raid, and Second Lieutenant Rebbeck left with his men to start training with the 9th Durhams.

That afternoon the 9th Durhams carried out a full dress rehearsal of the raid in its practice trenches, watched by Wilkinson, Cameron, and several senior officers including the commander of VI Corps, Lieutenant General Sir Aylmer Haldane, and the commander of Third Army, General the Honourable Sir Julian Byng; clearly, Wilkinson wished to demonstrate either the techniques for raiding in his division, or Bradford's qualities as a leader, or both. Later that day, Brigadier General Cameron issued the final instructions for the raid, sensibly ordering that the 9th Durhams would receive eight extra stretcher bearers from each of his other battalions. On the following morning Karslake released the date and times for the raid, the third phase of which remained only an option.

There was already some concern from VI Corps's gunners about the poor weather and bad visibility, typical of the late summer and early autumn of 1917. On 12 September the weather broke altogether, and it was cold and damp. C Company of the 8th Durhams had their final trial over the practice trenches while the 9th Durhams rested, taking a form of solace in an extra evening church parade at which, almost certainly, 'Abide With Me' was sung. The 8th Durhams preferred an extra film show that evening. Early the next day the brigade returned to the trenches, and by 11.45 a.m. the 8th Durhams were back in the front lines opposite Chérisy, with the 9th Durhams in the brigade reserve camp behind them. That night, the 8th Durhams sent out two-hour patrols into no man's land at 10 p.m. and 2 a.m. One patrol heard noises from the German trenches opposite – it sounded as if they might, after all, be building new defences in front of Narrow Trench.

By summer 1917 the German Army had already adopted the tactics of defence in depth, concentrating their main strength in the support trench and leaving the front-line trench only lightly held. On 13 September, the 1st Battalion

76th Reserve Infantry Regiment (abbreviated by the British to 1/76th Reserve Infantry), the regimental reserve in the village of Lecluse some distance from Chérisy (which after a summer of bombardment was little more than rubble and brickdust) paraded for a visit by the Mayor and Secretary of the Hamburg Senate. That night the battalions rotated: 3/76th Reserve Infantry came out of the front line into reserve, 1/76th Reserve Infantry moved from Lecluse to Chérisy, and 2/76th Reserve Infantry deployed its four companies in the dugouts of Narrow Support, each company sending one platoon forward to hold Narrow Trench. The front-line trench had no dugouts, only shelter holes (called 'funk holes' by the British), and German doctrine held that in an enemy attack these could be abandoned without a direct order. This change-over was the noise heard by the night patrol from the 8th Durhams, and by the following morning most of 2/76th Reserve Infantry were in their dugouts, asleep.[10]

Friday was very cold, and rain fell on and off throughout the day. That day, the next night, and on into the following morning the gunners and fire planners of 50th (Northumbrian) Division and VI Corps fought a slow, persistent, subtle war with the front-line platoons of the 2/76th Reserve Infantry, to prevent the gaps in the wire being repaired and the damaged machine-guns and mortars being replaced. The point of the game was that the Germans must lose without ever being allowed to guess that they were playing: too much shelling would alert their suspicions, not enough would mean that the raiders would find the defences too strong; either could result in a massacre. In the afternoon, C Company of the 8th Durhams retired inconspicuously from the front-line Bulfinch Trench and let the three companies of the 9th Durhams crowd in to take its place. Bradford and his men slept in the front-line trenches that night. To keep to routine, the 8th Durhams sent out night patrols, and with them went a patrol of the 9th Durhams which cut a series of gaps in the British wire, clearing the way for the attack the next day.

Saturday 15 September dawned to cold, mist, drizzle and the intermittent sound of shells bursting. A light wind from the south-west drifted smoke across the German trenches. By 10 a.m. the rain had stopped and the weather was clear. At midday a staff officer arrived from division with a vital piece of equipment

– a watch. He was bearing the correctly synchronized time, which was passed on down to the battalions in the trenches. The extra stretcher-bearers arrived, and the 9th Durhams prepared their raiding equipment. According to regulations, this was a lighter version of their normal fighting order, without gasmasks, haversacks, water bottles or entrenching tools. Each man fixed his bayonet to his rifle, discarded the scabbard, and collected two Mills bombs (the standard and reliable British hand grenade); in addition, many men may have carried unofficial weapons such as knives and clubs, often improvised from the detritus of the trenches. In the specialist bombing section of each platoon, the appointed grenade thrower carried five Mills bombs and the other members ten each. Each man of the rifle-bomber sections collected six rifle grenades, designed to be fired from the rifle for greater range by means of a blank cartridge and a special attachment. The grenade, with the bayonet, was the principal infantry weapon of trench warfare. One man in each section was given an MSK bomb (a type of smoke grenade) and sergeants and platoon commanders were given wire cutters. Except for the lead platoon in each company, the Lewis gunners in sections were leaving their machine-guns behind as too cumbersome, and taking only their rifles.

Meanwhile, at VI Corps, six batteries of 6-inch medium howitzers and one of 60-pounder medium guns were preparing to fire. Once the raid started they would attempt to cordon off the area from German reinforcements with a three-sided box or barrier of shellfire for which the French word *barrage* was already common usage. The divisional artillery would provide the fourth side of the box, moving ahead of the raiders as they attacked. Other guns and trench mortars finalized their roles in the raid, as did the Royal Engineers of 7th Field Company, strung out to the north and south of where William Rebbeck sat with his explosives and detonators. With no more that he could do, Lieutenant Colonel Rathbone went down into the trenches to join Cameron watching the raid.

Each of the five British Armies on the Western Front had its own Royal Flying Corps brigade, III Brigade in the case of Third Army. Part of this was 12 (Air) Wing, of which Number 12 Squadron was the chief reconnaissance squadron. In September 1917 the squadron was still adjusting to its new Royal Aircraft Factory RE8 aircraft with a top speed of just under 100 mph and the ability to fly safely at half that speed, often known as the 'Harry Tate' from a popular music hall comedian. Six of these aircraft were to fly as spotters for the guns during the raid, and the remainder to fly 'Contact Patrols', shooting at anything German in the air or on the ground. Aircraft 2767 was flown by Captain Donald F. Stevenson, who had volunteered for flying from the Northamptonshire Yeomanry in November 1915. His observer was Lieutenant John Webster, who had been commissioned into the Royal Flying Corps in March 1917, possibly after previous service with the infantry. Both men already held the Military Cross for bravery. The aircraft, in addition to its forward firing Vickers and observer's Lewis machine-guns, carried two 20-pound bombs beneath the wings, and an aerial reconnaissance camera mounted on its fuselage next to the observer's cockpit, pointed directly downwards. At 3.20 p.m. Stevenson and Webster took off from their airfield at Wagonlieu, west of Arras, and 40 minutes later they were airborne over Narrow Trench when the raid began.[11]

Since spring 1916, each brigade of a British infantry division had been allocated its own company of Vickers medium machine-guns, and in July 1917 a fourth divisional company was added. Normally, at least half these guns would be kept as replacements for wastage. For this special event, Karslake had concentrated every machine-gun in the division, plus more borrowed from neighbouring divisions, opposite the raiders' target. At 4 p.m. precisely, a total of 70 Vickers machine-guns, firing on high trajectory to clear their own front line, opened fire at 250 rounds a minute, their maximum sustained rate of fire. Simultaneously, 22 light mortars each began to fire off one round every four seconds, their own maximum rate; two heavy mortars and 18 mediums joined in with three rounds a minute. Cameron, watching from the trenches, would later describe this bombardment as 'perfect'. Also at the same time, 48 field guns and 17 howitzers started their own fire crashing down on Narrow Trench, in what was officially designated as 'intense' fire of one round per gun per minute onto the target, while the heavy guns of VI Corps started to build their barrage: five minutes of intense fire with 60-pound and 100-pound shells, mixed with smoke from 4.5-inch howitzers and Special Brigade's 4-inch smoke mortars. Even Number 12 Squadron joined in: flying at 800 feet, far too low for safety, Stevenson and Webster dropped their two bombs into the barrage and fired off 500 rounds in an all-too-successful attempt to attract hostile fire. Stevenson noticed that the barrage fell precisely, with no stray shells, a clearly defined and edged box of smoke and exploding metal. After two minutes the field guns lifted their fire from Narrow Trench and the line of explosions began to creep forward at a barely perceptible 100 yards a minute. At that moment, Bradford's men left Bulfinch Trench and, unable to see the enemy, launched themselves into the unknown. As they did so Stevenson, flying above C Company on the right, throttled back and Webster switched on his camera. The resulting sequence of photographs shows the running men as odd white flecks, throwing black shadows to the north, while light reflecting from helmets pinpoints a few Germans in Narrow Trench.

As rehearsed, the plan called for the three companies to attack in half-platoon waves. Each platoon formed two widely-spaced lines, each with its commander in the centre and NCOs on the flanks. In the lead platoons the Lewis machine-gunner stood beside the commander. After the first half-platoon wave had covered 15 yards, the second, with the company second in command, left the trenches. Then, after a further 10 yards, the first wave of the second platoons started, with the fourth wave a further 10 yards behind them, together with the company commanders and Rebbeck's demolition team. The third platoon of each company remained in the trenches. There was no overall commander in the advance. It appears that Bradford, like a good battalion commander, had asked for permission to lead his men, and Cameron, like a good brigade commander, had refused him. Instead, Bradford stood up on the parapet of Bulfinch Trench as the attack started, helping his men out of the trench and into no man's land, then ran across after them to check on their progress before doubling back to telephone through his report.[12]

The raiders of the 9th Durhams made progress as best they could across the short distance of no man's land, sliding around the shellholes and dodging German fire. Unlike some commanders, Cameron permitted his men to open fire on the approach, sacrificing maximum speed across no man's land. 'It improves our morale', he argued, 'lowers that of the enemy, and causes a certain number of casualties'. As the men of A Company left their trenches they came at once under fire from the new German machine-gun position, and scattered as they did so. The raiders had been well rehearsed for this moment. Quickly and professionally the bombers of the leading platoon worked towards the machine-gun team, throwing grenades to blind the machine-gunner's fire, making a few yards in a crawl. It was never established how the machine-gunner died, but Cameron believed that he was shot by an unnamed company officer. The men brought his machine-gun back with them as orders required. Three minutes after they had left their own trenches, the Durhams were all inside Narrow Trench, having lost – as far as anyone could later remember – just one casualty.

Seconds before the three companies left their trenches, at two points each half a mile to the north and south of Bulfinch Trench, flames were seen to billow and figures to move. Other British troops appeared above their parapets, while a barrage fell in support in front of them. Also visible to the south was the unmistakable lozenge shape of a Mark IV tank. German fire poured onto these targets. It was meant to do so: the flames came from burning straw, the figures were dummies, and the tank had been built from wood and canvas by 7th Field Company, who managed to haul it on pulleys a short distance into no man's land before it stuck. The deception plan to confuse the Germans about the extent and nature of the raid had begun.[13] As the field guns lifted their barrage, the 4.5-inch howitzers switched targets and joined the 4-inch mortars firing smoke in an effort to hide the SOS flares now rising over the German trenches, a signal to their own artillery that an enemy attack was in progress. If the British barrage failed to hide the German flares, a number of officers were strung out at regular intervals along the British line to north and south, each armed with a Very pistol and 250 coloured flares. Their job was to copy any flare pattern seen over the German trenches in the hope of duplicating the SOS signal and so attracting German fire away to the flanks of the raid.

Meanwhile, two special parties, each of an officer, a Lewis machine-gun team, two rifle bombers and two snipers, were moving to set up blocks in the trenches to cover the flanks of the raiders. Second Lieutenant Hall, commanding one of these flanking parties, was killed during the raid. But for a few precious minutes there was no SOS barrage, and in that time the Durhams took their first objective

– the length of Narrow Trench from the Chérisy Road to its first dog-leg, where it became Night Trench. For a while at least, the Germans believed that they were facing a full scale assault, and the 3/76th Reserve Infantry Regiment was moved up from Lecluse in case the British broke through. The first German SOS fire began to fall about four minutes after the attack started, and few of the gunners knew their exact targets. No more than 12 batteries out of a potential 26 available joined in a bombardment described by VI Corps as 'weak and ragged', by Stevenson, flying above it, as 'thin and scattered', and even by the 8th Durhams on whose trenches it was falling as 'doing considerable material but little personal damage'. There was one tragedy: a trench mortar battery on loan from 62nd (2nd West Yorkshire) Division, firing in a support trench, took a direct hit on its bomb dump, killing eight men. 'Few traces' wrote the divisional CRA, 'of piece or detachment could be found afterwards'. The luck of Stevenson and Webster had also run out. As they turned over the battlefield a bullet severed one of the RE8's elevator cables, which wrapped itself around the aircraft's tail. As best he could, Stevenson pointed his machine towards home and began to lose height.

As the raiders collected themselves in Narrow Trench, the second stage of the operation began. At 4.05 p.m. the machine-guns slowed their fire to one belt of 250 rounds every two minutes. Half the mortars ceased fire, the rest slowed to one round a minute for mediums and ten rounds a minute for lights. The heavy artillery switched to their own version of slow fire, with one round per battery per minute onto each target, including heat-generating Thermite shells fired under the supervision of Special Brigade into the smokescreen. At 4.07 p.m. the 18-pounders, having rolled their barrage out beyond Narrow Support, ceased fire. All the time, no one could see what was happening on the far side of no man's land. Then, at 4.18 p.m., two minutes before the machine-guns were due to cease fire, came the first flag signal from the German trenches that the raiders were safe.

The main force of the raid had fallen on 6th Company of 2/76th Reserve Infantry, whose men in Narrow Trench had quite properly fallen back when the attack came. The Durhams raced after them, using two of Rebbeck's charges to blast away wire blocks dropped across the communication saps. Aerial

reconnaissance and interpretation of photographs was not always an exact science in the war, and of the eight dugouts marked on the British maps only three
were found to exist, while two more were uncovered of which there was no
previous record. In the confusion, no one was afterwards sure if they had 12 or
11 shafts leading upwards. Most of 6th Company had been asleep underground
when the bombardment started and its violence, coupled with the speed of the
Durhams' advance, had trapped them below the surface. It was the most delic-
ate moment in trench warfare: while battle raged around them the infantry of
two opposing armies could not fight. The Germans could not come up one at a
time to be shot down, nor could the British venture one at a time underground.
The MSK smoke grenades circumvented this problem. Thrown into the dugouts,
they drove some of the defenders to the surface where they were taken prisoner,
coughing and choking. The other option open to the raiders was in keeping with
their stated aim of killing Germans, as recorded in the 7th Field Company diary:
'three of the dugouts destroyed were undoubtedly occupied by the enemy, who
in two instances tried to effect their escape, but were driven down by the demolition party and escort, the charges then being placed'.

To the north of the Narrow Trench dog-leg, other Germans, mainly from 5th
Company, left their dugouts in an attempt to counter-attack into the raiders'
flank. They emerged straight into the British barrage, including the burning
Thermite shells of Special Brigade. When the smoke cleared, a British pilot
estimated 50 bodies lying in the open. The Durhams never knew that it had
happened. Another German party tried to bomb its way up from the south,
but was driven off by the blocking party. Three men of 1/76th Reserve Infantry,
coming from Chérisy, managed to get through the barrage but achieved little
other than to be taken prisoner. At 4.30 p.m. the British machine-guns again
opened fire. Taking their wounded, their dead, their trophies and their prisoners,
9th Durhams began to retire back across no man's land. After five minutes the
rate of fire slowed; five more minutes and the German SOS bombardment had
died away. At 4.50 p.m. all British guns, machine-guns and mortars ceased fire,
as the raiders walked straight back down Foster Avenue and all the way back to
brigade reserve camp. The third platoons from each company remained holding

the line until 6.45 p.m. when C Company of the 8th Durhams relieved them. For Bradford's men the raid was over.

The pilot who had spotted the German dead around Narrow Trench was Captain Stevenson, once more airborne with Webster. Despite his lack of control Stevenson had landed safely at Wagonlieu at 4.25 p.m. and handed over his photographs. At 4.45 p.m. both men took off in another RE8 to resume patrol, having a near miss with three German Albatross scouts. Fifteen minutes later Webster spotted a German two-seater firing signal flares in an attempt to contact the men in Narrow Support below. The RE8 attacked and the German dived away below 200 feet, falling out of control. Convinced he had a kill, Stevenson pulled up and levelled out at 1,000 feet. Then, the luck of the two men ran out again: anti-aircraft shells punctured the aircraft's fuel tank. Had there been a spark, Stevenson and Webster would have faced the terrible First World War airmen's dilemma of jumping to death or burning to death. In the event Stevenson landed the RE8, leaking fuel, in a field about a mile north-east of Wancourt. The two fliers had been shot down twice in 90 minutes.

That evening, the 9th Durhams tallied their losses: one officer and five men had been killed, two officers and ten men had been seriously wounded, three officers and eight men were classed as 'walking wounded' and would stay with the battalion. But the roll call failed to account for two other men. Their names are not known, and their story can only be guessed from the record. The battalion listed them as missing to division, and pragmatically added them to its own list of dead. A further mystery was the fate of three German prisoners. The 9th Durhams believed that they had brought back 25 Germans, but only 22 reached Third Army prisoner-of-war cages. In the confusion, anything might have happened to the missing three men: they may have been hospitalized, escaped, been shot, or simply have never existed. Such was the power held by his captor over a prisoner of war in his first few hours.

The raiders later guessed that they had killed 70 Germans, a figure that gained the authority of repetition higher up the command chain. The exact German losses at this stage of the raid are not known, but for all practical purposes 6th Company had ceased to exist. The men of the 76th Reserve Infantry worked for three hours in the wreckage of the trenches, carrying away the wounded, burying the dead, and searching for those who had been buried alive. Watching them overhead, flying at a safe 2,000 feet, was another of Number 12 Squadron's RE8s. Then at 7.40 p.m. another barrage crashed down on the remains of Narrow Trench. The British were raiding again.

This was the main contribution of C Company of 8th Durhams to the raid, and it had only one stated aim, 'to kill Germans'. The target was the northern sector of the previous raid, and the time had been picked so that the raiders could retire in darkness. The scale was smaller, but otherwise the plan nearly identical:

Zero

7.40 p.m.	Infantry leaves trenches
	Artillery 4.5s open medium barrage
	18 pounder barrage opens
	M[achine-]G[un]s open at belt per minute
	T[rench] M[ortars] mediums open at gunfire [3 rounds per minute]
	Lights open at 15 [rounds] per minute
	Heavy artillery opens slow fire
7.41 p.m.	Dummies exposed
7.42 p.m.	18 pounder barrage lifts and creeps at 100 [yards] per min[ute]
7.44 p.m.	Infantry enter final objective
7.45 p.m.	MGs slow to one belt per 2 min[ute]s
7.47 p.m.	18 pounder barrage halts
8.05 p.m.	Infantry commence withdrawal
8.10 p.m.	Dummies cease
8.15 p.m.	Infantry withdrawal complete
	All covering fire ceases

Karslake and his planners were optimistic in thinking that they could bluff the Germans twice in one day. As soon as C Company reached the British wire the SOS barrage began to fall 'very intensely' on the British second line where again the mortar crews took casualties. Flying overhead in the fading light the British RE8 took notes of the German flare patterns, hoping to break their code. Meanwhile C Company reached Narrow Trench, defended by just five Germans, one of whom lived to be taken prisoner. Leaving one platoon to hold the trench, Captain Williams led his men down the communications saps and into the main communications trench of Neva Lane, which was known to the Germans as Recken Graben or Heroes' Trench. The Durhams claimed that they found no resistance, and followed Neva Lane to the outskirts of Chérisy itself. The German version was that 5th Company, attacking from the flank, drove the raiders out immediately. In the confusion of trench warfare both perceptions may have appeared true. C Company certainly found no difficulty in withdrawing.

One of Captain Williams' men was killed in this second raid and 11 men were seriously wounded. Three German prisoners had been taken, but only one survived the return journey across no man's land. Two machine-guns were brought back, one of which soon vanished from the records. C Company listed 12 Germans 'definitely dead' and estimated a further ten bodies, including the occupants of a funk hole: 'five Germans who refused to come out', as Cameron wrote, 'they were left dead'. Also left behind were 40 copies of a pamphlet describing the delights of being a prisoner of war in Britain. But C Company did bring back the two men missing from the previous raid. They had been wounded and had managed to hide, probably in shell holes in no man's land. They were too badly injured to return to the 9th Durhams, which continued to list them as dead, and were passed rapidly back to a base hospital. Episodes like this could result in a family at home getting a War Office telegram notifying them of a soldier's death, only to have him turn up alive later, so that for a while there was always some hope. Unluckily, the 8th Durhams' own battalion doctor, Captain M. J. McNiff of the Royal Army Medical Corps (RAMC), was also wounded in the head by shrapnel and had to be hospitalized.[14]

The night, in trench warfare, was for reconstruction and routine. Karslake and his planners had other ideas. There is, and of course there was meant to be, something frightening about the relentless brutality to which they subjected the men in the trenches before Chérisy. At 4.04 a.m. on the morning of Sunday 16 September, J Company of Special Brigade fired off its Livens projectors. These were a special type of mortar, simple tubes of metal sunk into the earth with an explosive charge at the bottom, which, when detonated by an electrical contact, threw into the air a 65-pound bomb, 30 pounds of which was liquefied phosgene gas.[15] Firing in salvoes, the Livens projectors delivered 552 gas bombs onto the German trenches, with only 20 of the projectors failing to fire. The British sat for 10 minutes waiting for the German stretcher bearers to arrive, then for a further 10 minutes every machine-gun, mortar, gun and howitzer in 50th (Northumbrian) Division fired into the gas cloud. When this bombardment stopped, the raid was over at last.

That evening, the 8th Durhams sent out their usual patrols into no man's land. They found, on approaching Narrow Trench, that it was empty; the 76th Reserve Infantry Regiment was making no attempt to hold it. This, in trench warfare, represented the ultimate low point of morale. Already, at 9.45 p.m. on the previous day, General Headquarters in France had issued a statement on the raid to the press, following British practice in mentioning the regiment involved for reasons of home morale, but not including the battalion. 'This afternoon, Durham troops successfully raided the enemy trenches west of Chérisy and captured 22 prisoners. Our casualties were slight.' At 10.35 a.m. the next day a second statement was released: 'Following on their successful raid yesterday afternoon west of Chérisy our troops raided the enemy's trenches in this neighbourhood a second time last night and penetrated the German position as far as the western outskirts of Chérisy'. No public mention was ever made of the final gas attack.[16]

Also on 16 September, British wireless posts intercepted a German official statement on the raid, which makes an interesting contrast:

S.E. of Arras the enemy artillery activity became intense in the afternoon. Under cover of a smoke cloud the British attacked at Chérisy on a front of 1500 metres. Tanks and flame projectors cleared the way for the assaulting troops, but our excellent resistance by artillery and machine-guns broke down the attack. In those places where the enemy penetrated into our lines they were ejected in hand-to-hand fighting by our infantry. Towards evening the enemy again attacked at the same point. This undertaking also failed and they were driven back with great loss.[17]

Copies of this circulated among the 50th (Northumbrian) Division staff. Lieutenant Colonel Karslake, in particular, seems to have appreciated what was a very great compliment to his deception plan.

Three men of the 7th Field Company, seven of the 8th Durhams, and 18 of the 9th Durhams received the Military Medal for bravery in the raid, and Captain Williams received the Military Cross for his leadership of C Company. Captain Stevenson got a bar to his Military Cross for the two flights above Narrow Trench; Webster got nothing. Two days after the raid, Karslake left 50th (Northumbrian) Division to become the GSO1 of 4th Division; an appointment as the chief staff officer of a Regular Army division, which counted as a promotion. In August 1918 he took over as chief staff officer of the Tank Corps in succession to the celebrated J. F. C. 'Boney' Fuller, and it was Karslake rather than Fuller who led the Tank Corps staff through the Battle of Amiens and the Hundred Days campaign to end the war. He was to retire between the wars as a lieutenant general. Brigadier General Cameron was promoted in October 1917 to command 49th (1st West Yorkshire) Division; after the war he reverted to his substantive rank of lieutenant colonel, and fulfilled his lifetime ambition by commanding the 1st Cameron Highlanders; he was to retire as a major general. In February 1918 the ageing Major General Wilkinson was relieved of command of the 50th (Northumbrian) Division while on leave in Britain, and finished the war as Inspector General of Musketry.

On 5 October, Roland Bradford was promoted to brigadier general commanding 186 Infantry Brigade of 62nd (2nd West Yorkshire) Division, as the youngest general in the British Army, a record that is likely to endure.[18] After leading his brigade successfully through the Battle of Cambrai, on 29 November he left his brigade headquarters alone for a tour of the trenches as was his custom, and next morning he was found to have been killed by a chance shell. In April 1918 his eldest brother George was killed winning the family's second Victoria Cross in the Royal Navy's raid on Zeebrugge. Without the famous Bradford to protect them, in spring 1918 the 9th Durhams suffered the indignity of being downgraded to a pioneer battalion for the rest of the war; but they continued to teach newcomers the tradition of singing 'Abide With Me', which became the regimental hymn of the Durham Light Infantry.

William Rebbeck died in a military hospital in France on 4 November 1918, of the influenza epidemic that swept Europe. There is a heartbreaking correspondence in his personnel file detailing his widow's attempts to recover his kit and personal effects, which had quite probably been stolen, although the War Office could never admit this. (Army humour held that RAMC stood for 'rob all my comrades'.)[19] Webster has been tentatively identified as the Lieutenant John Webster MC of the Royal Flying Corps who was killed in action on 21 September 1918.[20] Everyone else mentioned by name is believed to have survived the war, although this is not certain. The raid on Narrow Trench, although quite large and elaborate, was only part of the routine of trench warfare on the Western Front.

NOTES

1 The main sources for the raid are after-action reports written at battalion, brigade, and divisional levels, all kept in the relevant TNA WO files. These files contain several duplicate documents, notably the comprehensive report written by Brigadier General Cameron. Rather than cite them all for each point, notes below refer only to factual information which comes primarily from other sources. The relevant documents are:

WO 95/2840 War Diary 9th Durham Light Infantry April 1915–January 1918

WO 95/2841 War Diary 8th Durham Light Infantry April 1915–September 1917

WO 95/2839 War Diary Headquarters 151 Infantry Brigade September 1917

WO 95/2810 War Diary 50th Division General Staff April–December 1917

WO 95/2814 War Diary 50th Division Commander Royal Artillery January 1917 –June 1919

WO 95/2821 War Diary 7th Field Company Royal Engineers May 1915–May 1919

WO 95/366 War Diary Third Army General Staff September–October 1917

WO 95/771 War Diary VI Corps General Staff June–September 1917

WO 95/785 War Diary VI Corps Commander Heavy Artillery July–September 1917.

2 The best analysis of trench raids and their purpose remains Ashworth, T. (1980), *Trench Warfare 1914–1918: The Live and Let Live System*. London: Macmillan, *passim*; *see also* Spagnoly, T. (1991), *The Anatomy of a Raid: Australia at Celtic Wood 9 October 1917*. London: Multidream.

3 The sequence of photographs can be found at the Imperial War Museum, London [hereafter IWM], Department of Photographs, starting with photograph Q58653. The annotations on the top right-hand corner of the negatives confirm that they were originally numbered as photographs 1014 onwards, taken by an aircraft of 12 Light Bomber Squadron Royal Flying Corps, at grid reference 51B.026.c on 15 September 1917 at 4 p.m. (the British Army did not adopt the 24-hour clock until 1918). Other copies of these photographs are held at the Durham Light Infantry Museum at Aykley Heads, Durham.

4 Some of these details come from an analysis of Martin's personnel file, held as TNA WO 339/24116.

5 Additional material for this description come in part from Moses, H. (2003), *The Fighting Bradfords: Northern Heroes of World War One*. Durham: County Durham Books and Shannon, S. D. (1998), *Beyond Praise: The Durham Light Infantrymen Who Were Awarded the Victoria Cross*. Durham: County Durham Books.

6 Details of the 76th Reserve Infantry Regiment in summer and autumn 1917 can

be found in the regimental history, Gropp, H. (no date), *Hanseaten im Kampf*. Hamburg: Klindworth und Neuenhausen, pp. 250–3.

7   TNA WO 95/2820 War Diary 250 Brigade Royal Field Artillery (50th Division) January 1917–June 1919, entry for the week ending 15/16 September 1917.

8   For the Special Brigade *see* Foulkes, C. H. (1934), *Gas! The Story of the Special Brigade*. London: Blackwood; there is no specific reference to the raid in this book.

9   Trench map 1:10,000 51BSW2 Vis-en-Artois Edition 6A correct to 30 August 1917, copy held by the IWM Department of Printed Books.

10 Gropp (no date) op. cit., p. 252.

11 The main source for Stevenson's and Webster's involvement in the raid is TNA AIR 1/2240/209/42/9 War Diary III Brigade Royal Flying Corps September 1917 and AIR 1 1515/204/58/50 III Brigade Royal Flying Corps Recommendations for honours and awards June 1917 to March 1918.

12 This is according to an anonymous eyewitness, quoted in Moses (2003) op. cit., p. 89.

13 The detail of burning straw being used to create smoke and flames in this way comes from the personal account of George Cole, who on the day of the raid was a signaller with 250 Brigade Royal Field Artillery and acted as a runner between Bradford and the artillery brigade headquarters. Mr Cole attended a version of this talk given at the Durham Light Infantry Museum in September 1984, and his account was recorded by Stephen D. Shannon.

14 TNA WO 95/2815 War Diary Assistant Divisional Medical Services 50th Division April 1915 to June 1919, entry for 15 September 1917.

15 For details of the Livens Projector *see* Foulkes (1934) op. cit., pp. 159–73 and pp. 206–7.

16 Both statements appear in *The Times*, page 8C, 17 September 1917.

17 This particular translation of the German statement is in TNA WO 95/2823 War Diary 245th Machine-Gun Company 50th Division July 1917 to March 1918. A slightly different translation appears in the IWM Department of Documents, Papers of Lieutenant General Henry Karslake. This is the only reference to the raid in the Karslake Papers.

18 The point is unavoidable that, however remarkable in itself, Bradford's achievement hinges on a technicality. In the British Army of the time, 'brigadier general' was an appointment rather than a rank, and his correct rank was acting full colonel with the appointment of brigadier general. In 1922 the appointment of brigadier general was replaced in the British Army by the rank of 'colonel commandant', and in 1928 the name of this rank was changed to 'brigadier'. Most other armies since that time have regarded British brigadiers as generals, but officially British general officer ranks start with major general.

19 Rebbeck's personnel file is TNA WO 339/98107.

20 This personnel file is TNA WO 339/3085, but the identification is not certain beyond doubt.

7

The Press, Propaganda and Passchendaele 1917
with Philip M. Taylor

If, as Lord Reith later put it so memorably, news is the shocktroops of propaganda,[1] and war reporting has come to provide the 'first rough draft of history', then by the summer of 1917 these two ostensibly contradictory axioms were found wanting by the British. Modern warfare has been accompanied by the need to address morale from the battle front to the home front and, as the twentieth century unfolded against the backdrop of the communications revolution, governmental propaganda had a profound effect on the media 'record' of events such as battles. Third Ypres was an exception, but not in any obvious or straightforward sense. The official wartime British organizations for the release of news, and thereby for the conduct of official propaganda, had by that time achieved their most important initial objective; namely, the entry of the United States into the war on the Allied side. But, as a result, they were undergoing a major re-organization of both their aims and their structure that was not completed until several months after Third Ypres had ended, and so they were unusually poorly placed to influence public perceptions about 'Passchendaele' (as the battle is usually known). Consequently, the media record – which might be assumed to have affected public understanding of the battle down to the present day – in fact says far more about the propaganda performance within the wider political context of the time than it provides a useful historical record of the battle itself.

This is apparent only with hindsight. The campaign against American neutrality had been chiefly conducted, with great success, by the clandestine organization based at Wellington House and headed by Charles Masterman, a body that worked under close Foreign Office supervision. Even though its approach had been a news- and information-based strategy rooted in a commitment to 'factual' information, the careful selection (and therefore omission) of which facts would help the Allied cause while damaging that of the Central Powers gradually emerged as a professional wartime responsibility of government – and the way the British developed it was to earn the admiration of friends and enemies alike.[2]

It must be remembered that the term 'propaganda' had not been widely used before the First World War, and it did not acquire its largely negative connotation until more than a decade later. Its pioneers saw themselves not as purveyors of lies or distortion, but as professional persuaders trying to attract potential supporters through the force of their convictions and arguments. The guiding principle, described by Masterman himself as 'the propaganda of facts', was the presentation of a reasonable case for British wartime policies and actions, as distinct from those of Germany.[3] Wellington House's methods were politically sophisticated, chiefly indirect, and very much in the Liberal political tradition, focusing on elite opinion in neutral countries largely through written articles and pamphlets and personal contacts. In other words, this was not a direct appeal to public opinion itself, but rather to the opinion-makers, including the newspaper men and the newly emerging cinematographic professionals, whose coverage of events would shape the wider public impression of what was going on. But by 1917, the third summer of the war, the military stalemate was such that no news was better for the military than the good news desired by the politicians, and bad news was what all wanted to avoid. Military censorship, or the absence of news, had become the real shock troops of propaganda. As a result the media record was nothing like 'reality' but rather an illusion of reality, in that what was *not* being said counted for far more in shaping popular perceptions than the type of positive campaign that had been tried and tested in the United States. It would be for the historians to re-write the resultant flawed first rough draft, to fill in the enormous gaps, and for hindsight to expose the real horrors of the war.

After the United States' declaration of war against Germany on 6 April 1917, Wellington House and its successor organizations continued their attempts to strengthen American support for the war and to influence other countries. The scale of this activity was phenomenal, even though it was to be minimized subsequently by those who were to take charge of the official propaganda machinery in the months that followed. In any given month of 1917 (for example, July, when the Third Ypres offensive began), Wellington House in London produced about 150 different book and pamphlet titles in various languages, with a print run of around 2.5 million copies, of which 500,000 were despatched abroad. A monthly print run of a further one million books and pamphlets was produced by overseas branches, together with ten illustrated newspaper titles. By the time of the Third Ypres, the New York outlet for Wellington House material, the British Information Bureau, was sending out pamphlets regularly to a mailing list of 170,000 influential American citizens (rising to 260,000 by the war's end). Nonetheless, the precise extent of British propaganda directed overseas remains hard to estimate since, in keeping with its indirect style, Wellington House was to commission or produce work which in most cases appeared to have originated with independent citizens or informal committees, and positive propaganda masqueraded as simple patriotism. For example, throughout 1917 every Catholic priest in the United States and Canada received a monthly letter from an apparently independent British Catholic committee, while a Protestant committee sent similar letters to pastors in the United States, the Netherlands and Scandinavia. Cloaked in such anonymity, a considerable amount of British propaganda material also managed to circulate within Germany. Later, this type of activity would be defined as 'black' or covert propaganda; namely, that which appears to originate from a source that is different from its true origin.

At home, British propaganda aimed at domestic audiences emerged in a far less planned manner. It was more the result of official initiatives to encourage the work of the numerous local or unofficial patriotic organizations that sprang into existence at the start of the war. The semi-official Central Committee for National Patriotic Organizations (CCNPO), with the prime minister as the honorary president and the editor of *The Pall Mall Gazette* and former Unionist MP Henry Cuts as chairman, functioned as a central co-ordinating body.[4] Whereas an important part of the British governmental approach to propaganda was the trustworthiness and general respectability of official pronouncements, such unofficial or semi-official propaganda, often in the forms of newspaper reports and editorials, was characteristically much more outspoken. Indeed, it was a principle of

British propaganda from the outbreak of the war that the press should be largely self-regulating. Much of the 'hate propaganda' of the war was the product not of deliberate government policy, but of an almost spontaneous outburst of emotions on the part of wide and disparate segments of the population.

It is a widely held belief about the war on the Western Front generally, that no contemporary civilians understood its reality. In the strictest sense this is true, as many veterans felt a reluctance or inability to describe their experiences to those who had not shared them. However, given the relatively positive nature of British government news and propaganda policies, an average working-class adult, newspaper-reading and cinema-going, with friends or relatives in the Army, would have had to have been remarkably obtuse not to have had some idea about the likely course and effects of a major British offensive by July 1917, including the conditions in which it would be fought and the likely losses. The basic structure of Western Front reporting had been in place since roughly a year after the war's start. In June 1915, the Press Section was established at GHQ in France with a group of five reporters uniformed as captains, who were joined by two American reporters after April 1917. Inevitably, the sense of mutual identification that these arrangements created encouraged the phenomenon of what would later be termed 'bonding', namely an increased media awareness of, and empathy for, what the soldiers were going through, including their hopes and fears, which had a tendency to undermine the journalistic ideal of objectivity. A pool despatch from the official correspondents printed in *The Times* on 28 September 1917 at the height of Third Ypres proclaimed happily that, 'It is another lovely day, and the British Army would like you to know that it is in the best of spirits, thank you, and enormously contented with the results of the last two days' fighting – as it has a right to be'. As mentioned in other chapters, the first two official Western Front cinematographers (who wore uniforms but could be technically civilians until 1918), arrived at GHQ in November 1915, and the first official Western Front photographer, with the rank of second lieutenant, arrived in March 1916. Putting these reporters in uniform also increased the sense of shared destiny, even though all forms of war reporting remained subject to field censorship at GHQ. The members of the Press Section soon worked out what was acceptable practice for the Army as well as to their employers. The reporters continued to work directly for their respective newspapers; the cinematographers, two of whom filmed the Third Ypres offensive, were employed directly by the War Office Cinema Committee (WOCC) from November 1916; and the still photographers, two of whom photographed Third Ypres, worked for Wellington House. In addition, Australian involvement in the offensive was covered by two still photographers and one cine-cameraman, employed by the Australian War Records Section. The Canadian involvement in the last stages of Third Ypres was covered by one still photographer and one cine-cameraman employed by the Canadian War Records Office. The New Zealand Division had its own cameraman, who took both still pictures and cine film.[5]

This was an elite group that sometimes produced vivid prose and images, but it was hardly an adequate number of reporters and cameramen to do justice to an Army of more than 60 divisions. However, it has to be said that if it had been left to most senior officers in 1917 there would have been even less of a Press presence (or, better still, none at all). Stories of William Howard Russell of *The Times* during the Crimean War still rankled among officers who saw the Press as a potential enemy within its gates, capable of undermining civilian support by exposing the true nature of modern war. They need not have worried. The Press Section came under the Intelligence Branch at GHQ and Brigadier General John Charteris, who viewed its members with barely concealed disdain. Charteris' view was that the role of the Press Section was to provide a 'steadying' effect on the home population, and he encouraged the kind of upbeat purple prose that by the end of 1916 had in fact brought the reporters into disrepute with many serving soldiers.[6] Although the Press Section's senior conducting officer, Major the Honourable Neville Lytton, hoped to encourage more realistic reporting in 1917, he also expected the reporters to help promote good relations with the French.[7] Field Marshal Haig does not appear to have issued either specific instructions or a briefing to the Press Section for Third Ypres, but he undoubtedly remained true to his basic press principles, issued before the Somme offensive of the previous year.[8] In keeping with Haig's own quiet but formidable determination, these principles were that the press should explain the justice of the British cause to the

Home Front and the Army alike, together with the need for a hard struggle and victory going to the side with the greatest endurance. This was to be the real task of the war correspondents, and they duly obliged in their comparatively lavish French chateaux billets (leading to them being often known, along with the GHQ staff as 'chateaux warriors'). Haig's state of mind during Third Ypres is perhaps reflected by the fact that, quite unusually, he sat (on horseback) for official photographs twice during the offensive, on 12 September and again on 11 October. Significantly, he never lost his high opinion of the reporters of the Press Section for what he saw as their unflinching support throughout the period of his command and, as already related, at the war's end he conferred on each of them the reward of his handshake and a small Union Jack flag.[9] Haig appreciated that the full realities of Passchendaele would never reach the public via a Press Section that identified so patriotically and co-operatively with the high command.

With the United States in the war, the chief role of the British propaganda organizations changed from trying to influence elite opinion overseas to maintaining popular support for the war (described as 'high morale') on the Home Front and in the Army. Britain may have been in advance of some of the other Great Powers in her parliamentary system, but the country was by no means a democracy in the modern sense. Mobilizing 'public opinion' in support of the war was a complex equation for the Lloyd George government, in which the influence of various elites weighed very heavily. Other than their own instincts, politicians and propagandists had virtually no means of measuring opinion in the mass, and would not have until the introduction of sample-based opinion polls shortly before the Second World War. Being used mainly to communicate their ideas to the public through newspaper contacts, they tended to give disproportional influence to editors and owners of the major national newspapers in assessing public attitudes. With popular morale deemed to be falling after three years of Total War, the age of the 'Press Baron' was about to flower, and they would play a critical role in what has been termed the 'remobilization' of the British public in order to cope with the strains of the second half of the war.

By the time of Third Ypres, the need for propaganda to strengthen morale on the Home Front for this remobilization process was self-evident. The low point in wartime morale came between March 1917 and February 1918, and there were only limited actions that the government could take to redress this decline, which had all the appearance of being related specifically to the events of the war rather than to the impact of propaganda on either side. Although the entry of the United States into the war held out the promise of victory in the long term, this was offset by the initial Russian collapse in February 1917, the costly and limited victory of Arras in April, the failure of the Nivelle offensive and the early successes of the German submarine campaign. To state the obvious, the government's problem would have been more than solved by a successful breakthrough in Flanders of the kind originally promised by Haig.

Winter 1916–1917 had been unusually cold and harsh, making severe demands upon domestic fuel and affecting food production. The impact of the war on the home economy, including rising prices and taxes, and food shortages as the German submarine campaign began to take effect, was felt particularly by craftsmen and skilled workers in reserved occupations. The first serious wave of unofficial strikes since 1914 began at the end of March 1917, particularly among munitions workers, spreading to 58 towns and involving 200,000 men before it died away at the end of May, with the loss of 2.5 million working days. Industrial relations remained poor, and a fresh outbreak of strikes took place beginning in August.[10] In September, King George V paid an official visit to 'Red Clydeside' in an attempt to ease the situation, an event which was turned into a 30-minute official propaganda film, *H. M. The King on the Clyde*. An analysis of complaints by the government in April gave worsening food shortages as the strikers' major grievance, along with profiteering. Government actions against this problem, including the introduction of the convoy system in June and the establishment of proper rationing, would require some time to have any obvious effect.

The state of morale of the Army on the Western Front in 1917 is harder to judge, despite being better documented through the military censors' analysis of soldiers' letters home. The factors that make up a soldier's morale frequently have far more to do with his immediate surroundings and conditions than with wider considerations, and could fluctuate considerably over short periods. Nevertheless, there was a marked and general drop in Army morale in May, increasing war-weariness during the period July–August, and by October an almost universal longing for peace. But the only serious mutiny of any size suffered by the British Army on the Western Front was at Etaples in September 1917, and a final and thorough censor's analysis in December concluded that the morale of the Army was still basically sound, in the sense that large-scale mutiny was not likely.[11]

Again self-evidently, British official propaganda policy for 1917 had, as its principal objective, the raising of morale both on the Home Front and in the Army in France and Flanders, while attacking German morale. The characteristic 'propaganda of facts' approach that year can be seen from the emphasis on certain themes in official press statements, cinema films, and photographs. These were the arrival of United States' forces into the war, British successes against German submarines, improved Home Front food production and organization, and continuing good relations with the French, but not necessarily the promise of a great victory on the Western Front. The propagandists and their close associates were themselves Whitehall politicians, and they directed their policies accordingly, rather than in keeping with the views of GHQ in France. Historians have noted Lloyd George's distancing of himself from the Third Ypres offensive in Autumn 1917.[12] The most plausible explanation of Lloyd George's behaviour, apart from his limited freedom of action, is that he was resigned to the offensive's failure, and was preparing the political ground for Haig's dismissal at the end of the year, as well as that of Sir William Robertson. But in challenging Haig even indirectly after the Nivelle fiasco, Lloyd George's own position as prime minister was at risk, and Whitehall was full of manoeuvres and shifting alliances by ambitious politicians and kingmakers waiting to see which way the wind would blow. Unfortunately – if inevitably – at the critical time of Third Ypres, British propaganda also got caught up in these internal political games.

For the first two years of the war the main organizational problems facing British propaganda derived from the familiar turf wars of Whitehall ministries – in this case the Foreign Office, Home Office and War Office (and to a lesser extent the Admiralty) each claiming the right of control. Given that the main official propaganda effort during this period was directed overseas, the Foreign

Office tended to win. But as has been recounted already, the inter-departmental in-fighting had produced the curious arrangement that the official cine-cameramen and photographers, who worked together in pairs on the Western Front and shared GHQ transport facilities, came under the separate organizations of Wellington House and the War Office Cinema Committee. In December 1916, as Prime Minister, Lloyd George had just come from the War Office and was inclined to back its position that a completely new organization was needed. With Lloyd George himself very much on the populist wing of the Liberal Party, his supporters also included newspapermen and entrepreneurs who portrayed themselves as populists and professionals in the art of propaganda, in contrast to what they saw as the elitist amateurism of the civil servants who continued to dominate the machinery until 1917.[13]

Lloyd George's determination to wrestle influence from the Foreign Office has been well documented and, as has also been recounted, one of his first actions as prime minister was to commission Robert Donald, editor of the *Daily Chronicle*, to provide a highly critical report into British propaganda. Indeed, evidence suggests that Donald's finding had already been largely pre-determined by the new prime minister.[14] Another report on reorganization was commissioned, this time by Lieutenant Colonel John Buchan, a protégé of Lord Milner as well as already famous as a novelist.[15] The result was the formation in February 1917 – a few days after the notorious Calais Conference leading to the Nivelle Offensive – of the Department of Information (DoI) under Buchan. Although technically still a branch of the Foreign Office, the DoI (which absorbed Wellington House) had far greater independence and Buchan reported directly to Lloyd George. The DoI also greatly increased overt propaganda directed at enemy countries and their armed forces, including the use of balloons on the Western Front to distribute propaganda leaflets over the German rear areas. By the time of Third Ypres, British trench-raiding parties habitually left behind pamphlets in German describing the advantages of surrendering and the good treatment given to prisoners of war.[16]

As an important part of the move towards a more overt and populist propaganda style (and also as a way of by-passing Whitehall), Buchan pressed for centralized direction of the domestic informal and regional patriotic committee structure. This culminated on 4 August 1917 – a few days after the start of the Pilckem Ridge battle with which Third Ypres commenced – in the formation of the inappropriately named National War Aims Committee (NWAC) with Lloyd George as its chairman and Buchan on its executive committee, absorbing the CCNPO and the multitude of smaller committees which went with it, and with them the overall direction of rallies and public speeches at a regional level. In one 14-day period during Third Ypres (25 September–10 October, the height of the British successes at Polygon Wood and Broodseinde), a total of 889 meetings took place around the country under NWAC auspices.[17] The same populist style was reflected in the NWAC's employment as a touring speaker of the demagogue and former Liberal MP Horatio Bottomley, who was sent to visit both the Army in France and the Grand Fleet. In the same spirit, in May the WOCC invited the famous Hollywood film director D. W. Griffith to visit the Western Front in order to gain inspiration and scout for locations for a planned anti-German feature film to be known as *Hearts of the World*.[18] It is perhaps a reflection of the same policy change that it was also in May 1917 that, on the only major occasion in the war, the British government broke its own rules by officially promoting a propaganda atrocity story, the notorious German 'Corpse Factory' affair. The idea that the Germans, starved by the blockade, were so desperate that they were prepared to melt down the corpses of the fallen for recycling into substances such as glycerine and soap seemed so ludicrous that most soldiers would have laughed at it. Back home, however, the climate of hate propaganda was sufficiently unreal that even Foreign Secretary Arthur Balfour, upon reviewing the evidence, found that 'there does not, in view of the many atrocities of which the Germans have been guilty, appear to be any reason why it should not be true'.[19] Masterman, who had remained in charge of Wellington House despite the fact that it had been reduced in status to little more than a printing operation within the DoI, reluctantly went ahead with producing the resulting four-page pamphlet.[20]

A major complication in British propaganda following Lloyd George's rise to become prime minister was the dual role played by Lord Beaverbrook as head of the Canadian War Records Office (CWRO) and as the dominant figure in the War Office Cinema Committee (WOCC). Beaverbrook's dual responsibility meant that there were constant complaints from both the Australians and some British officers that the Canadians on the Western Front were getting a disproportionate amount of publicity. The overwhelming majority of motion pictures made and shown in Great Britain between 1914 and 1918 were fictional, and were intended to provide relief from the war rather than information about it. However, from the start, British government policy had been keen to market its official factual films of the Western Front as a commercial operation, with any profits going to War Office charities. As has been recounted, this led first to the success of *The Battle of the Somme*, followed by *The King Visits His Armies in the Great Advance*, and *The Battle of the Ancre and the Advance of the Tanks* and *The German Retreat and the Battle of Arras*. The large 'big battle' format of hour-long films lasted until the five-part series *Sons of our Empire*, was released in Great Britain in March and April 1918, but by that point the bottom had largely fallen out of the market. *The Battle of the Somme* and *The Battle of the Ancre* had between them earned the WOCC at least £65,000 in their first three months of release. But from January 1917 to June 1918, domestic revenues from all other British official films came to only a further £35,000.[21] There are numerous possible explanations for this collapse in popularity, including the combined impact of the new Entertainment Tax for cinemas and the cutbacks in domestic spending, which also produced the May 1917 strikes. While audiences had flocked to see the first 'big battle' films, probably out of some degree of curiosity about what the Western Front looked like as much as from any other motive, that curiosity had, by 1917, been more than satisfied. Also, just as the big offensives themselves had failed to produce correspondingly major victories, so the 'big battle' format no longer seemed appropriate to the war in 1917. The explanation favoured by the British propaganda organizations for the public lack of interest was linked directly to the new populist policy. 'The public is jaded', wrote Beaverbrook, 'and we have to tickle its palate with something a little more dramatic in the future if we are to maintain our sales'.[22]

The WOCC continued to produce films of the Western Front throughout 1917, characteristically between 10 and 30 minutes in length. Although many of these have survived, lack of written documentation precludes our certain knowledge of their release dates, and in most cases they were probably shown to the public a month or more after they were taken, robbing them of any immediate propaganda value. For example, although King George V remained a central figure in British official propaganda, the hour-long film of his visit to the Western Front on 13–14 July 1916 was not released until October. For the rest, although British and Dominion cameramen filmed Third Ypres from its first day, their method of doing so marked an admission of failure on the part of the British propaganda authorities. It had been acknowledged almost from the start of the war that the difficulties and dangers of the front line made it quite impractical to film or photograph infantry fighting. The earlier 'big battle' films had concentrated quite heavily on scenes of the dead and wounded, which made up almost 13 per cent of the content of *The Battle of the Somme* and *The Battle of the Ancre*. But these scenes virtually ceased to appear in official films after spring 1917, making up only two per cent of *The Battle of Arras*, with the implication that this was a deliberate change in propaganda policy.[23] By the end of 1917, the War Office had also issued orders to GHQ in France for still photographers not to take pictures of dead or seriously wounded soldiers.[24] From the summer of 1917, British official filming was virtually confined to the rear areas, with a new emphasis on the picturesque, the unusual and the personal. This was typified by films of the overseas Labour Contingents from China, Egypt and South Africa (mainly Zulus), and particularly by what became known as the *British Regiments Series* of more than 20 films, released between December 1917 and March 1918. Each of these lasted for about five minutes, and depicted an unidentified but supposedly typical battalion of each regiment at rest in the rear areas, with a heavy concentration on individual soldiers' faces.

This is not to denigrate the work of the Western Front cameramen, who got as far forward with their cumbersome equipment as often as they could. In that respect, their record is better than that of many of their print counterparts. One film in particular, possibly never released in the form in which it exists today, *Ypres: The Shell-Shattered City of Flanders* (with additional material added to a 1916 film of the same name), has provided later viewers with many of the classic images of the battlefield. But while the in-fighting over propaganda organization continued in London, the cameramen were without anyone to support them effectively against the War Office back home and GHQ in France. Their first difficulty was getting transport from the GHQ motor pool, which they could usually manage only on two days out of five. According to the cameraman Bertram Brooks-Carrington, filming was largely at the discretion of the WOCC's operations manager at GHQ, Lieutenant Colonel J. H. C. Faunthorpe:

> He'd say, "Well, there's not much doing today. Just scout around and see what you can find," or else, "There might be a bit of a show at So-and so. Go up there." You went out, and if there was anything worth shooting you shot it; if there wasn't, you came back without anything at all. As soon as you got back, the war correspondents, who had been sitting back there all the time, would come up to the cameramen wanting stories. Quite a number of them used to do that, including some very famous names.[25]

Shortly after the start of Third Ypres, Buchan expressed concern to Brade that 'the [camera] operators on the Western Front need more direction than they get under present circumstances'.[26]

A further problem for the cameraman was that increasingly during 1917 the Army took the view that any man fit enough to serve on the Western Front should do so as a combatant, and it proved difficult to recruit cameramen who were both technically unfit and willing to face the danger. By July 1917, the senior British cameraman J. B. McDowell had been in France for more than a year. The other British cameraman to film Third Ypres, Harry Raymond, arrived as a replacement for Geoffrey Malins in March 1917. But Brooks-Carrington, who had arrived at about the same time, had to be sent home with shell shock just before Third Ypres.[27] The two still photographers, Ernest Brooks and John Warwick Brooke, faced a similar situation with no apparent prospect of their being reinforced or replaced. Although they were all volunteers, it is hard to escape the conclusion that by the time of Third Ypres, like the rest of the Army, the cameramen and photographers were distinctly war-weary.

The major change in official film policy for 1917 – Beaverbrook's attempt to tickle the public's jaded palate – was the establishment of a cinema newsreel to show British, Canadian and Australian official films. This was achieved by the arrangement concluded on 28 May between the WOCC and William Jeapes, owner of the Topical Film Company, which produced the 5-minute Topical Budget newsreel twice weekly, and who accepted onto his staff Beaverbrook's appointee, Captain William Holt-White, of the CWRO. (Jeapes' brother Harold was sent out at the same time as the official cameraman for Egypt and Palestine.) The WOCC also concluded a reciprocal arrangement with the French government for their official newsreel, the *Annales de la Guerre*, material from which was incorporated into the *Topical Budget* newsreel, which as a symbol of its new authoritative status described itself from September 1917 onwards as the *War Office Official Topical Budget*. However, the arrangement proved a failure, with problems that were not solved until November when Beaverbrook bought the company outright for the WOCC and took complete control of the newsreel, by which time Third Ypres was virtually over.[28] One problem was the very low sales of the *Topical Budget*, which rose only from 78 to 82 issues sold between May and November, reaching an audience of barely 1.5 million. Another was a rapid breakdown in relations between Jeapes and Holt-White, who in keeping with the new policy stressed the need for the unusual, and for material other than from the Western Front. More important was the newsreel's topicality, which meant that it required film far faster than the official processing and censoring system between GHQ and London could supply it. This, together with the limitations of a newsreel that showed four or five items in each issue, each about a minute long, meant that the *War Office Official Topical Budget* barely covered the Third Ypres offensive. The surviving run of the newsreel indicates that coverage began with an item released on 25 July showing the preliminary bombardment. But thereafter the offensive received very little attention, except for occasional items on the difficulty of transport through the mud (released on 29 September, although presumably shot in August), and of Australians at Suicide Corner, released on 3 November. Generally, the official newsreel made more use of French official film material of the Western Front than British, presumably because of its novelty value.[29] Finally, the reality of the battle as recorded by the camera was simply not dramatic enough for the new policy. D. W. Griffith, on his own visits to the Western Front, made exactly this point. 'It is too colossal to be dramatic', he wrote,

'You might as well try to describe the ocean or the Milky Way. A very great writer could describe Waterloo. But who could describe the advance of Haig? No one saw it. No one saw a thousandth part of it'.[30] Certainly, with the technology of the time, no one could record it adequately on film.

A similar pattern of limitations and problems beset the official still photographers, as can be seen by the use made of their photographs by the *Daily Mirror*, owned by Lord Rothermere, which claimed the highest circulation of any national newspaper of the period. Typically, the *Daily Mirror*'s front page consisted of a major headline and up to five photographs, with the editorial and news inside. On 1 August the paper duly announced 'Successful Opening to the Great New "Push"', but the accompanying photographs were all from earlier battles, including one showing soldiers with caps rather than helmets, marking it as being either from well behind the lines or from the pre-1916 period. The first British official photograph of the battle appeared on 8 August, including troops on a light railway 'Cheering as They Go Forward'. The first Canadian official photograph appeared on 3 September, followed by a front page dominated by Canadian photographs the next day – despite the fact that Canadians were not involved in the battle at that stage! With Beaverbrook's protection, the Canadian official photographer, Lieutenant William Rider-Rider, frequently worked outside the Canadian area, and it was also not unknown for Beaverbrook to see that British official cameramen were sent to cover Canadian operations.

The *Daily Mirror* gave no further front page mention of Third Ypres or the Western Front until a spectacular front page given over to the battle on 6 September. Under the headline 'That Eternal Mud – Flanders: One Vast Quagmire' were four photographs, including one that became an instant classic, taken by John Warwick Brooke on 1 August, of seven men with a stretcher, struggling up to their knees in the mud.[31] The next mention of the battle was on 22 September as 'Complete Success in Battle of the Pill Boxes', and two days later 'Hope Unfulfilled – Failure of the "Pill Boxes"', with a mixture of British and Canadian pictures of the Battle of Menin Road Ridge. The newspaper seems to have caught some of GHQ's optimism over the Battle on Broodseinde with its headline on 5 October, 'Third "Push" in a Fortnight Opens Successfully', including the first use of Australian official photographs taken by Captain Hubert Wilkins and Captain Frank Hurley. The next day it ran with 'Haig's Smashing Blow – Splendid Welsh Troops', followed on 10 October with 'Haig Strikes Another Blow – French Also Attacking' for the Battle of Poelcappelle. However, the headline for 15 October (after the resumption of the attack on the previous day) included a much larger caption than usual set against a panorama shot of the battlefield, which illustrated both the openness and the limitations of reporting the battle:

> The public will be better able to realise the wonderful achievements of our Army when they see this Australian official photograph. It shows the quagmires over which our troops advanced in Flanders, with what in the background is a German strong point which fell into our hands. Despite bad weather we made another advance yesterday.[32]

After 16 October with the headline 'Moving Forward in the West – A Wrecked Pill Box', the battle did not appear again on the newspaper's front page. These were the only front-page references made by *The Daily Mirror* to Third Ypres while it was being fought; other newspapers with smaller circulations were equally patchy in their coverage. Subjects that did appear on *The Daily Mirror*'s front page in the same period included the collapse of the Russian Army and riots in Petrograd, Allenby's capture of Beersheba, the brief mutiny in the German High Seas Fleet, and domestic news including a nine-day-wonder murder trial.

While Third Ypres was being planned and then waged, the Whitehall fight for control of propaganda also continued, with a strong element of black farce. Soon after the formation of the DoI, Buchan concluded that the only solution was a cabinet member to represent propaganda, for which Beaverbrook was the obvious candidate. Beaverbrook, in turn, alternated between manoeuvring for a ministerial post for propaganda and dropping it altogether for something better. Lloyd George, meanwhile, was determined to remove Admiral Sir John Jellicoe as First Sea Lord, not least for the Admiralty's apparent inability to deal with the submarine threat and for Jellicoe's deeply pessimistic performance before the War Policy Committee on 20 June.[33] In order to remove Jellicoe, Lloyd George first needed another post for his political protector, First Lord of the Admiralty Sir Edward Carson, who was leader of the Ulster Unionists and a critical member of the coalition. Carson was appointed to the War Cabinet without portfolio, and in September took over control of propaganda, of which he had no experience. Within a month Buchan was pushing for another change.[34]

Buchan had already offered Beaverbrook control of photographs, in the form of a War Office Photographic Committee to run along identical lines to the WOCC, in order to improve the quality and distribution of photographs from the Western Front. From August through to the end of November – virtually the duration of Third Ypres – attempts were made to form such a committee, but the manoeuvre was firmly blocked by other Press magnates, particularly Sir George (later Lord) Riddell, owner of the *News of the World*, chairman of the Newspaper Proprietors Association, and another crucially important supporter of Lloyd George's rise to power. Riddell had no intention of giving Beaverbrook such a monopoly, arguing that the Press and 'certain interests' should be dominant in British propaganda.[35] After one more inconclusive meeting in which he had stressed the need for better coverage of the Western Front, Major Lytton of the GHQ Press Section recorded that:

> No one disagreed with our suggestions, but after the meeting I was informed privately that nothing could be done because Sir Reginald Brade was afraid to take any action independent of Lord Beaverbrook and that Lord Beaverbrook was expecting to be made Minister of Information (with portfolio) and until this appointment was ratified he refused to sanction any reforms no matter how urgently they were needed. It seemed to me a *non sequitur* that Sir Douglas Haig's armies should be kept short of photographers because Lord Beaverbrook wanted to be a Minister of the Crown.[36]

The issue was not resolved until the formation of a Ministry of Information in February 1918, incorporating the DoI with the WOCC, and the appointment of Beaverbrook as minister. This was long past the date that British propaganda could have had any effect on morale during Third Ypres. It has even been suggested that the appointment was part of the price paid by Lloyd George for the silence of the Beaverbrook newspapers over the resignation of Sir William Robertson.[37]

It is easier to point to the failings of British propaganda during Third Ypres than its successes, but it is extremely hard to evaluate its overall impact. Certainly, there is no evidence of German propaganda having any effect on British attitudes during this period, either on the Home Front or on the Army. No one in a position of authority attributed the low morale of the period to anything other than the circumstances of the war. Equally, there is no evidence of British propaganda having any visible effect either on the German Army or in Germany itself, where by autumn 1917 children were being taught by the sort of schoolmaster who functioned, 'in practice, as a propaganda agent of the state', including, in some cases, by reading the children the daily report of the Military High Command.[38] Put simply, in autumn 1917 both sides believed that Germany was winning the war, and neither side was prepared to negotiate. In these circumstances, there was very little that propaganda aimed at an enemy could do.

There is also little evidence that British propaganda during Third Ypres had a measurable effect on Army morale in France and Flanders, but its impact on the Home Front is much harder to assess. It has been convincingly argued that, despite the belief that flourished in the 1920s and later, the power of film propaganda in particular was grossly overestimated by the British during the war, and that public attitudes would have been much the same had organizations like the WOCC never existed.[39] But the weak and disorganized nature of the British propaganda organizations at the time of Third Ypres prevented them pursuing any coherent Home Front policy other than in very general terms. Without such guidance (or propaganda *with* facts) the media record was very patchy and erratic. Of course, we cannot be certain that a properly organized propaganda campaign might not have had a very different effect on Home Front morale, but the inescapable conclusion is that, like the Army in Flanders, the British propaganda organizations simply failed in their objectives at home in the autumn of 1917.

As for the truthfulness and accuracy of reporting Third Ypres from the Press section at GHQ, this is the full version of what Charles Masterman's wife recorded as an observation by Lord Rothermere at a private dinner party on 8 November, just as the Canadians were securing their final positions on Passchendaele ridge:

> We haven't the pluck of these young lieutenants who go over the top. We're telling lies, we daren't tell the public the truth, that we're losing more officers than the Germans, and

that it's impossible to get through on the Western Front. You've seen the correspondents shepherded by Charteris. They don't know the truth, they don't speak the truth, and we know that they don't.[40]

Apart from Rothermere's unconscious agreement with Bismarck's quip about humanity beginning with the rank of lieutenant, the implications of this remark were that 'the truth' about Third Ypres could be found not on the Western Front, nor among the people at home, but within the closed circles of Whitehall and its associated corridors of power. The belief held by the government, the newspaper proprietors and the propagandists was that the public was incapable of forming its own opinion and would take whatever perspective on the war it was given. It was not until a decade or so later that such simplistic views of the value of propaganda within a democracy began to change, at precisely the time that 'propaganda' was being discredited as a useful function of democratic government.

Finally, it has been argued that the First World War saw a major change in representing war in art and literature, with an emphasis on the continuing personal experience of the lowly individual soldier rather than on the commander, the battle, or the army as a mass, and that this critical development in Modernist thought was the product of the work of alienated individuals protesting against the existing social and political order during or after the war. This view neglects the impact made on our understanding of the role played by the British official propagandists during the war, as they made a similar change to their approach shortly before Third Ypres, for reasons that were largely political in nature. The priorities of propaganda had become mass persuasion rather than focusing mainly upon the elite. While there are entirely understandable technological, human and operational explanations for why the realities of war can never be portrayed contemporaneously by the mass media – by a hostile Press corps let alone a co-operative one – the lasting image of Passchendaele as an event of tragic human suffering could not have come from the contemporary media record of 1917; military control would have seen to that. Perhaps that was why Sir Douglas Haig gave each of the correspondents his own Union Jack.

NOTES

1 Reith, J. C. W. (1949), *Into the Wind*. London: Hodder & Stoughton, p. 354.

2 *See*, for example, Hitler, A. (1925), *Mein Kampf*. Munich, n.p. and numerous reprints); Hindenburg, P. von (1920), *Out of My Life*. London: Cassell; Ludendorff, E. (1920), *My War Memoirs 1914–1918*. London: Hutchinson. 'Admiration' is perhaps inappropriate in so far as the Americans were concerned; they were more alarmed at the skill of the British when post-war revelations showed the extent of the wartime campaign. *See* in particular Peterson, H. C. (1936), *Propaganda for War: The Campaign Against American Neutrality, 1914–1917*. New York: Kennikat Press, and for a discussion of the impact of the earlier campaign on the Second World War *see* Cull, N. J. (1995), *Selling War: The British Campaign against American 'Neutrality' in World War II*. Oxford: Oxford University Press.

3 For further details, *see* Sanders and Taylor (1982) op. cit.

4 Messinger (1992) op. cit., p. 47.

5 Reeves (1986) op. cit., pp. 9–88; Carmichael (1989), op. cit. pp. 52–61; Smither (1994) op. cit.

6 Grieves (1996) op. cit., p. 720.

7 Ibid., p. 728.

8 Haig Papers 3155.106 Diary for May 1916 'Memorandum on Policy for Press'.

9 Bourne (1989) op cit., p. 208; Smither (1994) op. cit., p. 134.

10 Bourne (1989) op. cit., pp. 209–10.

11 Sheffield, G. (1986), 'The morale of the British army on the Western Front 1914–1918', *Occasional Paper 2*, Institute for the Study of War and Society, De Montfort University (UK).

12 Prior, R. and Wilson, T. (1996), *Passchendaele: The Untold Story*. New Haven, CT: Yale University Press; Terraine, J. (1977), *The Road to Passchendaele: The Flanders Offensive of 1917 – a Study in Inevitability*. London: Leo Cooper.

13 McEwan, J. M. (1978), 'The press and the fall of Asquith', *Historical Journal*, 21, 863–3.

14 Warman, R. (1972), 'The erosion of Foreign Office influence in the making of foreign policy, 1916–1918', *Historical Journal*, 15, (1), 113–59.

15 Both reports are in TNA, INF 4 1/B.

16 Steed, A. (1996), 'British propaganda and the First World War', in I. Stewart, and S. L. Carruthers (eds), *War, Culture and the Media: Representations of the Military in Twentieth Century Britain*. London: Flicks Books, pp. 29–30.

17 Messinger (1992) op. cit., p. 130.

18 Brownlow (1979) op. cit., pp. 144–5; Smither (1994) op. cit., 39.

19 TNA FO 395/147, minute by A. J. Balfour, 26 April 1917.

20 Wellington House pamphlet [Anon] (1917), *A Corpse Conversion Factory* London: n. p.

21 Reeves, N. (1993), 'The power of film propaganda – myth or reality?' *Historical Journal of Film, Radio and Television*, 13, (2), 181–201.

22 Quoted in Reeves (1986) op. cit., p. 64; *see also* McKernan (1992) op. cit., p. 39.

23 Reeves (1993), op. cit., p. 193.

24 TNA HO 139/42, memorandum from MI7a to the Press Bureau, 5 December 1917.

25 Brownlow (1979), op. cit., p. 67.

26 House of Lords Record Office, Papers of Lord Beaverbrook, 'Cinema General': Buchan to Brade, 13 August 1917.

27 House of Lords Record Office, Papers of Lord Beaverbrook, Series E Box 'Cinema General': Buchan to Brade, 9 July 1917.

28 McKernan (1992), op. cit., pp. 38–47.

29 Smither (1994), op. cit., pp. 496–508.

30 Brownlow (1979), op. cit., p. 149.

31 Carmichael (1989), op. cit., p. 64.

32 *Daily Mirror*, 13 October 1917.

33 Terraine (1977), op. cit. pp. 154–8.

34 Steed (1996), op. cit., p. 33; Reeves (1986) op. cit., p. 291.

35 IWM (Photo) Papers Box 1, Riddell to Beaverbrook, 1 November 1917.

36 Lytton (1920), op. cit., p. 118.

37 Steed (1996), op. cit., p. 33.

38 Demm, E. (1996), 'German Teachers at War', in Cecil and Liddle (1996) op. cit., p. 709.

39 Reeves (1993), op. cit. pp. 197–8.

40 Masterman (1939), op. cit, p. 296.

8

The Missing Western Front: Politics, Propaganda and Strategy 1918

Within recent memory, pioneering research work into British politics and grand strategy in the First World War has greatly improved, if not transformed, historical understanding of this complex issue.[1] Substantial work has also been done by historians on the role of propaganda and the Press in the war.[2] Some studies of British politics and grand strategy mention the role of propaganda institutions in the events of 1918, and most make some use of press reporting and editorials as sources of evidence. But the media and their role has remained largely an addition to the narrative of events, rather than an intrinsic factor. What is offered here is – in part – a synthesis of this work on both strategy and propaganda, with the object of demonstrating how the actions of the 'high politics' of British grand strategy must be integrated with the 'low culture' of the role of propaganda and the media in order to understand events of 1918.

This research may also throw some illumination onto an important historical debate regarding both the First World War and the modern popular perception of its nature. On one side of this debate is historical investigation into the cultural meaning and symbolism of the Western Front, which is for most English-speaking people the most significant single aspect of the war. This investigation into cultural meaning has become a well-established field of history with its own distinctive view of the First World War as a uniquely terrible event, including the meaning given to its ending in 1918.[3] On the other side of the debate is the substantial change in historical understanding about the conduct of battle on the Western Front brought about in recent years through the extensive use of primary sources by military historians, particularly focusing on the British Army. The work of these revisionist military historians has challenged the modern popular view of the war as either uniquely terrible or incompetently conducted. For these revisionists, who stress the introduction of new technologies and tactics and a 'learning curve' in British war-fighting methods, 1918 is also a year of great importance, including the argument that by the end of the war the British Army on the Western Front was the decisive instrument of the Allied victory.[4] This revisionist position has conflicted with that of more traditional British military historians (or those seeking to preserve or revive the traditional position); with the historical tradition in Germany of the inherent superiority of the German Army even in defeat; and also with historians in the United States and Canada whose writings are very much derived from a German tradition, or who prefer to emphasize the role of the French Army and the American Expeditionary Force (AEF) in 1918. As has already been mentioned in previous chapters, the resulting difference in perspectives has been called the 'Two Western Fronts' debate: the Western Front of British military history against the Western Front of wider popular cultural understanding.[5]

The British revisionist position has gained wider acceptance among historians as it has accumulated more evidence, some of it drawn from the work on the culture of the war and from wider history.[6] It is now generally accepted that the highly critical perspective of a British cultural and social elite (including the more famous of the 'trench poets') during and after the war was not necessarily shared by the majority of participants. The next stage has been to link the findings of cultural history with those of battlefield history to produce a more complete picture of the war. How has it happened that the British Army's victory on the Western Front in 1918, one of the greatest and most important in British history, has somehow been forgotten in popular culture? Investigation has focused in particular upon the period of 'disillusionment' in the 1930s, and the period of social revolution in the 1960s. This represents an issue of considerable size and importance on a critical event in twentieth-century history.

Recent findings on the press and propaganda, taken together with those on British grand strategy, now make it possible to re-examine the events of 1918 and how the British government not only directed the war, but also directed the war's portrayal to its own people and others. In the German *Kaiserschlacht* spring offensive of 1918, the British (including forces of the Dominions of the

British Empire) played the leading role in defeating the last great German attack on the Western Front. In the 'Hundred Days', from the Battle of Amiens on 8 August to the Armistice on 11 November, the British Army may well have taken more German prisoners than all the other Allied armies on the Western Front combined, it dominated its enemy in the critical area of artillery tactics and it broke the formidable Hindenburg Line.[7] However much it may have been influenced by other events in subsequent decades, the British undervaluing of these achievements on the Western Front in 1918 has its origins in British propaganda policy of the year itself. The British government under Prime Minister David Lloyd George, its propaganda institutions, the British press, and Field Marshal Sir Douglas Haig's own GHQ in France, all pursued policies in 1918 that led to a propaganda neglect of the Western Front. While the British people welcomed the Armistice with enthusiasm and relief, they were not particularly aware of these British military victories. Also, at the end of the war, just as the British were in the process of disbanding their propaganda apparatus, the German Army contrived one of the most successful propaganda coups of the war, the foisting of the *Dolchstosslegende* ('Stab in the Back' myth) upon the German people, that also downplayed the British military triumph on the Western Front, leading swiftly to an outright German denial that their soldiers had ever been defeated at all.

The end of 1917 represented a low point for the British in the First World War, with the loss of Russia to revolution, mutinies in the French Army, and their own failure in Third Ypres. By this time, Lloyd George genuinely believed (with what accuracy it is still hard to judge) that he was facing a military faction led by Haig and by General Sir William Robertson as CIGS that represented a serious challenge to democracy in Britain, and that was orchestrating a press campaign against his government. The situation regarding manpower had changed utterly from that of 1916 when the Army, and specifically Haig's GHQ in France, had asserted and expected absolute priority on a virtually limitless supply of men.[8] From November 1917 onwards the new Ministry of National Service under Sir Auckland Geddes placed Army recruiting under civilian control as one part of a diminishing manpower pool. A direct result of this was the enforced reorganization and reduction of British divisions from 12 to 9 infantry battalions during winter 1917–1918, although Dominion divisions remained at the higher strength. In December 1917, Haig regarded only the Canadians and Australians among his reserve divisions as fit for front-line duty.

Over winter 1917–1918, Lloyd George both constructed a coherent British grand strategy for the future, and attempted to convince his War Cabinet colleagues, his Allies, and the British people of its merits. The reason for fighting on the Western Front at all was the familiar one of preserving Britain's security against a continental aggressor; but this was a defensive objective, if a critical one. Lloyd George, in a speech in Paris on 12 November 1917, had described the German line as 'an impenetrable barrier'. After the failure of the Third Ypres in July–November and the repulse of the initial success at Cambrai by the German counter-attack in November–December, the War Cabinet could be forgiven for concluding that there was no breakthrough for *either* side on the Western Front in 1918. Indeed, the War Cabinet at first expected the Germans to stand on the defensive in the West in 1918, and to exploit their success in the East. Since the manpower reserves for a major British offensive were no longer available, British troops on the Western Front should also go onto the defensive for a year or more, until the American arrival in force in 1919. In the interval, further British, Dominion, and Indian troops could be transferred to the campaign against Ottoman Turkey and to other projects in the East. The purpose of this was a double one: not only to win propaganda victories such as General Sir Edmund Allenby's spectacular capture of Jerusalem on 9 December 1917, as a way of boosting Home Front morale; but also to stake out positive British gains in the East, both in order to offset the German success against Russia and to provide an advantage if it came to a negotiated peace in the West.[9]

On 5 January 1918, at Caxton Hall in London, Lloyd George gave his first major policy speech on British war aims to a gathering of trade unionists. Coming only three days before President Woodrow Wilson's 'Fourteen Points' speech, this was clearly aimed at influencing the United States, while references to self-determination for the peoples of Austria-Hungary signalled the government's new strategy of concentration on the East. But the speech was aimed also at healing political rifts on the Home Front. Later in the month, new food regulations placed rationing in Britain on a more equitable basis, and the Ministry for National Service was given extended powers for 'combing out' manpower, with the Army placed last in the new priorities. Next month the new (and it was hoped also more equitable) Military Service Act passed into law, together with the Representation of the People Act, extending the franchise to all men over 21 years old and all women over 30 years old. All this contrasts strongly with the food riots and strikes that took place in Germany in January and February, as the German Home Front began to show signs of collapse.

In the absence of opinion polls and anything much more than anecdotal or indirect evidence, there is almost no way for historians to accurately assess the impact of these measures on British domestic morale and opinion. But most of the evidence available for attitudes on the Home Front, including the incidence and severity of strikes, suggests that public opinion was indeed 'remobilized', and rallied both to the government policy initiatives and also in the face of the threatened German victory. It has been well argued that, from the viewpoint of the British government and its propaganda, 'the Germans were in many ways the perfect enemy' since 'their conduct throughout the war seemed almost designed to offend British liberal sensibilities and to galvanize public opinion in support of the war effort'.[10] Although it cannot be proved, it is highly likely that the single greatest factor in unifying the British Home Front behind the war effort was the punitive nature of the Peace of Brest-Litovsk, announced on 3 March, only days before the German offensive in the West. This evidence of what a 'German peace' would mean was a gift to British propagandists, and one more example of strategic mistiming on Germany's part during the war.

Given Lloyd George's strategy of opportunism in the East, of minimizing and isolating Haig and the Western Front, and of maintaining the morale of the Home Front through a difficult year, it was logical that he should bring into his government the leading British newsmen. With a General Election constitutionally inevitable in 1918, regardless of whether the war had ended, it was also well understood at the time that Lloyd George, who had no majority support in any political party, needed the support of the London newspapers and their owners to survive in office.[11] Faced with the problem of identifying and directing public opinion in a new era of mass politics, British politicians of the First World War placed disproportionate faith in the press, and awarded its owners and editors considerable respect. Since 1916, Lloyd George had progressively involved several Press magnates and important editors with his government, including Sir George Riddell, Sir Robert Donald, Lord Beaverbrook and Lord Rothermere. Beaverbrook described the resulting Whitehall infighting as a conflict between self-made 'new men' like himself and the patricians of the Foreign Office, including his own particular Foreign Office *bête noire*, Lord Robert Cecil.[12]

As has already been described, in addition to owning the *Daily Express* and other newspapers, Beaverbrook's rise to dominate British propaganda at home had included founding the Canadian War Records Office in London in 1915, and chairing the War Office Cinema Committee from its creation in November 1916, as the fruit of his personal association with the Permanent Secretary at the War Office, Sir Reginald Brade. This committee had extended its authority by the end of 1917 to control all British filming of the fighting fronts and in Britain itself, including all Dominion filming, (to the annoyance of Dr Charles Bean, the official Australian war correspondent, whose claim to an *ex officio* place on the committee for an Australian representative was rejected). On 10 February 1918, Beaverbrook became Minister of Information, and also Chancellor of the Duchy of Lancaster, giving him a seat in the Cabinet. It is a measure of the importance that Lloyd George placed on propaganda in sustaining the Home Front throughout 1918 that he took such a political risk. The prominent Conservative Austen Chamberlain's reaction was that Beaverbrook's appointment 'can scarcely be described as a popular one. It adds to the prevalent feeling of irritation and soreness'.[13] Beaverbrook was himself warned by his friend Andrew Bonar Law that senior Conservative politicians and powerbrokers were prepared to tolerate in office either Beaverbrook himself or Lord Northcliffe, the owner of *The Times* and the *Daily Mail* and self-styled 'Ogre of Fleet Street', but not both. Nevertheless, Beaverbrook undertook to bring Northcliffe into the government with him.[14]

The Ministry of Information (MoI) was largely the work of Colonel John Buchan, head of the Department of Information (DoI) since its creation in

February 1917, and was itself created by amalgamating Buchan's DoI with the War Office Cinema Committee in early March. Beaverbrook owed his new position to some extent to Buchan's lobbying on behalf of the importance of propaganda, although Buchan would have entertained the idea of Northcliffe as minister if necessary. The new MoI shared its powers with the National War Aims Committee, created in August 1917 partly again through Buchan's work, and also chaired by Lloyd George; with the Official Press Bureau, which since 1914 had been responsible for daily Press censorship; and with MI7, the Directorate of Special Intelligence at the War Office.

Absent in the United States heading the British War Mission until November 1917, Northcliffe had been a strong supporter of the Army and of Haig against the government, as had his newspapers.[15] But as has been recounted in an earlier chapter, after some preliminary negotiations with Lloyd George on his return to London, Northcliffe's transfer of allegiance began on 7 December 1917, when on his visit to GHQ Haig showed boredom and indifference over Northcliffe's account of his achievements in the United States. The public effect of this switch was visible in the Northcliffe Press' attack on the British handling of the German counterattack at Cambrai that month. On 18 February 1918, co-incidentally the same day that Robertson departed as CIGS, Northcliffe took up a government post (although he maintained that, unlike Beaverbrook, he did not become a *member* of the government) as Director of the Department of Propaganda in Enemy Countries, with its headquarters at Crewe House in London. The London Headquarters of the British War Mission continued in existence, and in August all Northcliffe's responsibilities, including Crewe House, were placed in the Mission's name, although the resulting organization continued to be called simply 'Crewe House' for convenience. Although the British War Mission was strictly separate from the MoI, the relationship between Northcliffe and Beaverbrook was very close in a professional sense. On 21 February, Robert Donald, the editor of the *Daily Chronicle*, became director of the Department of Propaganda in Neutral Countries. The links between these various organizations were informal and personal as much as institutional, and their ability to dictate propaganda themes was, in practice, sometimes limited. The London Press in particular was

sufficiently powerful to be left as effectively self-regulating. Some sections, notably the *Morning Post* under H. A. Gwynne and the *Spectator* under John St Loe
Strachey, remained openly very critical both of the government and of Lloyd
George personally. In consequence, the abilities of Beaverbrook, Northcliffe and
Donald to influence the press in their private capacities was an important part
of their public and governmental power, as well as the target of acrimonious
complaints from Lloyd George's critics.

This new British propaganda apparatus, and the new and close relationship
between the Lloyd George government and what some called the 'Beavercliffe'
press, was put to the test with the *Kaiserschlacht*, starting with Operation
'Michael' on 21 March. The British government reaction to the crisis caused by
the initial success of 'Michael', and the reaction of British government propaganda, was an integral part of the much larger Allied crisis, deftly handled at
the Doullens Conference on 26 March at which Marshal Ferdinand Foch was
appointed Generalissimo of the Allied forces. From the German perspective
they had achieved a major victory, and indeed on 23 March First Quartermaster
General Erich Ludendorff advised Kaiser Wilhelm II that the war had been won.
The French perspective after 26 March was that they had rescued the British
from defeat and established their dominance over the Allied coalition, a dominance that was to last to the end of the war despite the weaknesses of the French
Army. But no British perspective on their own achievements was forthcoming
from the MoI, which failed to respond both to criticisms of British strategy and
to French claims of widespread British cowardice and desertion. According to
Major the Honourable Neville Lytton, the staff officer responsible for the French
and Allied press at GHQ, already in March there was 'beginning to be quite a
serious anti-British feeling in France. "Les Anglais f[outent] le camp" was on
every one's lips'.[16] British propaganda continued to fail to respond to the situation as the German attacks continued. 'In every city, town, village and hamlet
in France the story is told of how the soldiers of the British 5th Army ran away',
one eyewitness reported to the British government in June. 'Times out of number I have been asked how it happened, not if it were true'.[17] The Foreign Office
complained that its representatives had needed to go to MI7 at the War Office

to obtain briefings on the British government's position in the face of these accusations.

In his memoirs in 1956, Beaverbrook offered a very plausible explanation for the MoI's failure: that because of Foreign Office and War Office hostility to British propaganda the MoI was created from a blank slate in late February 1918, only a few days before the German offensive. 'There was no blueprint to work on', he wrote, 'no experience to guide the new department. There was no office, no staff. There was nothing but a decision of the War Cabinet decreeing that such a Ministry should be created and that I should be Minister.'[18] Beaverbrook's claim went substantially unchallenged at the time of publication, largely because little contemporary evidence existed on British wartime propaganda, as he well knew. As an investigation in 1938 concluded, the MoI's papers had been destroyed or had mysteriously vanished soon after December 1918 (some of them into Beaverbrook's own private collections).[19] It was not until after Beaverbrook's death in 1964 that historians were able to piece together the story, and expose his statement as a barefaced lie. Beaverbrook also seems to have left his biographer with the impression that the MoI had no part in propaganda aimed at the Home Front, which was also quite untrue, although overall management of Home Front propaganda was in the hands of the National War Aims Committee, not the MoI.[20]

The institutions of British propaganda were all in place in March 1918, but the failure of the MoI, rather than happening in isolation, reflected the shock within Whitehall at the impact of the German offensive – a very public piece of evidence on Whitehall attitudes that has not been given its full weight in the wider political history of 1918. The lack of any British propaganda plan shows clearly how complete a surprise the German attack had been in Whitehall. The substantial German gains did indeed look like a British defeat, especially to politicians who had come to expect the worst of their own generals; and in his speech to the House of Commons on 9 April, defending himself over the events of the 'Michael' offensive, Lloyd George appeared to give credence to the view that British troops had fled in large numbers. The focus of both official Whitehall and the London Press was entirely away from the Western Front at this time: on 21 March the

1et's chief topic for discussion was a possible Japanese intervention in
hile the Western Front hardly featured at all.[21] In a reflection of this,
on 23 March a leading article in the influential weekly *The Sphere* headlined not
the German advances on the Western Front, but 'The German Move Towards the
Western Asiatic Lands' of the central Caucasus.

A further reason for the MoI failure to deal effectively with the news and
propaganda implications of the German spring offensive was that Beaverbrook
and Northcliffe were preoccupied both with securing their immediate positions
and with their wider political ambitions. Throughout the year, both men were
also plagued by persistent ill-health. By late 1917 it was an open secret that Lloyd
George planned to replace Lord Derby as Secretary of State for War. In fact in
January he decided on Lord Milner, who succeeded to the post on 18 April.
But there were other candidates at the time, including both Beaverbrook and
Northcliffe, whose appointment Haig considered would be 'fatal to the Army
and the Empire'.[22] Northcliffe rejected the new Air Ministry in December 1917;
Beaverbrook claimed to have declined control of the Ministry of Munitions, and
his own candidacy for the War Office in February was real enough for the story to
reach Austen Chamberlain, whose reaction was 'I do not think that Lloyd George
yet desires to commit political suicide'.[23] Between February and August, repeated
threats by both Beaverbrook and Northcliffe to resign alternated with strident
demands from both men to Lloyd George that they should be protected from
parliamentary calls for their dismissal. Donald actually carried out his threat of
resignation in May, following this up by appointing Sir Frederick Maurice, author
of the notorious 'Maurice Letter' attacking Lloyd George, as military correspondent of the *Daily Chronicle*. After repeated criticisms of Lloyd George in the *Daily
Chronicle*, including that by Maurice, the paper was bought in October by a
syndicate of Lloyd George's backers headed by Sir Henry Dalziel and by Riddell,
and Donald resigned as editor.

The assessment of domestic political profit and loss for Lloyd George in cre-
ating the new MoI under Beaverbrook and the independent departments under
Northcliffe and Donald was therefore not at all straightforward. The support of
Northcliffe and Beaverbrook certainly helped Lloyd George with the dismissal

of Robertson, and later to survive the Maurice Letter crisis. It is also probable that the output of propaganda aimed at the Home Front did achieve something of what its purveyors hoped, in strengthening the morale of the British people. But what was achieved may have depended more on the ability of the various sub-departments to function without clear leadership from the top, which was generally not forthcoming. As for Northcliffe's Crewe House, it is doubtful if any of its propaganda contributed very much to the defeat of the German spring offensive. Its main contribution was probably no more than assistance with the production of propaganda leaflets aimed at German troops on the Western Front.

Lloyd George's political strategy of limiting Haig's power to challenge his own position, in step with his intention to downgrade the importance of the Western Front, was marked by the creation of the Allied Supreme War Council and the Air Ministry in November 1917, Robertson's replacement by General Sir Henry Wilson as CIGS in February and the creation of the independent RAF in April. An important part of this was the enforced replacement of General Sir Launcelot Kiggell as Haig's Chief Staff Officer, and Brigadier General John Charteris as his Chief of Intelligence (although Charteris remained at GHQ until August, attached to Transportation). Faced with these replacements, GHQ took the opportunity to restructure itself, in order both to better cope with the impending German offensive and to resist further incursions by Whitehall. This restructuring was again to play a significant part in the reporting of the events of 1918. Charteris' replacement, Brigadier General Edgar Cox, arrived at GHQ on 24 January, whereupon General Sir Herbert Lawrence, who had temporarily held the post, moved to replace Kiggell. Cox was fresh from heading MI3 at the War Office, the Intelligence section responsible for studying the structure and organization of the German Army, and was the principal author of the main Intelligence handbook on the subject.[24] Haig's strategy for defence against the forthcoming German offensive depended very heavily on Cox's skill in determining the fighting quality of the various German divisions; with his arrival GHQ ring-fenced Intelligence in order to concentrate on this role. Cox's only known involvement with the press was the decision to leak in advance the fact that GHQ knew the date of the German offensive to be 21 March, in the hope of disturbing German preparations.[25]

On 14 March, GHQ created a new Directorate of Staff Duties under Major General Guy Dawney, as a *portmanteau* for a number of GHQ functions now regarded as peripheral to Intelligence. One of these was the GHQ Press Section, transferred from Intelligence and renamed the Censorship and Publicity Section, which consequently suffered from the double neglect of losing an influential patron in Charteris, and the more mundane fact that Dawney himself took little interest in it.[26] It was widely agreed, both in London and in GHQ itself, that the number of official reporters, cine-cameramen and photographers in the new Censorship and Publicity Section was utterly inadequate to their task. But the political and administrative problems of creating even the very limited press structure that existed at GHQ had proved so great over three years that by 1918 even the major newspaper proprietors were more than content to leave well alone. There were by then usually about six British correspondents based at GHQ, together with a number of visiting reporters from other Allies, two or three official cameramen, and the same number of photographers, to cover an Army of more than 60 divisions across the entire British sector of the Western Front. The Canadians and Australians, and even the New Zealanders, were distinctly better off with their own propaganda and publicity organizations and their own cameramen.[27] The fact that the reporters were allowed to mention specific nationalities, such as the Australians, but not to identify British units, also led to Dominion troops receiving more than their fair share of British publicity.

This neglect of the press and propaganda was entirely in keeping with Haig's own personal command style. He had learned to trust a handful of the senior reporters at GHQ, but he engaged with the press only indirectly and with difficulty. The press was tolerated at GHQ, but only just; indeed, a group of staff officers, including Lieutenant Colonel James Edmonds (later the British official historian) regarded it as amusing to pass false information to the reporters as a test of their credulity, something of which Edmonds boasted to Charles Bean after the war.[28]

Both Northcliffe and Beaverbrook took the position that their respective organizations should control all aspects of propaganda, and they began to demand their own appointees within GHQ for that purpose.[29] The result was an institutional war to rival that going on in Whitehall, in which staff officers at GHQ used every device to block such appointments. Beaverbrook resorted to granting some of his men Canadian commissions, and temporarily paying their salaries from his own substantial private fortune. There was also an inevitable clash of cultures between the GHQ staff officers and these professional journalists: Harry Bartholomew, an experienced picture editor sent out to GHQ to oversee photographs, wrote to his superior in London in January: 'I would rather sweep a crossing than work with the crowd here'. In retaliation, Major Arthur Lee, one of the officers responsible for dealing with the press at GHQ, complained that 'the war correspondents were always prepared to find fault with anything and everything'.[30] Not until 16 August was the official establishment for the Censorship and Publicity Section agreed. It took Crewe House until September to get complete control of propaganda leaflets from MI7, and even then Major Lee confidently pronounced these to be not 'worth wasting balloons on', despite his own confessed inability to read either German or French.[31] The MoI's attempts to increase, even by a handful, the number of photographers and cameramen continued to be blocked well into October – even by the argument on one occasion that the GHQ officers' mess did not have enough waiters to serve them all. 'Do not think that I am depressed', Bartholomew wrote to London over this fiasco. 'I only wish the war would end, or a bomb drop on this establishment'.[32]

In covering the fighting on the Western Front in 1918, the British and Allied correspondents and cameramen faced the same problems as the troops themselves. The change in tactics and methods that had made breakthrough and a restoration of mobility on the Western Front possible in 1918 – itself a product of the 'learning curve' for all sides – produced wide, deep, confused and often infiltrated combat zones in which it was difficult to discover what had happened, and where the opposing forces actually were. Northcliffe was scathing about his own *Daily Mail* for publishing photographs entitled 'Street Snapshots at Maidenhead' on 23 March, as 'an absolute waste of space on the second day [*sic*] of the greatest battle in the world'.[33] Two days later GHQ introduced a ban on all visitors to the British Army on the Western Front, which was not eased until the middle of June. The daily difficulties of travelling out to a main battlefield perhaps 50 miles across, and then back to GHQ at Montreuil, led the reporters increasingly to fall back on GHQ briefings, while the photographers suffered similar problems. 'Out of 124 photographs received here of the offensive', an MoI official in London wrote to his subordinate at GHQ on 11 April, 'there is only one with any sign at all of actual warfare, and that is a distant shell burst'.[34] Haig's famous 'Backs to the Wall' order in April 1918, read out as a press release at his GHQ at Montreuil by his private secretary Major Philip Sassoon, was aimed as much at Home Front consumption as at the troops; and perhaps also, as one historian has suggested, at the history books in case of outright defeat.[35]

By late March, British losses as a result of the German spring offensive also led to the second Military Service Act, extending military service to men up to 50 years old, and sending 18-year-old boys and convalescents to the Western Front. The political impossibility of enforcing this Act's extension of conscription to Ireland led rapidly to the recognition at GHQ of the critical importance to the continued fighting effectiveness of the strong Canadian Corps and two Australian Corps, together with the New Zealand Division. From Whitehall the perspective was slightly different, but the need for the Dominions to maintain their forces at full strength became an increasingly important part of the Lloyd George strategy of lasting out 1918. In turn, this increased importance of Dominion troops became a main theme in British official propaganda. The assembly of Dominion leaders in London in June for the meetings of the Imperial War Cabinet consequently took on a new and much greater significance.

During the summer of 1918, British newspapers largely continued to reflect the main government propaganda themes of holding out on the Home Front, the importance of the Dominion and Imperial effort, the build-up of American troops, and opportunities in the East. As a populist, Beaverbrook also prided himself on a deliberate change of emphasis in propaganda directed at the Home Front from written to visual media, which became probably the most important aspect of Home Front propaganda in 1918. For official Whitehall it was still the London quality Press that mattered, but the mass of the people gained their

information from the picture-spreads of the tabloids such as the *Daily Mail*
and the *Daily Mirror*, together with the provincial press, and most importantly
newsreel film. The most visible sign of this policy (in more ways than one) was
the change to official film propaganda. In 1918, the very large minority of the
British people who attended the cinema as their principal source of entertainment and information were, from the propagandists' viewpoint, not quite the
ideal audience, as they included a majority of women and a significant number
of younger people and children, but they represented by far the largest single
working-class audience in the country.[36] The War Office Cinema Committee's
twice-weekly newsreel, *The War Office Official Topical Budget*, which competed
directly with commercial newsreels, reached an audience of about three million
for each issue by 1918, about three times the circulation of Northcliffe's *Daily
Mail.* According to his biographer, Beaverbrook claimed that, 'The Topical Budget
shown in every picture palace was the decisive factor in maintaining the moral
[*morale*] of the people during the black days of the early summer of 1918'.[37] Even
if it cannot be supported, this claim at least conveys the importance attached to
visual propaganda by the government at the time.

In February the newsreel underwent a name change to *The Pictorial News
(Official)*. This coincided with Beaverbrook becoming Minister of Information,
and marked his successful conclusion of a six-month battle to wrest complete
control of the newsreel, including its content and style, away from its original
commercial owners. Filming on the Western Front had, since its inception in
late 1915, been dogged by considerable technical and administrative problems,
including the impossibility of filming actual combat and the delays in the military censorship process. Some months *before* the change in government strategic
thinking which devalued the importance of the Western Front, but fitted per-
fectly within it, Beaverbrook and his propagandists had decided for entirely
practical and commercial reasons to emphasize the unusual and picturesque in
their newsreel, including particularly film of Palestine and Mesopotamia. The
newsreel's name change coincided with the dedication of an entire issue to the
newly arrived film of Allenby's entry into Jerusalem. By a synergy rather than a
coincidence, the film of this 'Christmas present to the British nation', released

on 23 February 1918, became the visible symbol of the new government strategy and propaganda policy.[38]

Other than the changes to the newsreel, the solution adopted by the film and photograph propagandists under Beaverbrook to the problem of obtaining good, authentic and topical images on the fighting fronts was largely to cease to try, which was very much in keeping with the response of the print journalists to their own problems. Although filming of the fighting fronts continued, in 1918 the MoI began instead to emphasize cartoons and short fictional films with far better production values. There was also a move away from a fact-based approach to overt hate-propaganda of a distinctly crude sort. One notorious short fictional film, *The Leopard's Spots* (often known as *Once A Hun, Always A Hun*) made by Hepworth for the MoI, drew criticism from Parliament in August, not so much for its portrayal of German soldiers as swaggering, drunken baby molesters, but for its proclamation that Britain would not buy German goods after the war.[39] A large part of the hostility felt within the Foreign Office in particular towards Beaverbrook and Northcliffe was the manner in which they openly intruded in political and strategic issues, going far beyond their notional roles as propagandists and publicists. But Beaverbrook saw no discrepancy in the MoI dictating post-war trade policy, or indeed wartime foreign policy, arguing that 'we have a diplomacy of our own to conduct, a popular diplomacy'.[40] Again, the impact of such rabble-rousing material on the British people cannot be assessed in any definite sense. What can be said is that the government itself believed firmly in the power of such images, and that British Home Front enthusiasm for the war finished in the last months of 1918 on a high point not seen since its beginning.[41]

The contribution of Crewe House to the image of the British performance on the Western Front in 1918 appears to have been negligible, although promoting British successes in enemy countries certainly fell within its remit. A frequent complaint from Crewe House was that propaganda must follow government policy, and that no policy towards either Germany or Austria-Hungary was forthcoming. Northcliffe used this as an excuse to generate his own policy, with propaganda towards Austria-Hungary going far beyond government policy on promises of self-determination. Claims for the importance of its role were made in 1920 with the publication of *Secrets of Crewe House* by Sir Campbell Stuart, one of Northcliffe's subordinates. In Germany in particular, Northcliffe enjoyed quasi-demonic status in 1918 as the 'Father of All Lies' and master propagandist.[42] Colonel E. M. House, President Wilson's personal envoy, wrote to Northcliffe in July quoting American diplomatic cables from neutral countries close to Germany, passing on a German fear of 'the propaganda which Lord Northcliffe is directing against us. The English are doing more to defeat us in this way than the armies in the field'.[43] But historical research has modified the view that Northcliffe and Crewe House played the dominating role in Allied propaganda against the Central Powers, or that this had a major effect on the German Home Front collapse. Certainly, Crewe House plans for a propaganda offensive against Germany existed, but Northcliffe's political and bureaucratic struggles, together with his own continual illnesses, meant that it was not until August–September that Crewe House became effective as a propaganda organization, and by that time the Central Powers were already collapsing, starting with Bulgaria. In keeping with government policy, and on the advice chiefly of Henry Wickham Steed, the main focus of Crewe House's efforts was not Germany but Austria-Hungary, where the role played by Italian propaganda both before Crewe House's involvement and through to the end of the war was probably more important.[44]

Well into summer 1918, both the British government and its propaganda apparatus continued to show the same indifference to the Western Front, and particularly to the role of the British Army. Leopold Amery, Assistant Secretary to the War Cabinet and a lifelong Imperialist, wrote to Lloyd George in early June in a way intended to delight him that, 'When this little "side show" in the West is over, whether the line gets stabilized or disappears altogether, we shall have to take the war for the mastery of Asia in hand seriously'.[45] Political attacks on both Lloyd George and on Beaverbrook and Northcliffe diminished significantly by the end of June, and it would be logical to associate this with a recognition in political London of the British success on the Western Front, but the evidence does not support this interpretation. Only a few days before the Battle of Amiens, the War Cabinet discussed halving Haig's army to 35 divisions or fewer, in order to conduct the war better elsewhere. Haig's reputation in Whitehall was in fact no higher in summer than in spring, and this was reflected in the press coverage, with its concentration on the East, on the increasing importance of the Americans and on the global nature of the war. In July the weekly *The Sphere*'s front covers featured the arrival of A. F. Kerensky in London, King George V's silver wedding, the King of the Belgians, and the Second Battle of the Marne. The *Illustrated London News* for the same month featured on its front covers the King's silver wedding, American soldiers, French soldiers, and Czech troops on the Western Front. Haig appeared on the front cover of the *Illustrated London News* just once in 1918 on 31 August in reference to the Battle of Amiens, while its Armistice edition featured on its front cover a picture of Marshal Foch.

All this provided the context for the remarkable under-reporting of the Battle of Amiens and the Hundred Days' advance by the BEF. A new concern with security meant that, in marked contrast to the Battle of the Somme in 1916, the press were not told of the forthcoming offensive, and the doyen of the GHQ press corps, Philip Gibbs, was actually at home in Britain resting from illness when the battle began.[46] The remaining reporters and cameramen were occupied covering one of King George V's periodic visits to the Western Front, which began on 5 August. (These royal visits received great publicity, in the belief that they boosted morale on the Home Front as much as in France.) In the next few months of the Hundred Days, the strain on the reporters at GHQ trying to cover the advance was easily as great as that on any of the divisional staffs. 'Three of my colleagues at one time could scarcely endure to enter a motor-car except under compulsion', wrote William Beach Thomas of the *Daily Mail*, 'so worn were their nerves'.[47] It is not surprising that most of the correspondents reported the last great British victories and the Armistice in a subdued manner, the re-invigorated Philip Gibbs being an exception. Moreover, and again entirely in keeping with government policy, during summer and early autumn 1918 the resources of Beaverbrook's MoI were principally directed not to promoting Haig's forces, but to publicizing the role of the American troops who were at last making an impact on the Western Front. British propaganda resources were also directed not only at the Dominion leaders present for the Imperial War Cabinet, but also at their own accompanying pressmen. On 21 July, Haig was asked by London to make the time to meet a party of

26 Canadian newspaper owners at his headquarters chateau at Montreuil, and a further party of Dominion journalists on 7 September.[48] Beaverbrook ruled it more important that the GHQ cameramen and photographers should cover this latter excursion than that they should be out filming the front. Nor was he above diverting British cameramen and photographers to cover the Canadian Corps, at a time when their numbers had dropped to only one or two to record the battles of the entire British Army on the Western Front.

A last chance to boost the public image of Haig's Army came in October, as both the possible end of the war and the British General Election loomed. On 3 October, just before the *Daily Chronicle* was bought by Lloyd George's friends, it carried an article by Sir Frederick Maurice pointing out that 'the British successes on the Western Front since 8th August are much the greatest in scale ever won by the British Army or a British general', but that the War Cabinet, which had sent official congratulations to General John J. Pershing and also to Allenby, had failed to do so to Haig.[49] Beaverbrook resigned as Minister of Information on 21 October, from ill-health due to swollen neck-glands, but also because it had become apparent to him that his ambition for the MoI to become a permanent peacetime organ of government stood no chance of becoming a reality, and that he would not be offered a government post of what he considered to be real power. Just before his resignation, Beaverbrook wrote to Northcliffe with the suggestion that he should take over as Minister of Information.[50] The MoI itself officially ceased to exist on the stroke of midnight on 31 December 1918, despite Beaverbrook's suggestion in October that it should be kept in existence at least until the signing of the peace treaties, in order to promote the British perspective.[51]

For Northcliffe the situation was rather different; from August onwards, he had been negotiating for, at least, a Cabinet seat in the next government, and a permanent and influential role for his British War Mission in any peace settlement. Beaverbrook put Northcliffe's ambition much higher, as 'a Lloyd George-Northcliffe administration', and on 3 October Northcliffe wrote to Riddell that he and his newspapers would not support a future Lloyd George government unless he knew 'definitely and in writing, and can conscientiously approve, the personal constitution of the Government', a suggestion that Lloyd George naturally rejected.[52]

This break between Northcliffe and Lloyd George became Haig's opportunity to win back Northcliffe's favour. Correspondence between Northcliffe and Major Sassoon resumed in September after a gap of several months, with a letter in which Northcliffe deplored the fact that Haig's name was hardly mentioned when the war was discussed in Britain.[53] Northcliffe continued to write to Haig through Sassoon, stressing the need for better publicity for Haig and his victories. Haig himself was usually absent from Montreuil at this stage of the war, preoccupied with directing his Armies from various temporary headquarters, or from his headquarters train. The first mention of the press in his diary for some time came on 12 October, when he recorded that he had received at his temporary headquarters in Arras 'six journalists from South Wales, who the propaganda department [sic] specially wanted me to see'. But on 17 October the editor of *The Times*, Geoffrey Dawson, came out to Haig's headquarters now based temporarily at Bertincourt, calling his attention to what Haig described as 'the very small support given by the English press to the British Army. Papers seem to vie with each other in cracking up the French, and running down British military methods and Generals!'[54] Dawson's behaviour reflected Northcliffe's change of allegiance away from Lloyd George only a few days earlier. The final break between the two men came on 3 November, when Lloyd George refused Northcliffe's demand for a seat at the Peace Conference. On 12 November Northcliffe resigned from the British War Mission, which was disbanded.

This change of heart and policy by Northcliffe only just before the Armistice was too late to change the propaganda themes and Home Front impressions of the year. From August to October, Haig himself had alternated between a belief that the war could be won in 1918 and a belief that the Germans might yet stabilize their line. In fact, the conclusion that the German Army had lost the war on the Western Front came much earlier to the German Great General Staff, after the defeat at Amiens on 8 August, Ludendorff's famous 'black day of the German Army'. The General Staff's response to the prospect of defeat was to work to ameliorate its effect on the German Army, rather than on Germany or its people, by the creation of the *Dolchstosslegende*. For the senior officers of the General Staff, this myth was an essential part of the mechanism of ending the war, by deflecting responsibility and criticism for Germany's defeat away from themselves and the German Army, and onto their political enemies.[55] As Hindenburg himself put it, with complete falsehood, 'Like Siegfried, stricken down by the treacherous spear of savage Hagen, our weary front collapsed'.[56] The belief that Crewe House had contrived the collapse of the German Home Front in 1918 was subsequently promoted in the 1920s by one of the strangest alliances of convenience in history: a mixture of British and European pacifists, boastful British journalists, League of Nations supporters, American isolationists and German proto-Nazis. But by then any official British government institutions that might have challenged the German claim to be undefeated on the Western Front had been disbanded, and their real work forgotten.

The achievement of the British Army on the Western Front in 1918 was undervalued at the time through the cumulative effect of several apparently unrelated decisions. Reduced in importance at the year's start by Lloyd George's grand strategy, Haig's GHQ reduced still further its own interest in publicity and propaganda. Beaverbrook's insistence on the shift to visual propaganda also played a part in reducing the impact on the public of a new and more technological style of fighting battles that was, by its very nature, neither as simple nor as accessible to reporters or cameramen as the methods of 1916, and not as picturesque as scenes of camels and ancient ruins in Palestine. Largely through the distractions caused by Northcliffe's vast political ambitions, Crewe House also failed to project an image of a British Army superior to its enemies. Taken altogether, the British Army's colossal victory on the Western Front in 1918 was a story that was not so much forgotten as just never properly told.

NOTES

1 *See* French, D (1986), *British Strategy and War Aims 1914–1916*. London: Allen & Unwin and French, D. (1995), *The Strategy of the Lloyd George Coalition 1916–1918*. Oxford: Clarendon Press; Millman, B. (2001), *Pessimism and British War Policy 1916–1918*. London: Frank Cass; Woodward (1983) op.cit.

2 Much has been done since the pioneering Sanders and Taylor (1982), op. cit., which still remains the best starting place for this subject. *See* Messinger (1992), op. cit., Farrar (1998), op. cit., Reeves (1986), op. cit., Carmichael (1989), op. cit., Smither (1994) op. cit, and Hiley, N. (1984), 'Making war: the British news media and government control 1914–1916', PhD Thesis, Open University. Important studies of the media and propaganda in other countries during the war include Welch, D. (2000), *Germany, Propaganda and Total War 1914–1918*. London: Athlone; Cornwall, M. (2000), *The Undermining of Austria-Hungary: The Battle for Hearts and Minds*. London: Macmillan; Williams, J. F. (1999), *ANZACs, The Media and the Great War*. Sydney: University of New South Wales Press.

3 Fussell (1975), op. cit., Eksteins (1989), op. cit., Winter (1995), op. cit., Hynes, S. (1990), *A War Imagined: The First World War and English Culture*. London: Bodley Head, Bourke, J. (1996), *Dismembering the Male: Men's Bodies, Britain and the Great War*. London: Reaktion; Robb, G. (2002), *British Culture and the First World War*. London: Palgrave.

4 Sheffield, G. (2001), *Forgotten Victory: The First World War – Myths and Realities*. London: Headline; Griffith, P. (1994), *Battle Tactics of the Western Front: The British Army's Art of Attack 1916–1918*. New Haven, CT: Yale University Press; Simkins, P. (1999), 'Somme reprise: reflections on the fighting for Albert and Bapaume, August 1918', in B. Bond (ed.), *Look To Your Front: Studies in the First World War*. Steeplehurst: Spellmount; Bailey, J. B. A. (2001), 'The First World War and the birth of modern warfare', in M. Knox, and W. Murray (eds), *The Dynamics of Military Revolution 1300–2050*. Cambridge: Cambridge University Press, pp. 132–53, and Prior and Wilson (1992), op. cit.

5 The various arguments are well covered in Bond (2002), op. cit, and *see also* Bond, B. (ed.) (1991), *The First World War and British Military History*. Oxford: Clarendon Press; Todman, D. (2002), 'The reception of *The Great War* in the 1960s', *Historical Journal of Film, Radio and Television*, 22, (1), 29–36; and Todman (2005), op, cit.

6 Beckett, I. F. W. (2001), *The Great War 1914–1918*. London: Longman, especially pp. 158–79 and pp. 428–61; Howard, M. (2002), *The First World War*. Oxford: Oxford University Press, especially pp. 120–30.

7 Harris J. P., with Barr, N. (1998), *Amiens to the Armistice: The BEF in the Hundred*

Days' Campaign, 8 August–11 November 1918. London: Brassey's; Terraine, J. (1978), *To Win a War: 1918 the Year of Victory*. London: Sedgwick & Jackson.

8 For manpower issues the author has relied particularly on Grieves, K. (1988), *The Politics of Manpower 1914–1918*. Manchester: Manchester University Press. *See also* Adams, R. J. Q. and Poirier, P. P. (1987), *The Conscription Controversy in Great Britain 1900–1918*. London: Macmillan, pp. 205–44.

9 This summary is based in particular on French (1995), op. cit., pp. 193–212.

10 Bourne (1989), p. 210; *see also* the discussion of British propaganda and the press in the same work, pp. 202–9.

11 Thompson, J. L. (1999), *Politicians, The Press and Propaganda: Lord Northcliffe and the Great War 1914–1919*. Kent, OH: Kent State University Press, pp. 175–6.

12 *See* in particular, Taylor, P. M. (1999), *British Propaganda in the Twentieth Century: Selling Democracy*. Edinburgh: Edinburgh University Press, pp. 5–34.

13 Self, R. C. (ed.) (1995), *The Austen Chamberlain Diary Letters*. Cambridge: Royal Historical Society, p. 71.

14 For Beaverbrook's becoming minister *see* Taylor, A. J. P. (1974), *Beaverbrook*. London: Penguin edition, pp. 188–94 *et seq*. Northcliffe's involvement with Lloyd George and the war effort in 1918 is extensively discussed in Thompson (1999) op. cit., pp. 170–218.

15 For Northcliffe's involvement in propaganda in 1918 and his relationship with Haig and GHQ, *see* Pound and Harmsworth (1959), op. cit. p. 598 *et seq*.

16 Lytton (1920), op. cit., p. 152.

17 TNA, INF 4/6 'Confidential report on the need and form of British propaganda in France'.

18 Beaverbrook (1956), op. cit., p. 267.

19 TNA INF 4/1A and CAB 24/5 'Liquidation of the Ministry of Information' 20 December 1918. Some Ministry of Information documents exist in the Beaverbrook Papers in the House of Lords Record Office, and others have been found in Canadian collections. (The author is grateful to Roger Smither for this last information.)

20 Taylor (1974), op. cit., p. 198.

21 Woodward (1983), op. cit., pp. 282–6.

22 Blake (1952), op. cit., p. 287.

23 Self (1995), op. cit., p. 71; *see also* Riddell (1933), op. cit., p. 310.

24 Nash, D. (ed.) (1977), *German Army Handbook April 1918*. Reprinted London: Arms and Armour; for Cox's career *see* Davies and Maddocks (1995), op. cit., p. 56.

25 Lytton (1920), op. cit., p. 146.

26 Ibid, pp. 141–2.

27 Farrar (1998), op. cit., pp. 189–224; Reeves (1986), op. cit., pp. 77–88; Carmichael (1989), op. cit., pp. 46–75; Robertson (1978), op. cit., Bickel, L. (1980), *In Search of Frank Hurley*. Melbourne: Macmillan, pp. 55–72.

28 Australian War Memorial, Canberra, AWM 8 Papers of Charles E. W. Bean 3DL 7953/34 Letter from Edmonds to Bean 16 October 1928; *see also* the critical comments of Major A. N. Lee in IWM Department of Documents, Lee Papers.

29 Lytton (1920), op. cit., p. 140; IWM, Lee Papers, p. 172.

30 IWM (Photo) Bartholomew to Holt, 14 January 1918, Bartholomew File; Lee Papers, p. 137.

31 IWM, Lee Papers, pp. 180–1.

32 IWM (Photo), Bartholomew File, Letter Bartholomew to Roon, 22 October 1918.

33 Pound and Harmsworth (1959), op. cit., p. 628.

34 IWM (Film) 'The Ministry of Information 1918', Holt to Clough, 11 April 1918.

35 Millman (2001), op. cit., p. 251; not all of those in France who received this order were dismissive about it, and some found it inspirational.

36 Reeves, N. (1983), 'Film propaganda and its audience: the example of Britain's official films during the First World War', *Journal of Contemporary History*, 18, pp. 463–94; Hiley (1995), op. cit., pp. 160–70.

37 Taylor (1974), op. cit., p. 197 (Taylor attributes this quotation to Beaverbrook, but leaves it unreferenced); *see also* McKernan (1992), op.cit.

38 McKernan, L. (1993), '"The supreme moment of the war": General Allenby's entry into Jerusalem', *Historical Journal of Film, Radio and Television*, 13, (2), pp. 169–80; Hughes, M. (1999), *Allenby and British Strategy in the Middle East 1917–1919*. London: Frank Cass.

39 Messinger (1992), op. cit., pp. 137–8; Millman (2000), op. cit., pp. 240–5; Smither (1993) (ed.), op. cit., p. 449.

40 Taylor (1974), op. cit., p. 203.

41 Reeves (1993), op. cit., pp. 181–202.

42 Welch (2000), op. cit., pp. 229–32, Ludendorff (1920), op. cit., pp. 171–5, Stuart, C. (1920), *Secrets of Crewe House: The Story of a Famous Campaign*. London: Hodder & Stoughton; [Anon] (1952), *The History of The Times Volume IV: The 150th Anniversary and Beyond 1912–1948, Part 1, Chapters 1–XII, 1912–1920*. London: Times Publishing, pp. 350–66; Messinger (1992), op. cit., pp. 154–5, 169–83; Pound and Harmsworth (1959), op. cit., p. 671.

43 Pound and Harmsworth (1959), op. cit., p. 656.

44 Cornwall (2000), op. cit., Taylor (1999), op. cit., pp. 49–62, Messinger (1992), op. cit., pp. 162–83.

45 Quoted in Woodward (1983), op. cit., p. 315.

46 Gibbs, P. (1946), op. cit., p. 225.

47 Quoted in Farrar (1998), op. cit., p. 207.

48 Haig Papers 3155.107 Diary entries 21 July 1918 and 7 September 1918.

49 *Daily Chronicle*, 3 October 1918.

50 The reply, declining the offer, can be found in the House of Lords Record Office, Papers of Lord Beaverbrook, Northcliffe to Beaverbrook, 13 October 1918.

51 House of Lords Record Office, Papers of Lord Beaverbrook, File 'Memorandum to War Cabinet on the Setting Up of the Imperial News Wireless Service', Memorandum from Beaverbrook to the War Cabinet, 16 October 1918.

52 Beaverbrook (1956), op. cit., p. 88; Pound and Harmsworth (1959) op. cit, p. 666; Riddell (1933), op. cit., p. 366.

53 Thompson (1999), op. cit., p. 209.

54 Haig Papers, 3155.108 Diary entry 12 October 1918; Blake (1952) op. cit., p. 332.

55 Welch (2000), op. cit., p. 253; Herwig, H. H. (1997), *The First World War: Germany and Austria-Hungary 1914–1918*. London: Arnold, pp. 425–6; Moyer, L. V. (1995), *Victory Must Be Ours: Germany in the Great War 1914–1918*. London: Leo Cooper, pp. 276–83; Asprey, R. B. (1991), *The German High Command at War: Hindenburg and Ludendorff Conduct World War I*. New York: William Morrow, pp. 479–80.

56 Hindenburg (1920), op. cit., pp. 436–0.

Bibliography

OFFICIAL DOCUMENTS AND PRIVATE PAPERS

Australian War Memorial, Canberra
Bean Papers

Churchill Archive Centre, Churchill College, University of Cambridge
Rawlinson Papers

House of Lords Record Office, London
Beaverbrook Papers

Imperial War Museum, London
Chetwode Papers
Gwynne Papers
Karslake Papers
Lee Papers
Wilson Diary

Liddell Hart Centre for Military Archives, King's College, London
Allenby Papers

Liverpool Record Office
Derby Papers

The National Archives, Kew
AIR Series
CAB Series
FO Series
HO Series

INF Series
PRO Series – Kitchener Papers
WO Series

National Army Museum, London
Talbot-Rice Papers

National Library of Scotland, Edinburgh
Haig Papers

BOOKS AND ARTICLES

[Anon.] (1998), *Black-Adder: The Whole Damn Dynasty*. London: Michael Joseph.

[Anon.] (1917), *A Corpse Conversion Factory*. London: n. p.

[Anon.] (1952), *The History of The Times Volume IV. The 150th Anniversary and Beyond 1912–1948, Part I, Chapters 1–XII, 1912–1920*. London: Times Printing House.

[Anon.] (1929), *A Short History of the 1st King's Dragoon Guards*. Aldershot: Gale & Polden.

[Anon.] His Majesty's Stationery Office (1922), *Statistics of the Military Effort of the British Empire During the Great War 1914–1920*. London: HMSO.

Adams, R. J. Q. and Poirier, P. P. (1987), *The Conscription Controversy in Great Britain 1900–1918*. London: Macmillan.

Amery, L. S. (1953), *My Political Life: Volume I, England Before the Storm 1896–1914*. London: Hutchinson.

Asprey, R. B. (1991), *The German High Command at War: Hindenburg and Ludendorff Conduct World War I*. New York: William Morrow.

Asquith, [H. H.] Earl of Oxford and, (1928), *Memories and Reflections 1852–1927: Volume II*. London: Cassell.

Ashworth, T. (1980), *Trench Warfare 1914–1918: The Live and Let Live System*. London: Macmillan.

Badsey, S. (2007), 'The Boer War (1899–1902) and British cavalry doctrine: a re-evaluation', *The Journal of Military History*, 71, (1), 75–97.

—— (2008), *Doctrine and Reform in the British Cavalry 1880–1918*. London: Ashgate.

Bailey, J. B. A. (2001), 'The First World War and the birth of modern warfare', in M. Knox and W. Murray (eds), *The Dynamics of Military Revolution 1300–2050*. Cambridge: Cambridge University Press.

Barnett, C. (1972), *The Collapse of British Power*. London: Eyre Methuen.

Barrow, G. de S. (1941), *The Fire of Life*. London: Hutchinson.

Baynes, J. (1995), *Far From a Donkey: The Life of General Sir Ivor Maxse*. London: Brassey's.

Beaverbrook, [W. M.] Lord, (1956), *Men and Power 1917–1918*. London: Collins.

Beach, J. (intro.) (2008), *The Division in Attack 1918 SS 135 T/1635 40/ WO/7036*. Strategic and Combat Studies Institute Occasional Paper No 53. Shrivenham: SCSI.

Beckett, I. F. W. (2001), *The Great War 1914–1918*. London: Longman.

—— (2006), *Home Front 1914–1918: How Britain Survived the Great War*. Kew: The National Archives.

—— (ed.) (1986), *The Army and the Curragh Incident, 1914*. London: Army Records Society.

Berrisford Ellis, P. and Schofield, J. (1993), *Biggles: The Life Story of Captain W. E. Johns*. Godmanstone: Veloce.

Bickel, L. (1980), *In Search of Frank Hurley*. Melbourne: Macmillan.

Bidwell, S. and Graham, D. (1982), *Fire-Power: British Army Weapons and Theories of War 1904–1945*. London: Allen & Unwin.

Black, J. (2000), *War and the World: Military Power and the Fate of Continents 1450–2000*. London: Yale University Press.

Blair, D. (2001), *Dinkum Diggers: An Australian Battalion at War*. Melbourne: Melbourne University Press.

Blake, R. (1952), *The Private Papers of Douglas Haig 1914–1919*. London: Eyre and Spottiswoode.

Bond, B. (ed.) (1991), *The First World War and British Military History*. Oxford: Clarendon Press.

—— (2002), *The Unquiet Western Front: Britain's Role in Literature and History*. Cambridge: Cambridge University Press.

—— (1972), *The Victorian Army and the Staff College 1854–1914*. London: Eyre Methuen.

—— (1997), 'A victory worse than a defeat? British interpretations of the First

World War', Liddell Hart Centre for Military Archives Annual Lecture, King's College London, 20 November 1997.

Bourke, J. (1996), *Dismembering the Male: Men's Bodies, Britain and the Great War*. London: Reaktion.

Bourne, J. M. (1989), *Britain and the Great War 1914–1918*. London: Edward Arnold.

Brereton, J. M. (1982), *A History of the 4th/7th Royal Dragoon Guards 1685–1980*. Catterick: privately printed.

Brett-Smith, R. (1969), *The 11th Hussars (Prince Albert's Own)*. London: Leo Cooper.

Bridges, T. (1938), *Alarms and Excursions*. London: Longmans.

Bristow, A. (1995), *A Serious Disappointment: The Battle of Aubers Ridge 1915 and the Munitions Scandal*. London: Leo Cooper.

Broks, P. (1996), *Media Science Before the Great War*. London: Macmillan.

Brown, J. G. and Bridges, E. J. (1932), *Historical Records of the 14th (King's) Hussars, Volume II, 1900–1922*. London: RUSI.

Brown, M. (1978), *Tommy Goes To War*. London: J. M. Dent.

Brownlow, K. (1979), *The War, The West, and the Wilderness*. London: Secker & Warburg.

Brownrigg, D. (1920), *Indiscretions of the Naval Censor*. London: Cassell.

Bülow, Prince von, (1931), *Memoirs 1903–1909*. London: Putnam.

Burnett, C. (1926), *The Memoirs of the 18th (Queen Mary's Own) Royal Hussars 1906–1922*. Winchester: Warren & Son.

Callwell, C. E. (1927), *Field Marshal Sir Henry Wilson*, London: Cassell.

Carmichael, J. (1989), *First World War Photographers*. London: Routledge.

Cecil, H. and Liddle, P. H. (eds) (1996), *Facing Armageddon: The First World War Experienced*. London: Leo Cooper.

Charrington, H. V. S. (1927), *Where Cavalry Stands Today*. London: Gale and Polden.

Charteris, J. (1931), *At GHQ*. London: Cassell.

Churchill, W. S. (1960), *The World Crisis 1911–1918*. London: 4-Square Edition.

Clarke, I. F. (1992), *Voices Prophesying War: Future Wars 1763–3749*. Oxford: Oxford University Press.

Cohen, E. A. and Gooch, J. (1990), *Military Misfortunes: The Anatomy of Failure in War*. New York: The Free Press.

Collier, B. (1961), *Brasshat: A Biography of Field Marshal Sir Henry Wilson*. London: Secker & Warburg.

Cook, T. (2008), *Shock Troops: Canadians Fighting the Great War 1917–1918*. Toronto: Canadian Penguin Group.

Cornwall, M. (2000), *The Undermining of Austria-Hungary: The Battle for Hearts and Minds*. London: Macmillan.

Crichton, M. (1999), *Timeline*. New York: Ballantine.

Cull, N. J. (1995), *Selling War: The British Campaign Against American 'Neutrality' in World War II*. Oxford: Oxford University Press.

Davies, F. and Maddocks, G. (1995), *Bloody Red Tabs: General Officer Casualties of the Great War 1914–1918*. London: Leo Cooper.

De Groot, G. (1996), *Blighty: British Society in the Era of the Great War*. London: Longman.

—— (1988), *Douglas Haig 1861–1928*. London: Unwin Hyman.

Demm, E. (1996), 'German teachers at war', in H. Cecil and P. H. Liddle (eds), *Facing Armageddon, The First World War Experienced*. London: Leo Cooper.

Denison, G. T. (1868), *Modern Cavalry*. London: Thomas Bosworth.

Dixon, N. (1976), *On the Psychology of Military Incompetence*. London: Jonathan Cape.

Edmonds, J. E. (general ed.) (various dates), *The History of the Great War Based on Official Documents: Military Operations*. London: HMSO.

Eksteins, M. (1990), *Rites of Spring: The Great War and the Birth of the Modern Age*. London: Black Swan.

Ellis, J. (1975), *The Social History of the Machine-Gun*. London: Crosset.

'Eques' (pseudonym) (1908), 'Cavalry on the battlefield', *The Cavalry Journal*, 3, (10).

Esher, [O.] Viscount, (ed.) (1938), *Journals and Letters of Reginald Viscount Esher, 4 Volume 1916–1930*. London: Ivor Nicholson & Watson.

Evans, R. (1951), *The Story of the Fifth Royal Inniskilling Dragoon Guards*. Aldershot: Gale & Polden.

Farrar, M. J. (1998), *News From the Front, War Correspondents on the Western Front 1914–1918*. Thrupp: Sutton.

Forester, C. S. (1936), *The General*. London: Penguin.

Foulkes, C. H. (1934), *Gas! The Story of the Special Brigade*. London: Blackwood.

Fraser, A. H., Robertshaw, A. and Roberts, S. (2009), *Ghosts on the Somme: Filming the Great Battle, July 1916*. London: Pen & Sword.

Fraser, G. M. (1988), *The Hollywood History of the World: From One Million Years BC to Apocalypse Now*. New York: Beech Tree Books.

French, D. (1986), *British Strategy and War Aims 1914–1916*. London: Allen & Unwin.

—— (1995), *The Strategy of the Lloyd George Coalition 1916–1918*. Oxford: Clarendon Press.

Fussell, P. (1975), *The Great War and Modern Memory*. Oxford: Oxford University Press.

Gardner, B. (1965), *Allenby*. London: Cassell.

Gibbs, P. (1918), *From Bapaume to Passchendaele, 1917*. n.p.

—— (1946), *The Pageant of The Years*. London: William Heinemann.

—— (1920), *Realities of War*. London: William Heinemann.

Goldmann, C. S. (1902), *With General French and the Cavalry in South Africa*. London: Macmillan.

Gooch, J. (1974), *The Plans of War: The General Staff and British Military Strategy c.1900–1916*. London: Routledge & Kegan Paul.

Gough, H. (1931), *The Fifth Army*. London: Hodder & Stoughton.

Green, A. (2004), *Writing the Great War: Sir James Edmonds and the Official Histories 1915–1948*. London: Routledge.

Grieves, K. (1988), *The Politics of Manpower, 1914–1918*. Manchester: Manchester University Press.

—— (1996), 'War correspondents and conducting officers on the Western Front from 1915', in H. Cecil and P. H. Liddle (eds), *Facing Armageddon, The First World War Experienced*. London: Leo Cooper.

Griffith, P. (1994), *Battle Tactics of the Western Front: The British Army's Art of Attack 1916–1918*. New Haven, CT: Yale University Press.

Grodzinski, J. R. and McNorgan, M. R. (2000), ' "It's a charge, boys, it's a charge!" Cavalry action at Moreuil Wood, 30 March 1918', in D. E. Graves (ed.), *Fighting For Canada: Seven Battles, 1758–1945*. Toronto: Robin Brass Studio.

Gropp, H. (no date), *Hanseaten im Kampf*. Hamburg: Klindworth und Neuenhausen.

Haig, D. (1907), *Cavalry Studies*. London: Hugh Rees.

Hammond, B. (2008), *Cambrai 1917: The Myth of the First Great Tank Battle*. London: Weidenfeld & Nicholson.

Harris, J. P. (2008), *Douglas Haig and the First World War*. Cambridge: Cambridge University Press.

Harris J. P. with Barr, N. (1998), *Amiens to the Armistice: The BEF in the Hundred Days' Campaign, 8 August–11 November 1918*. London: Brassey's.

Harvey, J. R. and Cape, H. A. (1923), *The History of the 5th (Royal Irish) Regiment of Dragoons from 1689 to 1797 and Afterwards The Fifth Royal Irish Lancers from 1858 to 1921*. London: Gale & Polden.

Haste, C. (1977), *Keep the Home Fires Burning: Propaganda in the First World War*. London: Allen Lane.

Herwig, H. H. (1997), *The First World War: Germany and Austria-Hungary 1914–1918*. London: Arnold.

Higgins, D. S. (ed.) (1980), *The Private Diaries of Sir Henry Rider Haggard*. London: Cassell.

Hiley, N. (1995), 'The British cinema auditorium', in K. Dibbets and B. Hogenkamp (eds), *Film and the First World War*. Amsterdam: Amsterdam University Press.

—— (1993), 'Hilton de Witt Girdwood and the origins of British Official Filming', *The Historical Journal of Film, Radio and Television*, 13, (2), 129–48.

—— (1984), 'Making war: the British news media and government control 1914–1916', PhD Thesis, Open University.

Hindenburg, P. von (1920), *Out of My Life*. London: Cassell.

Hitler, A. (1925), *Mein Kampf*. Munich, n.p.

Hoare, P. (1997), *Wilde's Last Stand: Decadence, Conspiracy and the First World War*. London: Duckworth.

Hodgkins, J. (2008), 'Hearts and minds and bodies: reconsidering the cinematic language of the Battle of the Somme', *Film and History*, 38, (1), 9–19.

Holmes, R. (1981), *The Little Field Marshal: Sir John French*. London: Jonathan Cape.

—— (2004), *Tommy: The British Soldier on the Western Front 1914–1918*. London: HarperCollins.

Howard, M. (2002), *The First World War*. Oxford: Oxford University Press.

—— (intro.) (2008), *A Part of History: Aspects of the British Experience of the First World War*. London: Continuum.

Hughes, M. (1999), *Allenby and British Strategy in the Middle East 1917–1919*. London: Frank Cass.

Hussey, J. (1999), 'Portrait of a Commander in Chief', in B. Bond and N. Cave (eds), *Haig: A Reappraisal 70 Years On*. London: Leo Cooper.

Hynes, S. (1990), *A War Imagined: The First World War and English Culture*. London: Bodley Head.

Jackson, S. (1968), *The Sassoons*. London: Heinemann.

Keegan, J. (1976), *The Face of Battle*. London: Jonathan Cape.

—— (1998), *The First World War*. London: Hutchinson.

Kelly, A. (1997), *Cinema and the Great War*. London: Routledge.

Knightley, P. (1982), *The First Casualty*. London: Quartet.

Lewis, C. (1936), *Sagittarius Rising*. London: Peter Davies.

Liddell Hart, B. H. (1972), *History of the First World War*. London: Pan Edition.

Lloyd, R. A. (1938), *A Trooper in the Tins*. London: Hurst & Blackett.

Lloyd George, D. (1936), *The War Memoirs of David Lloyd George*. London: Odhams Press.

Low, R. (1950), *A History of British Film, Volume IV, 1914–1918*. London: George Allen & Unwin.

Ludendorff, E. (1920), *My War Memoirs 1914–1918*. London: Hutchinson.

Lumley, L. R. (1936), *History of the 11th Hussars (Prince Albert's Own) 1908–1934*. London: RUSI.

Lytton, N. (1920), *The Press and the General Staff*. London: Collins.

Malins, G. (1920), *How I Filmed the War*. London: Herbert Jenkins.

Marshall-Cornwall, J. (1973), *Haig as Military Commander*. London: B. T. Batsford.

Massie, R. K. (1991), *Dreadnought: Britain, Germany and the Coming of the Great War*. New York: Random House.

Masterman, L. (1939), *C. F .C. Masterman: A Biography*. London: Nicholson and Watson.

McEwan, J. M. (1978), 'The press and the fall of Asquith', *Historical Journal*, 21, 863–3.

McKernan, L. (1993), '"The supreme moment of the war": General Allenby's entry into Jerusalem', *Historical Journal of Film, Radio and Television*, 13, (2), 169–80.

—— (1992), *Topical Budget: The Great British News Film*. London: BFI
  Publishing.

Messenger, C. (1976), *The Art of Blitzkrieg*. London: Ian Allen.

Messinger, G. S. (1992), *British Propaganda and the State in the First World War*.
  Manchester: Manchester University Press.

Middlebrook, M. (1971), *The First Day on the Somme*. London: Allen Lane.

Millman, B. (2001), *Pessimism and British War Policy 1916–1918*. London:
  Frank Cass.

Montgomery, A. (1919), *The Story of the Fourth Army in the Battles of the
  Hundred Days, August 8th to November 11th 1918*. London: Hodder &
  Stoughton.

Moore, W. (1988), *A Wood Called Bourlon: The Cover-Up After Cambrai 1917*.
  London: Leo Cooper.

Moses, H. (2003), *The Fighting Bradfords: Northern Heroes of World War One*.
  Durham: County Durham Books.

Moyer, L. V. (1995), *Victory Must Be Ours: Germany in the Great War
  1914–1918*. London: Leo Cooper.

Nash, D. (ed.) (1977), *German Army Handbook April 1918*. Reprinted London:
  Arms and Armour.

Neiberg, M. S. (2004), 'Cromwell on the bed stand: Allied civil-military
  relations in World War I', in J. Macleod, and P. Purseigle (eds), *Uncovered
  Fields: Perspectives in First World War Studies*. Leiden: Brill.

Norman, T. (1984), *The Hell They Called High Wood*. London: William
  Kimber.

Oats, L. B. (1966), *I Serve: The Regimental History of the 3rd Carabineers*.
  Norwich: Jarold & Son.

Orwell, G. (1962), *Inside the Whale and Other Essays*. London: Penguin.

Peterson, H. C. (1936), *Propaganda for War: The Campaign Against American
  Neutrality, 1914–1917*. New York: Kennikat Press.

Phillips, G. (2002), 'The obsolescence of the *Arme Blanche* and technological
  determinism in British military history', *War in History*, 9, (1), 39–59.

—— (2007), 'Scapegoat arm: twentieth-century cavalry in anglophone
  historiography', *The Journal of Military History*, 70, (1), 37–74.

Pomeroy, R. L. (1938), *History of the Scots Greys (The Second Dragoons) August
  1914–March 1919*. London: privately printed.

—— (1924), *The Story of a Regiment of Horse: Being the Regimental History from 1685 to 1922 of the 5th Princess Charlotte of Wales's Dragoon Guards*, Edinburgh: Blackwood.

Pound, R. and Harmsworth, G. (1959), *Northcliffe*. London: Cassell.

Preston, R. M. P. (1921), *The Desert Mounted Corps*. London: Constable.

Prior, R. and Wilson, T. (1992), *Command on the Western Front: The Military Career of Sir Henry Rawlinson 1914–1918*. Oxford: Blackwell.

—— (1996), *Passchendaele: The Untold Story*. New Haven, CT: Yale University Press.

—— (1994), 'Paul Fussell at war', *War in History*, I, (1), 63–80.

—— (2005), *The Somme*. New Haven, CT: Yale University Press.

Reeves, N. (1983), 'Film propaganda and its audience: the example of Britain's official films during the First World War', *Journal of Contemporary History*, 18, 463–94.

—— (1986), *Official British Film Propaganda During the First World War*. London: Croom Helm.

—— (1993), 'The power of film propaganda – myth or reality?' *Historical Journal of Film, Radio and Television*, 13, (2), 181–201.

—— (1996), 'Through the eye of the camera: contemporary cinema audiences and their experience of war in the film "Battle of the Somme"', in H. Cecil, and P. H. Liddle (eds), *Facing Armageddon: The First World War Experienced*. London: Leo Cooper.

Reith, J. C. W. (1949), *Into the Wind*. London: Hodder & Stoughton.

Renne, J., *et* Ford, C. (1961), *Le Cinema et la Presse 1895–1960*. Paris: Armande Colin.

Repington, C à C. (1920), *The First World War*. London: Constable, London.

Riddell, [G.] Lord, (1933), *Lord Riddell's War Diary 1914–1918*. London: Ivor Nicolson & Watson.

Robb, G. (2002), *British Culture and the First World War*. London: Palgrave.

Robertson, P. (1978), 'Canadian photojournalism in the First World War', *History of Photography*, 2, (1).

Rogers, H. C. B. (1959), *The Mounted Troops of the British Army 1066–1945*. London: Seely Service.

Sanders, M. L. (1975), 'Wellington House and British propaganda during the First World War', *The Historical Journal*, XVIII, (I), 119–46.

Sanders, M. L. and Taylor, P. M. (1982), *British Propaganda During the First World War*. London: Macmillan.

Sassoon, S. (1930), *Memoirs of an Infantry Officer*. London: Faber & Faber.

Seely, J. E. B. (1930), *Adventure*. London: Heinemann.

Self, R. C. (ed.) (1995), *The Austen Chamberlain Diary Letters*. Cambridge: Royal Historical Society.

Sellar, W. C. and Yeatman, R. J. (1930), *1066 and All That: A Memorable History of England*. London: Methuen.

Shannon, S. D. (1998), *Beyond Praise: The Durham Light Infantrymen Who Were Awarded the Victoria Cross*. Durham: County Durham Books.

Sheffield, G. (2001), *Forgotten Victory: The First World War – Myths and Realities*. London: Headline.

—— (1986), 'The morale of the British Army on the Western Front 1914–1918', *Occasional Paper 2*, Institute for the Study of War and Society, De Montfort University (UK).

—— (1996), '"Oh! What a futile war": representations of the Western Front in modern British media and popular culture', in I. Stewart and S. L. Carruthers (eds), *War, Culture and the Media*. Trowbridge: Flicks Books.

Sheffield, G. and Bourne, J. (eds) (2005), *Douglas Haig: War Diaries and Letters 1914–1918*. London: Weidenfeld and Nicholson

Sheppard, E. W. (1939), *The Ninth Queen's Royal Lancers 1715–1936*. London: Gale & Polden.

Shy, J. (2008), 'History, and the history of war', *The Journal of Military History*, 72, (4), 1033–1046.

Simkins, P. (1999), 'Somme reprise: reflections on the fighting for Albert and Bapaume, August 1918', in B. Bond (ed.), *Look To Your Front: Studies in the First World War*. Steeplehurst: Spellmount.

Smith, F. (1898), 'The effects of the Lee-Metford bullet on the bones of horses', *Journal of the Royal United Services Institute*.

Smither, R. (1993), '"A wonderful idea of the fighting": the question of fakes in *The Battle of the Somme*', *The Historical Journal of Film, Radio and Television*. 13, (2), 149–68.

Smither, R. (ed.) (1994), *Imperial War Museum Film Catalogue, Volume I: the First World War Archive*. Trowbridge: Flicks Books.

Spagnoly, T. (1991), *The Anatomy of a Raid: Australia at Celtic Wood 9 October 1917*. London: Multidream.

Spears, E. L. (1967), *The Picnic Basket*. London: Secker and Warburg.

—— (1939), *Prelude To Victory*. London: Jonathan Cape.

Spiers, E. M. (1977), 'The British cavalry 1902–1914', *Journal of the Society for Army Historical Research*, 57, 71–9.

Steed, A. (1996), 'British propaganda and the First World War', in I. Stewart and S. L. Carruthers (eds), *War, Culture and the Media: Representations of the Military in Twentieth Century Britain*. London: Flicks Books.

Steiner, Z. (1977), *Britain and the Origins of the First World War*. London: Macmillan.

Stone, N. (1975), *The Eastern Front 1914–1917*. London: Hodder & Stoughton.

Stuart, C. (1920), *Secrets of Crewe House: The Story of a Famous Campaign*. London: Hodder & Stoughton.

Taylor, A. J. P. (1974), *Beaverbrook*. London: Penguin edition.

—— (1963), *The First World War: An Illustrated History*. London: Hamish Hamilton.

Taylor, P. M. (1999), *British Propaganda in the Twentieth Century: Selling Democracy*. Edinburgh: Edinburgh University Press.

Tennant, E. (1939), *The Royal Deccan Horse in the Great War*. Aldershot: Gale & Polden.

Terraine, J. (1963), *Douglas Haig: The Educated Soldier*. London: Hutchinson.

—— (1977), *The Road to Passchendaele: The Flanders Offensive of 1917 – a Study in Inevitability*. London: Leo Cooper.

—— (1992), *The Smoke and the Fire: Myths and Anti-Myths of War*. London: Leo Cooper.

—— (1978), *To Win a War: 1918 the Year of Victory*. London: Sedgwick & Jackson.

Thompson, J. L. (1999), *Politicians, The Press and Propaganda: Lord Northcliffe and the Great War 1914–1919*. Kent, OH: Kent State University Press.

Todman, D. (2005), *The Great War: Myth and Memory*. London: Hambledon & London.

—— (2002), 'The reception of *The Great War* in the 1960s', *Historical Journal of Film, Radio and Television*, 22, (1), 29–36.

Towle, P. (1975), 'The debate on wartime censorship in Britain 1902–1914', in B. Bond and I. Roy, (eds), *War and Society, A Yearbook of Military History*. London: Croom Helm.

Travers, T. (1992), *How the War Was Won: Command and Technology in the British Army on the Western Front 1917–1918*. London: Routledge.

—— (1987), *The Killing Ground: The British Army, The Western Front, and the Emergence of Modern Warfare 1900–1918*. London: Unwin Hyman.

Tuchman, B. (1962), *The Guns of August*. New York: Macmillan.

Vaughan, J. (1954), *Cavalry and Sporting Memories*. Bala: The Bala Press.

Warman, R. (1972), 'The erosion of Foreign Office influence in the making of foreign policy 1916–1918', *Historical Journal*, 15, (1), 133–59.

Wavell, A. (1940), *Allenby: A Study in Greatness*. London: Harrap.

Wilhelm II, Kaiser, (1922), *My Memoirs 1878–1918*. London: Cassell.

Welch, D. (2000), *Germany, Propaganda and Total War 1914–1918*. London: Athlone.

Willcox, W. T. (1925), *The 3rd (King's Own) Hussars in the Great War (1914–1919)*. London: John Murray.

Williams, J. (1983), *Byng of Vimy: General and Governor-General*. London: Leo Cooper.

Williams, J. F. (1999), *ANZACs, The Media and the Great War*. Sydney: University of New South Wales Press.

Wilson, T. (1986), *The Myriad Faces of War: Britain and the Great War 1914–1918*. London: Polity Press.

Winter, J. (1995), *Sites of Memory, Sites of Mourning: The Great War in European Cultural History*. Cambridge: Cambridge University Press.

Wolff, L. (1958), *In Flanders Fields*. London: Longman & Green.

Woolcombe, R. (1967), *The First Tank Battle: Cambrai 1917*. London: Arthur Barker.

Woodward, D. R. (1983), *Lloyd George and the Generals*. London: University of Delaware Press.

—— (ed.) (1989), *The Military Correspondence of Field Marshal Sir William Robertson, Chief of the Imperial General Staff December 1915–February 1918*. London: Army Records Society.

Index

Lightning Source UK Ltd.
Milton Keynes UK
UKOW06f0334030817

306596UK00003B/97/P